HELEN HALL LIBRARY

D0473276

Word 2013 and 2010 for SENIORS

HELEN HALL LIBRARY
100 Walker St
League City, TX 77573

OCT 1 5

Studio Visual Steps

Word 2013 and 2010 for SENIORS

Learn step by step how to work with Microsoft Word

DISCARD

HELEN HALL LIBRARY
100 WEST WALKER
LEAGUE CITY,TX 77573

www.visualsteps.com

This book has been written using the Visual Steps™ method.
Cover design by Studio Willemien Haagsma bNO

© 2014 Visual Steps
Author: Studio Visual Steps

First printing: May 2014
ISBN 978 90 5905 110 2

All rights reserved. No part of this publication may be reproduced, stored in a retrieval system or transmitted in any form or by any means, electronic, mechanical, photocopying, recording, scanning or otherwise, except as permitted under Sections 107 or 108 of the 1976 United States Copyright Act, without the prior written permission of the Publisher.

LIMIT OF LIABILITY/DISCLAIMER OF WARRANTY: While the publisher and author have used their best efforts in preparing this book, they make no representations or warranties with respect to the accuracy or completeness of the contents of this book and specifically disclaim any implied warranties of merchantability or fitness for a particular purpose. No warranty may be created or extended by sales representatives or written sales materials. The advice and strategies contained herein may not be suitable for your situation. You should consult with a professional where appropriate. Neither the publisher nor author shall be liable for any loss of profit or any other commercial damages, including but not limited to special, incidental, consequential or other damages.

Trademarks: This book contains names of registered trademarks. iPad is a registered trademark of Apple, Inc. All other trademarks are the property of their respective owners. Visual Steps Publishing is not associated with any product or vendor mentioned in this book.
In the text of this book, these names are not indicated by their trademark symbol, because they are solely used for identifying the products which are mentioned in the text. In no way does this constitute an infringement on the rights of the trademark owners.

Resources used: Some of the computer terms and definitions seen here in this book have been taken from descriptions found online at the Windows Help and Support website.

Do you have questions or suggestions?
Email: info@visualsteps.com

Would you like more information?
www.visualsteps.com

Website for this book:
www.visualsteps.com/word2013

Subscribe to the free Visual Steps Newsletter:
www.visualsteps.com/newsletter

Table of Contents

Foreword

Nowadays, being able to work with *Word* from *Microsoft's Office* suite has become a standard requirement for many computer users. Employees, pupils, and students alike are expected to know the program and be able to use it to create professional looking documents.

In this book we will discuss many of the popular features and frequently used options found in *Word 2013* and *Word 2010*. Among other things, this book shows you step by step how to enter and format text, work with styles and page layout, insert pictures, and create lists and tables. You will learn how to use standard letters, templates and wizards. You will be able to apply finishing touches to documents by adding tables of contents, indexes and source references.

We wish you lots of fun with this book,

Studio Visual Steps

P.S.
We welcome all your comments and suggestions regarding this book.
Our email address is: info@visualsteps.com

Newsletter

All Visual Steps books follow the same methodology: clear and concise step-by-step instructions with screenshots to demonstrate each task.
A complete list of all our books can be found on our website **www.visualsteps.com**
You can also sign up to receive our **free Visual Steps Newsletter**.
In this Newsletter you will receive periodic information by email regarding:
- the latest titles and previously released books;
- special offers, supplemental chapters, tips and free informative booklets.
Also, our Newsletter subscribers may download any of the documents listed on the web page **www.visualsteps.com/info_downloads**

When you subscribe to our Newsletter you can be assured that we will never use your email address for any purpose other than sending you the information as previously described. We will not share this address with any third-party. Each Newsletter also contains a one-click link to unsubscribe.

Introduction to Visual Steps™

The Visual Steps handbooks and manuals are the best instructional materials available for learning how to work with the computer, mobile devices and software applications. Nowhere else will you find better support for getting started with a *Windows or Mac* computer, an iPad or other tablet, iPhone, the Internet or various software applications.

Characteristics of the Visual Steps books:
- **Comprehensible contents**
  Every book takes into account the wishes, knowledge and skills of computer users, beginners as well as more advanced users.
- **Clear structure**
  Every book is set up as an entire course, which you can easily follow, step by step.
- **Screenshots of every step**
  You will be guided by simple instructions and screenshots. You will immediately see what to do next.
- **Get started right away**
  All you have to do is place the book next to your keyboard and perform each operation as indicated on your own computer.
- **Layout**
  The text is printed in a large size font and is clearly legible.

In short, I believe these manuals will be excellent guides for you.

Dr. H. van der Meij
Faculty of Applied Education, Department of Instructional Technology, University of Twente, the Netherlands

Website

This book is accompanied by the website **www.visualsteps.com/word2013**
Be sure to check this website from time to time, to see if we have added any additional information or errata for this book.
You can also download the practice files used throughout this book from this website.

What You Will Need

To be able to work through this book, you will need a number of things:

 The main requirement for working with this book is to have **Microsoft Word 2013** or **Microsoft Word 2010** installed on your computer.
It does not make a difference if you use the stand alone *Word* application or *Word* as part of the *Office* suite. You can also use this book if you are a subscriber to *Office 365*, the subscription-based online service from *Microsoft Office*.

 Your computer needs to have *Windows 8.1, 7* or *Vista* installed.
Word 2013 will only work on computers with the *Windows 8.1* or *Windows 7* operating system. *Word 2010* is suitable for *Windows 8.1, 7 and Vista*.

 You will need an active Internet connection in order to download the practice files and bonus chapters from the website that accompanies this book.

 Some of the exercises require the use of a printer. If you do not own a printer you can skip these exercises.

Your Basic Knowledge

This book has been written for computer users who already have some experience using *Windows* and have acquired basic text editing skills. To work through this book successfully, you should be able to do the following:

Windows:
- start and stop *Windows*;
- click, right-click, double-click, and drag with the mouse;
- open and close programs;
- use a scroll bar;
- use tabs.

***Basic text editing skills*:**
- type a text;
- correct errors;
- create and delete a new line;
- move the cursor;
- select text;
- save a document and open it again;
- create a new document.

If you do not have these skills, you can use one of our beginner's books. For more information about our current titles, visit the catalog page on our website: **www.visualsteps.com**

How to Use This Book

This book has been written using the Visual Steps™ method. The method is simple: just place the book next to your computer or laptop and perform each task step by step, directly on your own device. With the clear instructions and the multitude of screenshots, you will always know exactly what to do next. This is the quickest way to become familiar with the many features and options in *Word 2013* or *Word 2010*.

In this Visual Steps™ book, you will see various icons. This is what they mean:

Techniques
These icons indicate an action to be carried out:

The mouse icon means you need to do something with the mouse.

The keyboard icon means you should type something on your keyboard.

The hand icon means you should do something else, for example, turn on the computer or carry out a task previously learned.

In some areas of this book additional icons indicate warnings or helpful hints. These help you to avoid making mistakes and alert you when a decision needs to be made.

Help
These icons indicate that extra help is available:

The arrow icon warns you about something.

 The bandage icon will help you if something has gone wrong.

The hand is also used with the exercises. Doing these exercises helps to reinforce what you have learned.

1 Have you forgotten how to do something? The number next to the footsteps tells you where to look it up at the end of the book in the appendix *How Do I Do That Again?*

The following icons indicate general information or tips about *Word 2013* and *Word 2010*. This information is displayed in separate boxes.

Extra information
Information boxes are denoted by these icons:

 The book icon gives you extra background information that you can read at your convenience. This extra information is not necessary for working through the book.

 The light bulb icon indicates an extra tip for using a program or service.

Test Your Knowledge

After you have worked through this book, you can test your knowledge online, on the **www.ccforseniors.com** website. By answering a number of multiple choice questions you will be able to test your knowledge of *Word*. If you pass the test, you can also receive a free *Computer Certificate* by email.
Participating in the test is **free of charge**. The computer certificate website is a free service from Visual Steps.

For Teachers

This book is designed as a self-study guide. It is also well suited for use in a group or a classroom setting. For this purpose, we offer a free teacher's manual containing information about how to prepare for the course (including didactic teaching methods) and testing materials. You can download the teacher's manual (PDF file) from the website which accompanies this book: **www.visualsteps.com/word2013**

More about Other Office Programs

Word is one of the programs included in the *Microsoft Office* suite. One of the other programs in this suite is the *Excel* spreadsheet program, for which the same type of step-by-step book is available. See **www.visualsteps.com/excel2013**

The Screenshots

The screenshots used in this book indicate which button, folder, file or hyperlink you need to click on your computer screen. In the instruction text (in **bold** letters) you will see a small image of the item you need to click. The black line will point you to the right place on your screen.
The small screenshots that are printed in this book are not meant to be completely legible all the time. This is not necessary, as you will see these images on your own computer screen in real size and fully legible.

Here you see an example of an instruction text and a screenshot. The black line indicates where to find this item on your own computer screen:

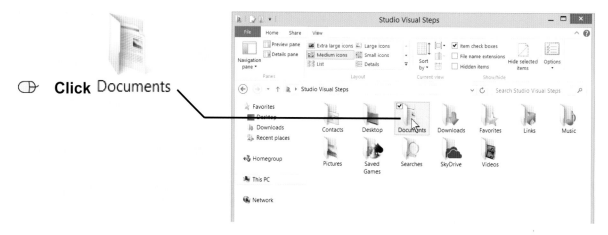

Sometimes the screenshot shows only a portion of a window. Here is an example:

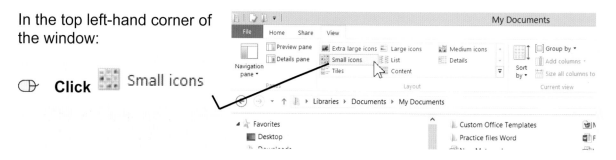

It really will **not be necessary** for you to read all the information in the screenshots in this book. Always use the screenshots in combination with the image you see on your own computer screen.

1. Starting with Word

Word is a versatile text editor. Along with the many options available for editing and creating text files, you can also adjust many of the program's settings to better fit the way you work.

When you open *Word* for the first time, you will be using the program's default settings. You may be quite happy with these settings at first, but after you have gained some experience, you may want to change some of them. This can improve your workflow and allow you to create documents more quickly and efficiently. In this chapter you will become acquainted with a number of the settings that can be adjusted to fit your needs.

In this chapter you will learn how to:

- open *Word*;
- set up the *Quick Access* toolbar;
- adjust the ribbon;
- display the ruler;
- set the line spacing and paragraph spacing;
- set the font type and font size;
- Undo changes;
- open a document;
- display hidden symbols;
- print a text;
- close a text and close *Word*.

 Please note:

In order to perform the exercises in this chapter, you need to download the practice files from the website accompanying this book **www.visualsteps.com/word2013** and save them to the (*My*) *Documents* folder on your computer. In *Appendix B Downloading the Practice Files* you can read how to do this.

1.1 Opening Word

In *Windows 8.1*, you can open *Microsoft Word 2013* or *Word 2010* from the Start screen:

⬧ **Click** **or**

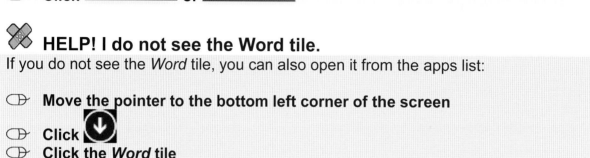

HELP! I do not see the Word tile.
If you do not see the *Word* tile, you can also open it from the apps list:

⬧ **Move the pointer to the bottom left corner of the screen**
⬧ **Click** ⬇
⬧ **Click the *Word* tile**

In *Windows 7* and *Vista*:

⬧ **Click** ⊞ , ▶ **All Programs** , 📁 **Microsoft Office** , W〰 **Word 2013** **or** W〰 **Microsoft Word 2010**

When you open *Word 2013*, you will see this window:

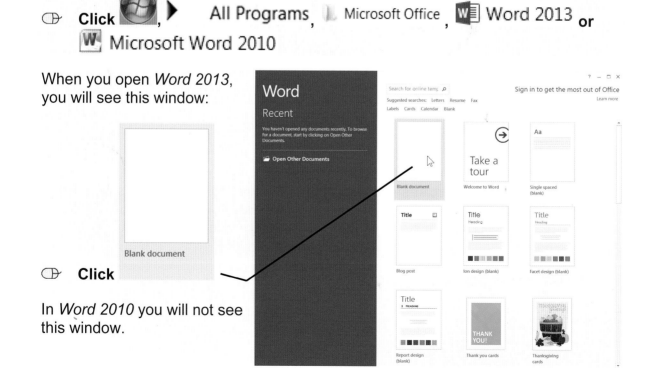

⬧ **Click**

In *Word 2010* you will not see this window.

A new, blank *Word* document will be opened.

In the title bar you will see the name of the document: ‐‐‐

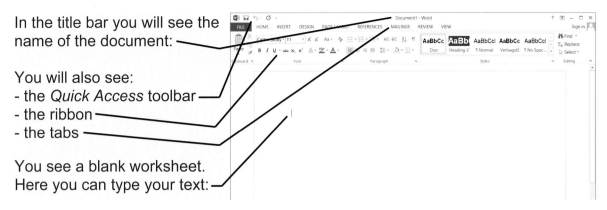

You will also see:
- the *Quick Access* toolbar ‐‐‐‐
- the ribbon ‐‐‐‐
- the tabs ‐‐‐‐

You see a blank worksheet. Here you can type your text: ‐‐‐

 HELP! I see different windows.

When you open a program from the *Office* suite for the first time, you will see different windows.

Only in *Word 2010*:

 **Click the radio button** ⊙ **by** U̲se Recommended Settings

 **Click** [🛡 OK]

You can choose whether you want to send information:

 **Click the radio button** ● **by** N̲o thanks

 **Click** [A̲ccept]

Select the default file format. **Office Open XML formats** is the most frequently applied format:

 **Click the radio button** ⦿ **by** **Office Open XML formats**

 **Click** [OK]

Close the welcome window that is displayed:

 **Click** ✕

1.2 The Ribbon

The ribbon has been designed to help you quickly find the commands you need to use while working with your documents. The commands have been arranged into logical groups on separate tabs. Each tab relates to a specific type of activity, such as text fonts or style, or page layout.

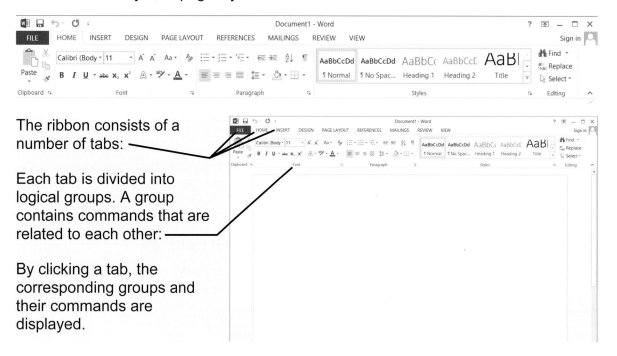

The ribbon consists of a number of tabs:

Each tab is divided into logical groups. A group contains commands that are related to each other:

By clicking a tab, the corresponding groups and their commands are displayed.

If you need more space, you can temporarily minimize the ribbon by collapsing it.

☞ **Right-click the**
    HOME **tab**

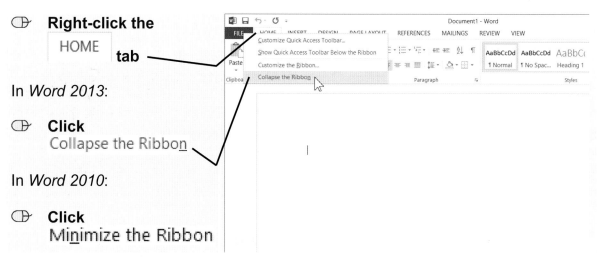

In *Word 2013*:

☞ **Click**
    Collapse the Ribbon

In *Word 2010*:

☞ **Click**
    Minimize the Ribbon

Here you see that the ribbon has almost disappeared:

Just the names of the tabs are displayed.

You can easily restore the ribbon again:

 Right-click the HOME **tab**

 Click ✓ Collapse the Ribbon (*Word 2013*) **or**

✓ Minimize the Ribbon (*Word 2010*)

Now the ribbon has regained its original size.

💡 **Tip**
Minimize the ribbon with another button
You can also minimize the ribbon with the ⌄ button in the top right-hand corner of the ribbon:

Click ⌄

HELP! The ribbon on my screen looks different.
The display of the commands in the ribbon is automatically adapted to the size of your screen, the resolution that has been selected and the size of the *Word* window. The bigger your screen and the higher the resolution, the more information the ribbon can contain.

On a large monitor – with a width of 1280 pixels – the ribbon will be fully displayed:

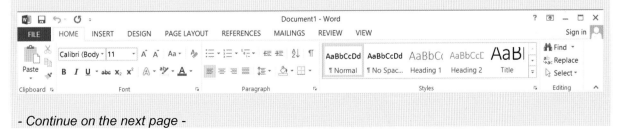

- Continue on the next page -

On a somewhat smaller monitor – with a width of 1024 pixels – the ribbon looks a bit different:

Here you see that all the groups still exist, but the view has changed and different information is displayed.

The screenshots in this book have been made on a screen with a width of 1280 pixels. If you are using a different resolution, the ribbon on your screen will look different. You may need to click a few more times, in order to display all the commands in a specific group.

1.3 Adjusting the Quick Access Toolbar

If you want to use a command on the ribbon, you usually need to click twice: first you click the tab, and then the command. This can get a little tiresome, if you use some of these commands very often. There is a special toolbar you can use that is very useful, called *Quick Access* 🔒 ↻ ↺ ⹀. By adding frequently used commands to this toolbar, you can access them with just one mouse-click.

You see the *Quick Access* toolbar at the top of the *Word* window:

You can decide which commands to add to the *Quick Access* toolbar. You can also remove a command that you do not use very often, if you want:

👆 **Click** ⹀

You will see a menu with several frequently used commands:

👆 **Click** ✓ Redo

Now you see that the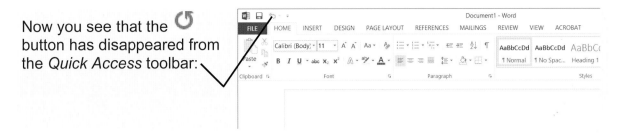
button has disappeared from
the *Quick Access* toolbar:

In the same way, you can add a button to the *Quick Access* toolbar:

☞ **Click** ▼, Open

Now the *Quick Access* toolbar looks like this: 💾 ↩ ▾ 📁 .

You can also change the location of the *Quick Access* toolbar. You can position it
below the ribbon instead of above the ribbon, for example:

☞ **Click** ▼, Show Below the Ribbon

Now the *Quick Access*
toolbar is displayed below the
ribbon:

You can revert back to the *Quick Access* toolbar's original position like this:

☞ **Click** ▼, Show Above the Ribbon

Now the *Quick Access* toolbar is displayed above the ribbon in its original position.

1.4 Adjusting the Ribbon

The ribbon can also be adapted to better fit the way you work. For instance, you can
create your own tab and group the commands you frequently use on this tab.

☞ **Click the** FILE **tab**

Click **Options**

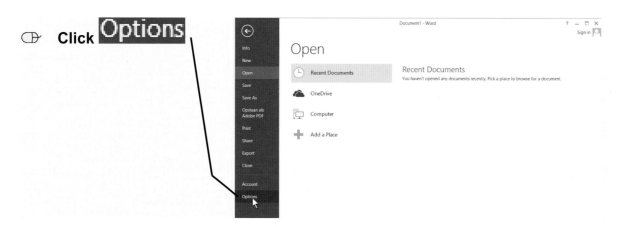

Now the *Word Options* window is opened. This is where you can change all sorts of settings for *Word*. If you would like to customize the ribbon, for instance:

Click
Customize Ribbon

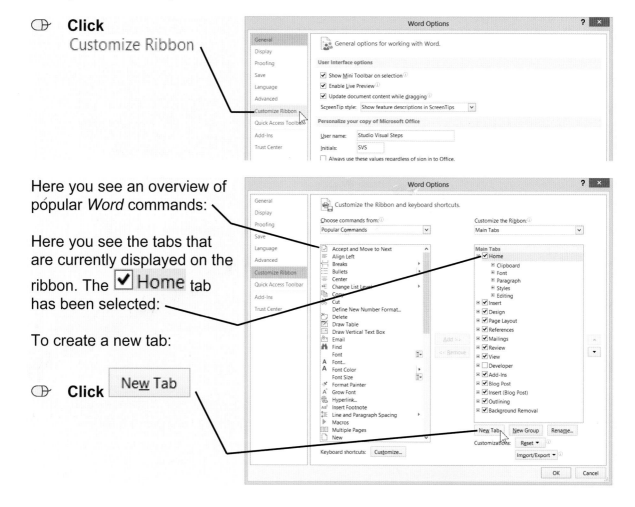

Here you see an overview of popular *Word* commands:

Here you see the tabs that are currently displayed on the ribbon. The ☑ **Home** tab has been selected:

To create a new tab:

Click New Tab

The new tab called
New Tab (Custom) has been
added below the ☑ Home
tab: ─────────

And a new group called
New Group (Custom) has
also been added to the tab:

With the Rename... button
you can change the name of
a selected tab. For now this
will not be necessary.

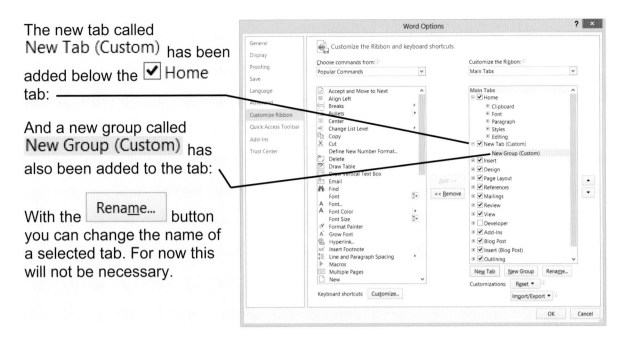

This is how you add a command to the new tab:

👉 **For example, click**
   Pictures...

👉 **Click** Add >>

👉 **Click** OK

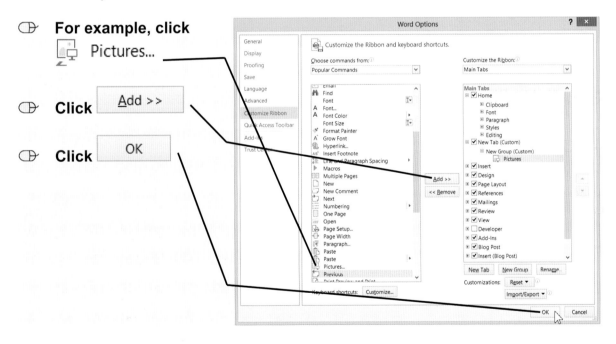

Now the new tab has been added to the ribbon:

⊕ **Click**

Here you can find the
command that you have
added to the tab:

You can just as easily delete the new tab. This is also another method for opening
the *Word Options* window:

⊕ **Right-click** New Tab

⊕ **Click** Customize the Ribbon...

This is how you delete the new tab:

⊕ **Right-click**
  New Tab (Custom)

⊕ **Click** Remove

⊕ **Click** OK

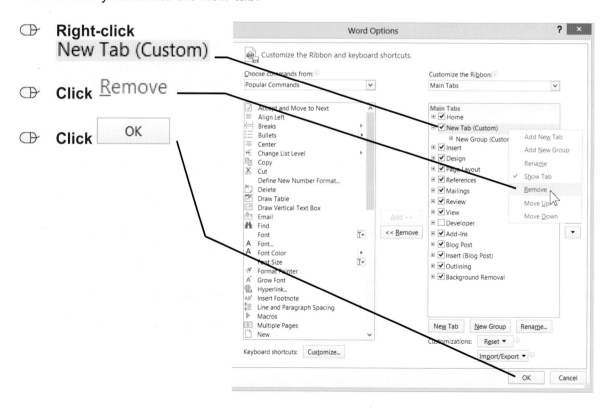

Now the ribbon has been restored to its original state.

1.5 The Ruler

When you are formatting text, it is sometimes useful to have the ruler displayed:

If you do not see the ruler, you can display it like this:

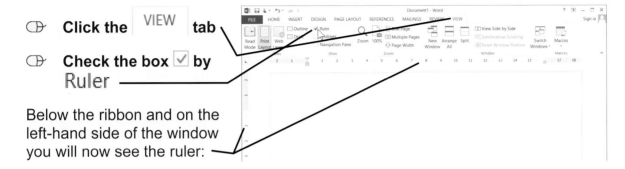

☞ **Click the** VIEW **tab**

☞ **Check the box** ☑ **by Ruler**

Below the ribbon and on the left-hand side of the window you will now see the ruler:

1.6 Line Spacing and Paragraph Spacing

In *Word 2013*, the default line space is set to *Multiple 1.08 pts*. The space between the paragraphs is set to *8 pts.* In *Word 2010*, the default line space is set to *Multiple 1.15 pts*. The space between the paragraphs is set to *10 pts*. If you would like to change these settings, you can do that like this:

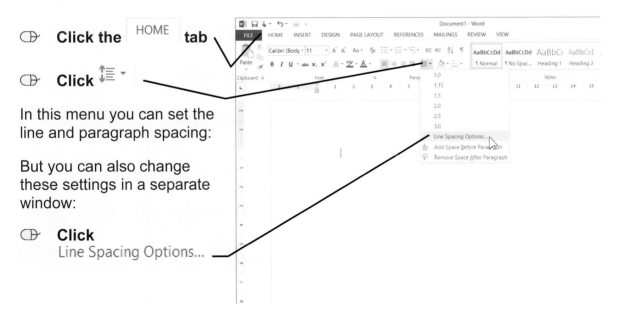

☞ **Click the** HOME **tab**

☞ **Click** ⬇☰ ▾

In this menu you can set the line and paragraph spacing:

But you can also change these settings in a separate window:

☞ **Click** Line Spacing Options...

If you do not want to set a space after a paragraph:

 By After:**, click** ⏷ **until you see** 0 pt

To change the line spacing to 1 pt:

 By Line spacing:**, select** Single

At the bottom of the window:

 Click | OK |

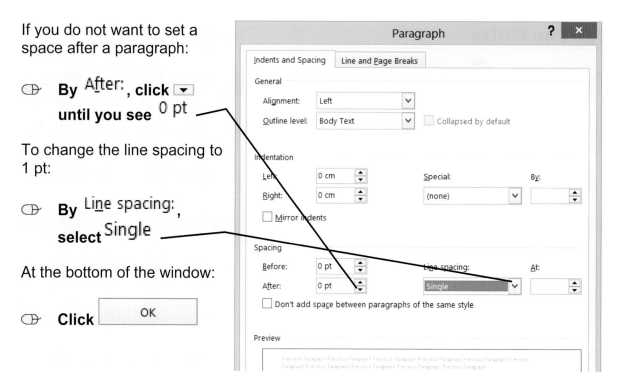

💡 **Tip**

Set the line and paragraph spacing afterwards
If you have a document that was already created and want to adjust the line and paragraph spacing in it, you can select the entire text with the key combination:

Ctrl + **A**. Then adjust the settings in the same way as explained above.

You don't need the ruler at this point. You can disable it like this:

 Click the tab | VIEW |

 Uncheck the box ☑ **by** Ruler

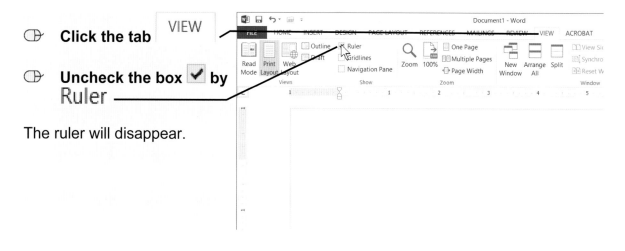

The ruler will disappear.

1.7 Formatting the Font

Selecting a font is done in the same way as many other text editors. *Word* uses the *Calibri* font by default with a size of *11 points*. If you would like to set the font to *Arial*:

⊕ **Click the tab** HOME

⊕ **By** Calibri (Body, **click**

⊕ **Click** O Arial

This is how you change the font size:

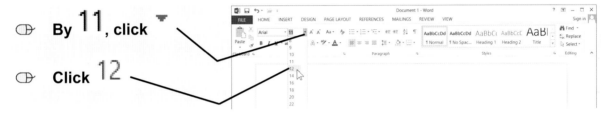

⊕ **By** 11, **click**

⊕ **Click** 12

Now the font type and size are set to *Arial, 12 pts*.

 Tip

More character styles and effects
Besides using different fonts, there are many other options you can set. You can underline a text, use boldface or italics and change the color of the letters. You can even add various effects to the text. Here you can see the various options:

1.8 Undo

You can always undo an action you just made. To demonstrate that, you can type a little bit of text:

 Type: `This is a text with fonts`

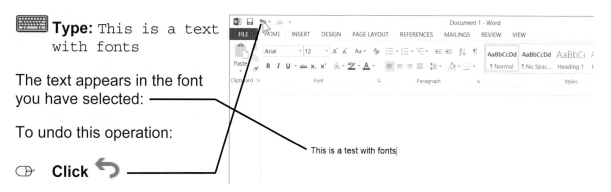

The text appears in the font you have selected:

To undo this operation:

☞ **Click** ↶

The text you just typed will be deleted.

💡 **Tip**
Undo multiple actions
You can also undo multiple actions at once. To do that:

☞ **By** ↶ **, click** ▾

In the list that appears, you can select any of the actions shown, or all of them at once. The starting point for undoing any subsequent actions will be reset.

☞ **Click the edit**

1.9 Opening a Sample Text

This is how you open a document in *Word*:

☞ **Click the** FILE **tab**

You will see a number of commands:

☞ **Click**

You will see the *Open* window. If you have downloaded the practice files from the website, they are stored in the (*My*) *Document* folder.

☞ **Open the folder named *Practice files Word*** ✂⁴

The All Word Documents option has been selected:

In this window you see all the *Word* documents.

☞ **Click the document named**

The Internet conne[

☞ **Click** Open ▼

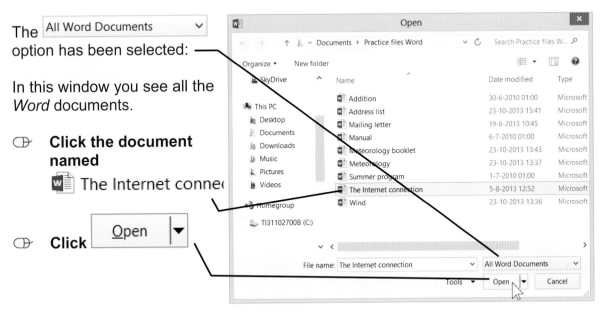

💡 **Tip**

Use the Quick Access toolbar to open a file

You can also open a file using the *Quick Access* toolbar 🖬 ↺ ▾ 📁 ▾.

By clicking the 📁 button, the *Open* window will open.

A new window is opened. You will see the document containing text:

If you open a document that has been downloaded from the Internet, it will often be displayed in *Safe mode*. This means you will only be able to read this document.

If you want to edit it:

☞ **Click** Enable Editing

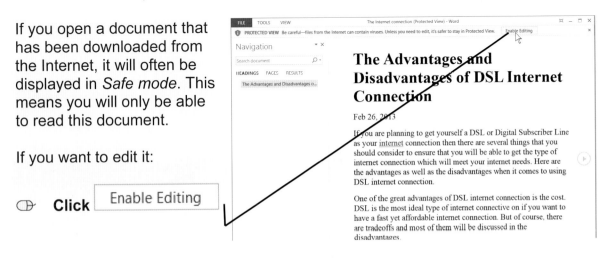

You might see a navigation pane at the left-hand side of the window:

You can close it like this:

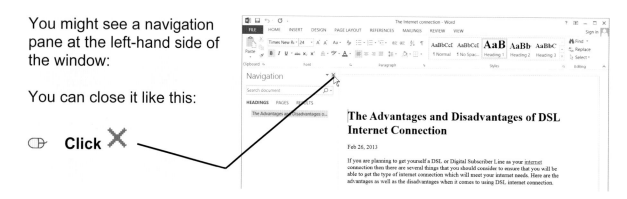

⬚ **Click** ✗

1.10 Hidden Symbols

Word contains a number of symbols that you usually do not see and which are also not printed. For instance, there are symbols that indicate the end of a paragraph and those that show where tabs have been used. When you are formatting text it can be very useful to know how to display these hidden symbols. You do that like this:

⬚ **Click** ¶

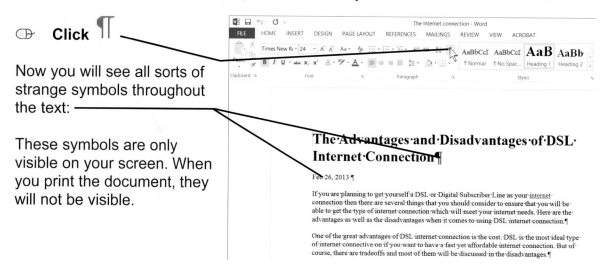

Now you will see all sorts of strange symbols throughout the text:

These symbols are only visible on your screen. When you print the document, they will not be visible.

These are the main symbols used in this book:

a blank space (a dot ·)	**Internet·Connection**
an end-of-paragraph marker	¶
an end-of-line marker	↵
the tab symbol	→

You can hide these hidden symbols again:

⬚ **Click**

1.11 Printing Text

In this section, you will practice printing a document.

 Please note:
It is important that you always check whether your printer is ready for use (turned on) before you enter a print command.

 HELP! I do not have a printer.
You can still carry out a number of the following steps. The only thing you cannot do is actually give the command to print the text.

Before you print the text, you can take a look at what the actual print will look like. This is called the *print preview*.

☞ **Click the** FILE **tab**

☞ **Click** Print

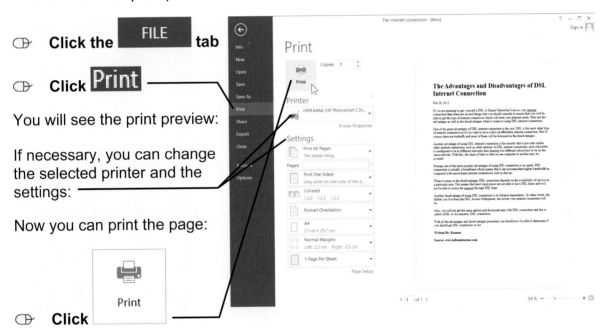

You will see the print preview:

If necessary, you can change the selected printer and the settings:

Now you can print the page:

☞ **Click**

Your text will be printed.

In *Word 2013*:

☞ **In the top left-hand corner, click**

1.12 Closing a Text

Now you can close the window containing the text:

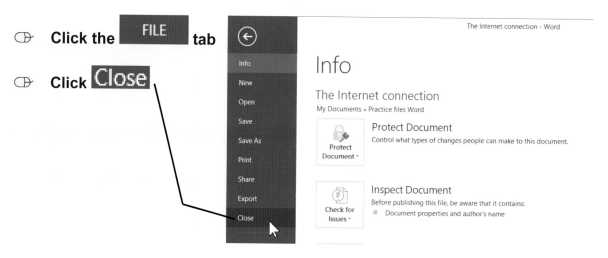

☞   **Click the FILE tab**

☞   **Click Close**

The window is closed and you will see the blank document again.

1.13 Closing Word

Now you can close *Word* too. You do that like this:

☞   **Click ✕ (*Word 2013*)**
    or ✕ (*Word 2010*)

You will be asked if you want to save the changes. For now, this will not be necessary:

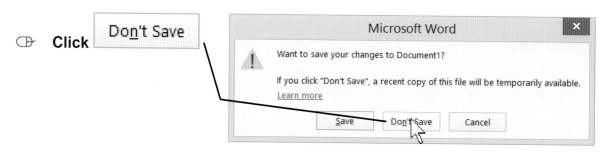

☞   **Click Don't Save**

In the following exercises you can repeat the operations explained in this chapter.

1.14 Excercises

Have you forgotten how to do something? Use the number beside the footsteps to look it up in the appendix *How Do I Do That Again?* at the end of the book.

Exercise 1: Setting the Font and Line Spacing

☞ Open *Word*. ❦[1]

☞ Set the line spacing to *Single*. ❦[5]

☞ Set the paragraph spacing to *0 points*. ❦[6]

Exercise 2: Toolbar

In this exercise you will add a command to the *Quick Access* toolbar and adjust its position.

☞ Add the *Quick Print* button to the *Quick Access* toolbar. ❦[7]

☞ Place the *Quick Access* toolbar below the ribbon. ❦[8]

☞ Place the *Quick Access* toolbar above the ribbon. ❦[8]

☞ Remove the *Quick Print* button from the *Quick Access* toolbar. ❦[9]

☞ Close the document and do not save the changes. ❦[3]

Exercise 2: Printing

In this exercise you will print a document.

☞ Open the *Meteorology* document in the *Practice files Word* folder. ❦[10]

☞ If necessary, enable editing ❦[82]

☞ Print the text. ❦[11]

☞ Close *Word*. ❦[2]

1.15 Background Information

Dictionary

Command	A specific function in *Word*.
End of line marker	A marker that is displayed at the end of a line.
End of paragraph marker	A marker that is displayed at the end of a paragraph.
Formatting symbol	A symbol that indicates a certain formatting code within the text. For example, an end marker.
Group	Part of a tab, consisting of a group of related commands.
Hidden text	Invisible text that will become visible when you display the formatting symbols.
Open window	Window that is used to open text documents.
Print preview	A view which displays the page as it will look when it is printed.
Quick Access toolbar	A toolbar that displays frequently used commands.
Ribbon	The collection of tabs, groups and commands.
Ruler	A ruler that is displayed below the ribbon. You can use it to set certain dimensions when you are formatting the text.
Space	The blank space between two words
Tab	Each tab refers to a certain type of activity in *Word*, such as writing text or formatting a page.
Temporary hyphen	A symbol that separates syllables.
Text editor	Program that is used to write and format text.

Source: Word 2013, Word 2010 and Windows Help and Support

1.16 Tips

 Tip

Keyboard shortcuts

With these keys or key combinations you can enter various commands.

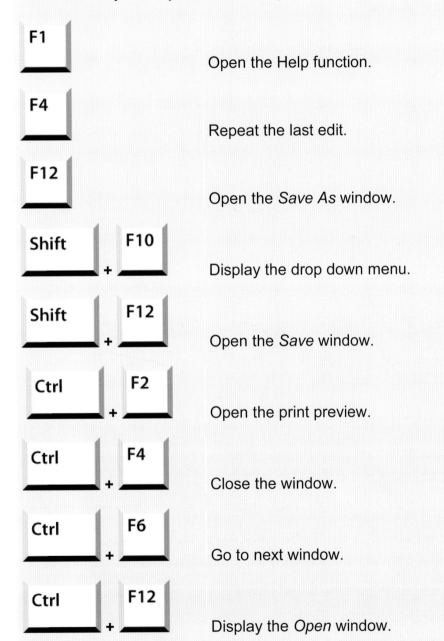

F1	Open the Help function.
F4	Repeat the last edit.
F12	Open the *Save As* window.
Shift + F10	Display the drop down menu.
Shift + F12	Open the *Save* window.
Ctrl + F2	Open the print preview.
Ctrl + F4	Close the window.
Ctrl + F6	Go to next window.
Ctrl + F12	Display the *Open* window.

- Continue on the next page -

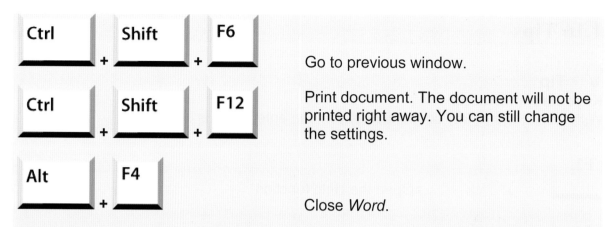

Go to previous window.

Print document. The document will not be printed right away. You can still change the settings.

Close *Word*.

Please note: some types of keyboards require you to press a special button first, in order to activate the F-keys. If necessary, consult your computer manual about how to use the function keys (F-keys).

  Tip
Add additional commands to the Quick Access toolbar
You can easily add more commands to the *Quick Access* toolbar. You do that like this:

☞ **Right-click a command**

☞ **Click**
Add to Quick Access Toolba

The command will be added.

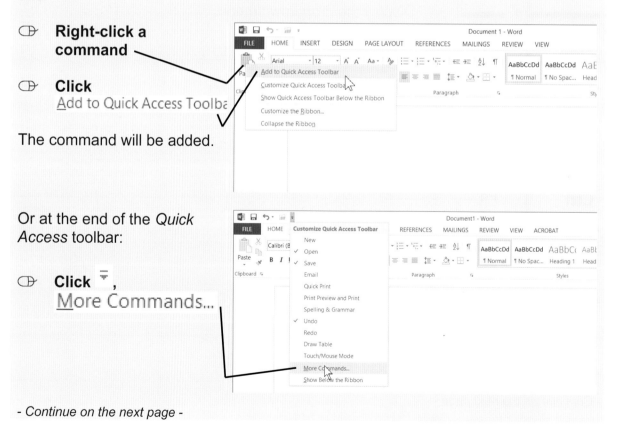

Or at the end of the *Quick Access* toolbar:

☞ **Click** ⁼ ,
More Commands...

- Continue on the next page -

☞ **By**
   Choose commands from
   select the
   All Commands
   option

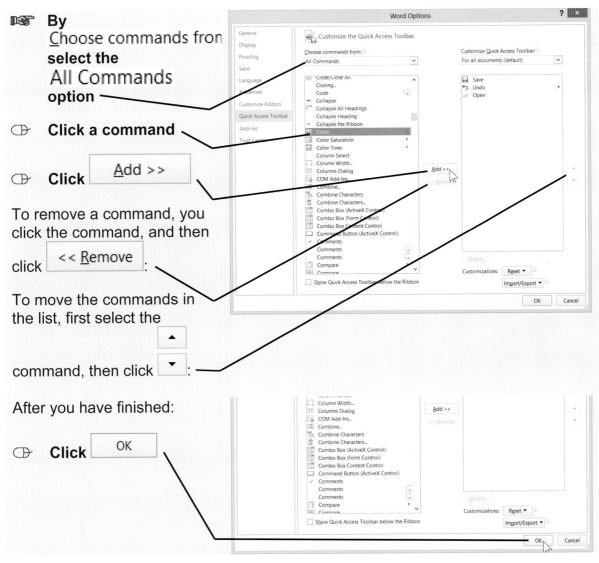

⊕ **Click a command**

⊕ **Click** [Add >>]

To remove a command, you
click the command, and then
click [<< Remove]:

To move the commands in
the list, first select the [▲]

command, then click [▼]:

After you have finished:

⊕ **Click** [OK]

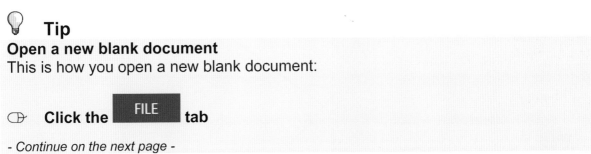

💡 **Tip**

Open a new blank document
This is how you open a new blank document:

⊕ **Click the** [FILE] **tab**

- Continue on the next page -

Click **New**

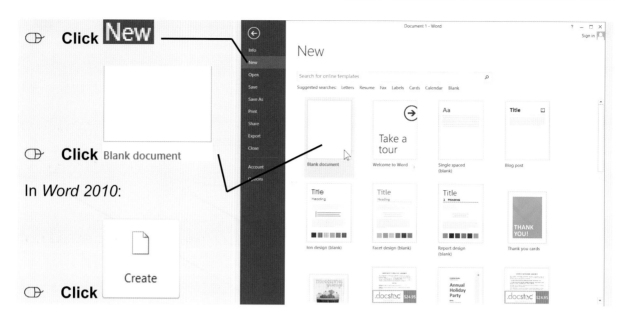

Click **Blank document**

In *Word 2010*:

Click **Create**

💡 Tip

Scale a document

If you want to print a document that has not been created for the letter size format (8.5 x 11) on letter sized paper, you can scale the document:

Click the **FILE** tab

Click **Print**

Click **1 Page Per Sheet**

Click **Scale to Paper Size**

Click **Letter 8.5" x 11"**

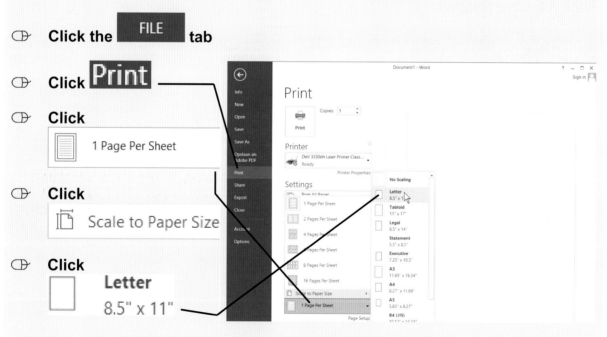

Now the page will be printed (and scaled) to the regular letter paper size (8.5 x 11). With the scaling function you can easily create smaller sample prints of larger print formats. You can print a document that eventually has to be printed, for example on an A3 printer, on your regular letter-sized printer.

2. Entering Text

When you start typing in *Word* for the very first time, you may see all sorts of strange symbols. A weird, zigzag line may appear below some of the words, and 1st will automatically be changed to '1ˢᵗ. *Word* tries to help you by checking the text as you type and applies automatic error correction when indicated.

These spelling and grammar tools can be very useful if you know how to use them and have them set up properly. If you don't think they are very useful, you can always disable them or turn them off.

In this chapter you will learn how to:

- type text;
- work with the automatic spell checker;
- work with synonyms;
- work with *AutoCorrect*;
- set up automatic text functions;
- insert symbols;
- change the spelling;
- save a document;
- work with hyphens;
- insert fixed blank spaces;
- save a document with a different name.

 Please note:

In order to perform the exercises in this chapter, you need to download the practice files from the website accompanying this book **www.visualsteps.com/word2013** and save them to the (*My*) *Documents* folder on your computer. In *Appendix B Downloading the Practice Files* you can read how to do this.

2.1 Typing Text

This book assumes you are already somewhat familiar with the keyboard. In any case, you should be able to perform the following actions:

Type letters, blank spaces, and numbers.

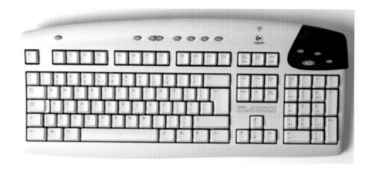

Type capital letters and punctuation marks.

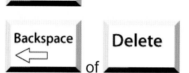

Delete a typing error (typo).

 of

Add a new line.

Type special characters and accents.

Type quotation marks.

☞ **Open** *Word* 👣[1]

2.2 Automatic Spell Checker

Word contains various built-in functions that can help you while you are typing text. Just take a look at some of them:

 Type: if you type a text,

You will see that *Word* immediately replaces the first letter with a capital letter:

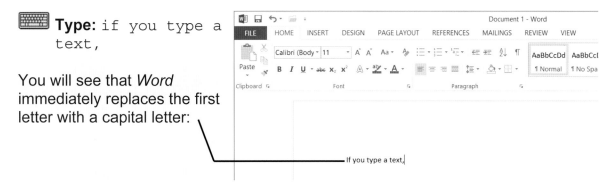

HELP! No capital letter.

If the capital letter does not appear on your screen, *Word's* automatic correction option may have been disabled in your program. In *section 2.5 Setting Up the Automatic Functions* you can read how to adjust these settings.

Word immediately checks the text as you type for spelling errors. Just try it:

Type a blank space

Type: than it will be cheked right away.

Press Enter

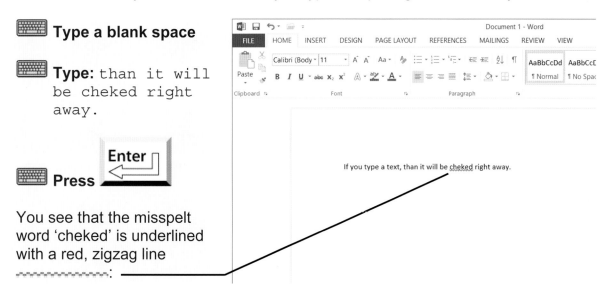

You see that the misspelt word 'cheked' is underlined with a red, zigzag line:

Note that not all errors will be recognized at once. For example, 'than' (instead of 'then') is not recognized. This is because 'than' is also a regular English word.

HELP! No spell checker.

If you do not see the red, zigzag line below 'cheked', *Word's* automatic correction option may have been disabled in your program. For the moment, this does not matter. You can just continue. More about the spell checker comes a little later on.

 Tip

No capital letter at the beginning?
Do you want the word to begin with a lower case letter, instead of a capital letter? Then you can simply delete this capital letter and replace it by a lower case letter.

2.3 Synonyms

Word can also help you write an adequate text. The list of synonyms in *Word*, for example, can be very useful in helping you find alternatives for certain words.

 Type: London is a renowned

☞ **Right-click the word 'renowned'**

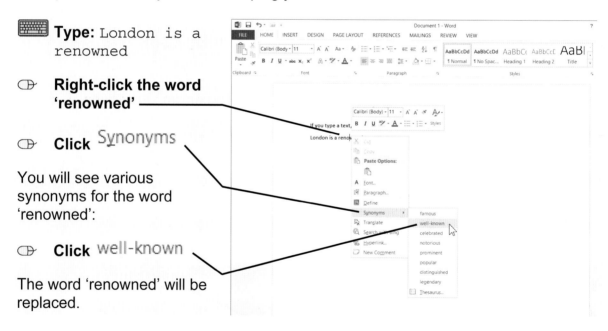

☞ **Click** Synonyms

You will see various synonyms for the word 'renowned':

☞ **Click** well-known

The word 'renowned' will be replaced.

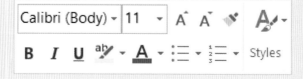 **Please note:**

After you have right-clicked, you will see two windows:

The smallest window contains a number of frequently used commands on the ribbon.

- Continue on the next page -

The larger window includes commands for copying and pasting, changing the font and finding synonyms:

✂ Cut

▤ Copy

📋 **Paste Options:**

📋

A Font...

▤ Paragraph...

🔍 Define

Synonyms ▸

🔤 Translate

🌐 Search with Bing

🌐 Hyperlink...

🗨 New Comment

2.4 AutoCorrect

Word has a function that tries to correct typos and misspelled words at once. Just give it a try:

👉 **Place the cursor next to the word 'well-known'** ────

⌨ **Type a blank space**

⌨ **Type:** `city`

⌨ **Type a blank space**

Now you can insert a typing error:

⌨ **Type:** `ont he`

⌨ **Type a blank space**

You will see that 'ont he' is corrected and changed into 'on the': ────

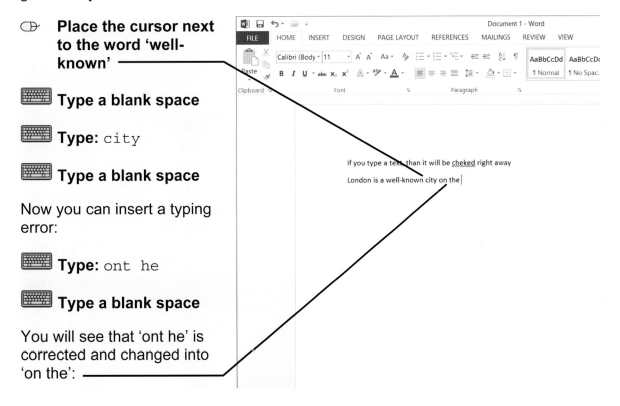

If you type a text, than it will be cheked right away

London is a well-known city on the

Sometimes, *Word* will add typographical elements as well. Just try this:

Type: 1 / 2

Type a blank space

Now you see that '1/2' is corrected, and instead the ½ symbol appears:

Not everyone is in favor of these automatic functions. It may seem like you have no control over your own text as you write. We will discuss this in the next section.

2.5 Setting Up the Automatic Functions

You can change the settings of the automatic functions and adapt them to suit your own preferences. It is a good idea to take a look at the automatic functions in *Word* beforehand. This may stop you from becoming irritated, when you get the feeling that *Word* is not behaving in the manner that you would like.

☞ **Click the** FILE **tab, and then** Options

☞ **Click** Proofing

Here you see the settings *Word* uses when it performs text correction:

☞ **Click**
AutoCorrect Options...

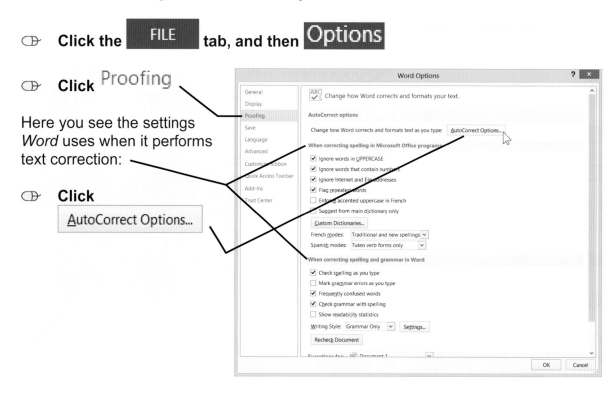

Now you will see this window:

In the case of two initial capitals: the second letter will be displayed in lower case:

The first letter of each sentence is capitalized automatically:

Certain words will be replaced by other words, taken from the list:

 Take a look at the list of combinations

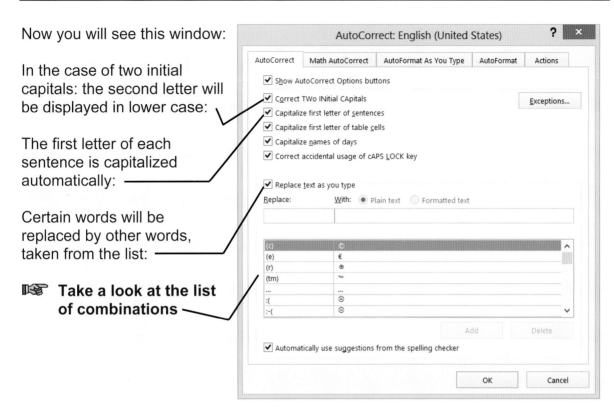

💡 **Tip**

Check spelling while typing

On the AutoCorrect tab at the bottom, you will see the option labeled ☑ Automatically use suggestions from the spelling checker. This function will automatically replace typing errors with words from the spelling checker dictionary. If you do not think this is useful, you can disable this function.

In this window you can set up the automatic formatting of certain symbols as well:

☞ **Click the**

AutoFormat **tab**

Here you see the substitutions that are applied as you type. These include ½ and 1st:

☞ **Change the settings, if you wish**

You can close this window now.

☞ **Click** OK

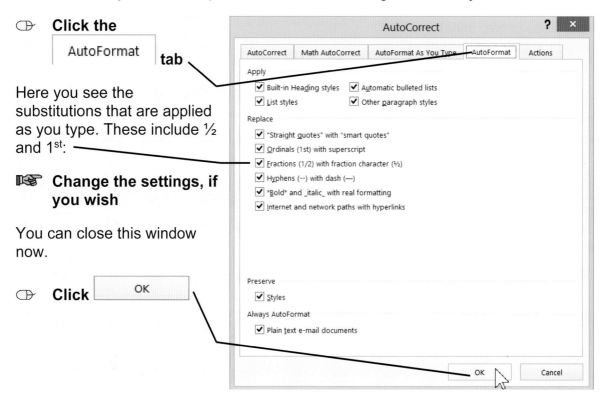

In the *Word Options* windows:

☞ **Click** OK

2.6 Inserting Symbols

There is another way to enter various symbols in your text. You can access it by using the ribbon:

☞ **Click the** INSERT **tab**

☞ **Click** Ω Symbol ▾

You will see various symbols that can be inserted into the text:

☞ **For example, click** ©

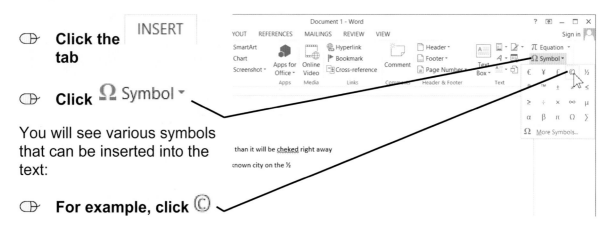

The copyright symbol has been inserted into the text. There are lots of other symbols you can use:

☞ **Click** Ω Symbol ▾, Ω More Symbols...

Font: has been set to (normal text):

You see many other symbols you can insert into the text:

☞ **For instance, click** £

☞ **Click** Insert

Please note: you might see other symbols than the symbols in this example.

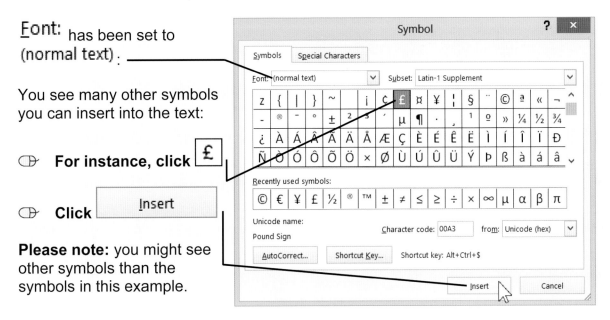

The symbol is inserted. You can use the same window to select multiple symbols or special characters at once:

☞ **Click the** Special Characters **tab**

☞ **Click** § Section

☞ **Click** Insert

The symbol is inserted.

☞ **Click** Close

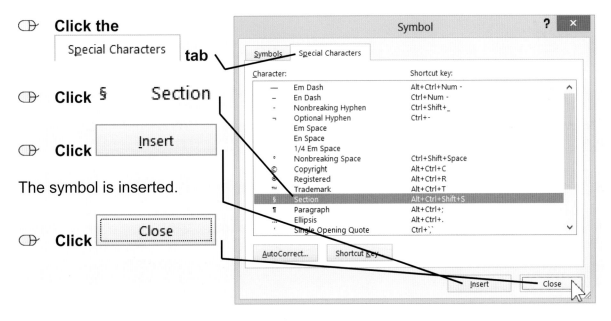

2.7 Using Capitals

There is another method you can use to convert a lower case letter to a capital letter. Give it a try:

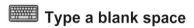 **Type a blank space**

 Type: thames

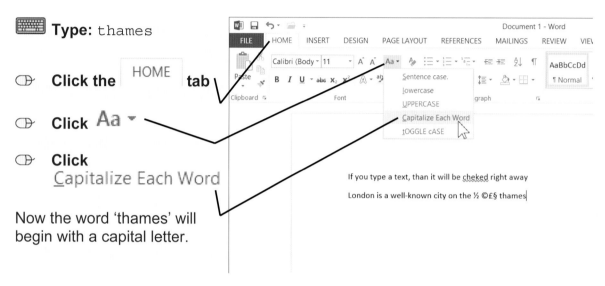

⊕ **Click the** HOME **tab**

⊕ **Click** Aa ▾

⊕ **Click**
Capitalize Each Word

Now the word 'thames' will begin with a capital letter.

2.8 Changing the Spelling

Before you close your document, you can correct the spelling error in the word 'cheked'. Here is how you do that.

⊕ **Right-click the word 'cheked'**

You will see a list of suggestions:

⊕ **Click** checked

Now the word 'cheked' has been replaced by 'checked'.

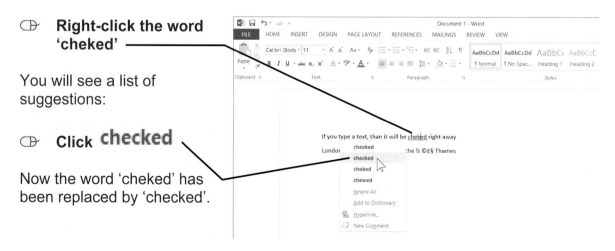

2.9 Saving a Document

This is how you save a document:

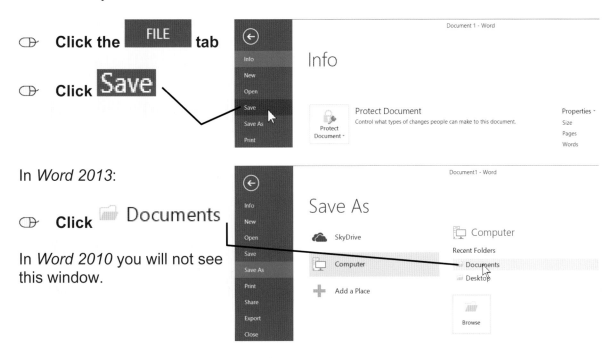

Click the FILE **tab**

Click Save

In *Word 2013*:

Click Documents

In *Word 2010* you will not see this window.

Word always enters a name for a file. This name consists of the first words in the text. You can see this name in the box next to File name:. You can change this name.

Type: First text

The file is saved in the (*My*) *Documents* folder:

The file will be saved as a Word Document. It can be opened and edited in *Word 2013, 2010* and *Word 2007*:

Click Save

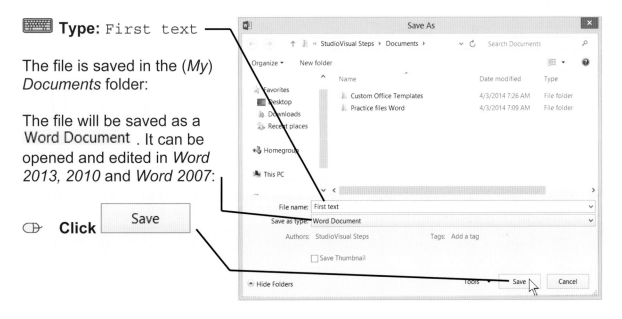

HELP! My window looks different.

You may you see a smaller window like the one shown here. To enlarge the window:

⊕ **Click**

⊙ **▼ Browse Folders**

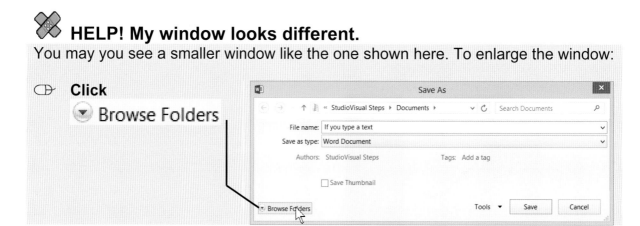

Now the text is stored on your computer. You can open the document later on, if you want to continue working on it.

HELP! I see another window.

Do you see this window? This means that a document with the same name already exists. If you are sure you want to replace the existing document with the current one you have been working on, you can replace it now.

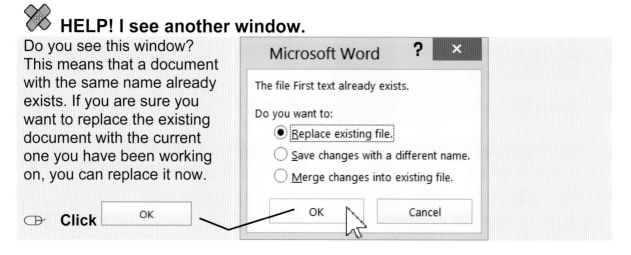

⊕ **Click** [OK]

In the *Background Information* at the end of this chapter you can find additional information about saving files.

2.10 Hyphens

As you type text, you can allow *Word* to split a longer word that occurs at the end of a line. In this way the lines will be neatly aligned and evenly spaced. You can see how this works with one of the practice files from the *Practice files Word* folder:

☞ **Open the document called** 📄 Meteorology 👣10

The document is opened in a new window. You can close the window with the *First text* document:

☞ **Close the *First text* document** 👣³

Now you can let *Word* split the words in this text. Here is how you do that:

👉 **If necessary, click** Enable Editing

👉 **Click the** PAGE LAYOUT **tab**

👉 **Click** bc̲ᵃ⁻ Hyphenation ▾

👉 **Click** bc̲ᵃ⁻ Hyphenation Options.

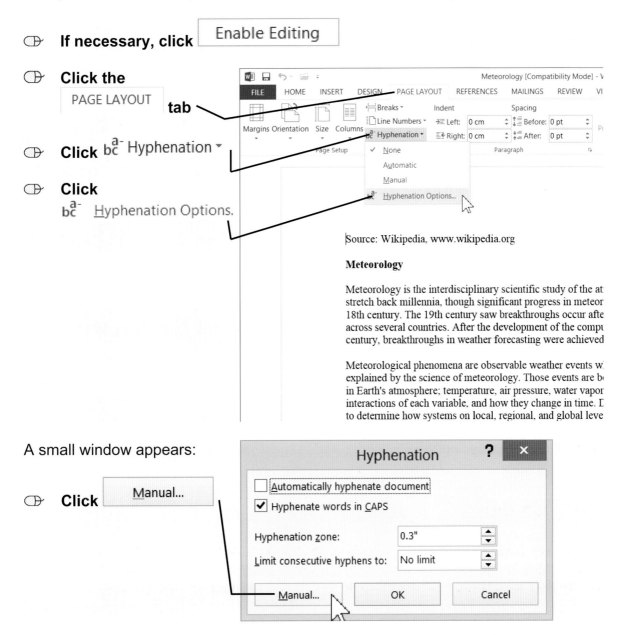

A small window appears:

👉 **Click** Manual...

Word will start looking for words in the text that can be split (hyphenated). The first word that qualifies is 'explained'.

A black rectangle is placed where the hyphen will occur. This is the preferred spot to split the word. If the words contain more than two syllables, you can select a different spot by clicking it. Automatically hyphenating words will not be perfect all the time, but if you use this method, you can decide for yourself exactly where the words will be split.

☞ **Click**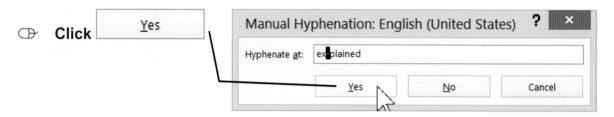

The next suggestion is less pretty: 'de-ter-mine'. You can choose not to hyphenate this word:

☞ **Click**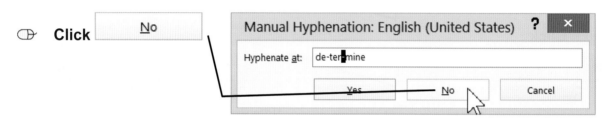

You do not need to go through all the hyphenations in the document:

☞ **Click**

 Tip
Temporary hyphens
Word always inserts so-called *temporary hyphens*. If, in due course and after several edits, the full word fits on the line again, these hyphens are automatically removed.

This will not happen when you have inserted a hyphen with the 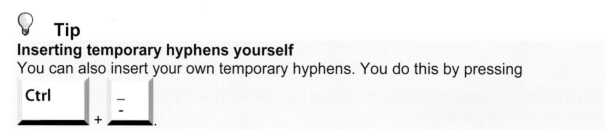 key.
This is a so-called *hard hyphen* that will remain visible in the text even if the full word fits on the line again.

 Tip
Inserting temporary hyphens yourself
You can also insert your own temporary hyphens. You do this by pressing

Ctrl ⊞ + ⊟ .

Tip

Fixed hyphens

Word knows yet another type of hyphen, the so-called *fixed hyphen*. This is a hyphen that is not perceived as a hyphen.

For example, the hyphen in the word *re-sign*. By using a fixed hyphen you can prevent the program from splitting the word after the *re-* in *re-sign*. You can insert a

fixed hyphen by pressing 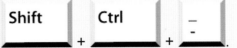.

 Tip

Delete hyphens

You can delete temporary or fixed hyphens with the  key.

2.11 Fixed spaces

A fixed space is a special character you can use to keep two words together at all times. For instance, a name such as John Paul.

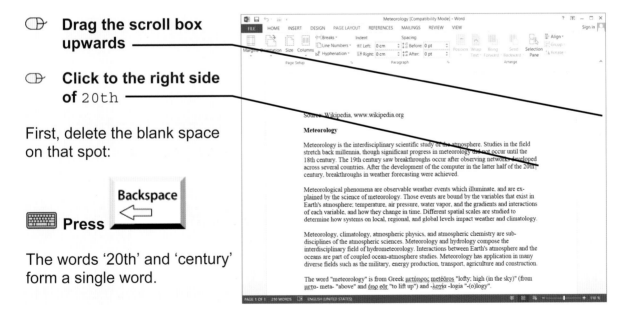

☞ **Drag the scroll box upwards**

☞ **Click to the right side of** `20th`

First, delete the blank space on that spot:

⌨ **Press** Backspace

The words '20th' and 'century' form a single word.

Now you can insert the fixed space:

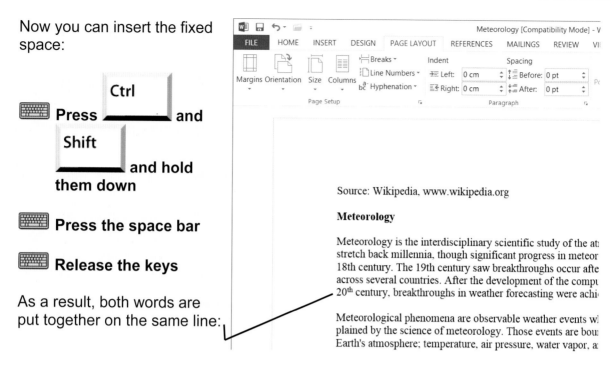

Press *Ctrl* **and** *Shift* **and hold them down**

Press the space bar

Release the keys

As a result, both words are put together on the same line:

In this way you can keep two or more words together on the same line.

2.12 Saving a Document with Save As

By now you have applied a few edits to the *Meteorology* document.
You can also save a document with a different name, or in another file format. When you do this, the original file will remain unchanged while you also save the edited file. Here is how you do that:

Click the FILE **tab, and then** **Save As**

You will see the *Save As* window. You can save the file in the (*My*) *Documents* folder:

In *Word 2013*:

Click Documents

In *Word 2010* you will not see this window.

You can save the file as a Word 97-2003 document. These type of files can also be opened in many other text editing programs.

☞ **If necessary, by** 🖥 **This PC** **, click** ▷

☞ **If necessary, click** 🚪 Documents ——

☞ **By** Save as type: **, click** Word Document

☞ **Click** Word 97-2003 Document

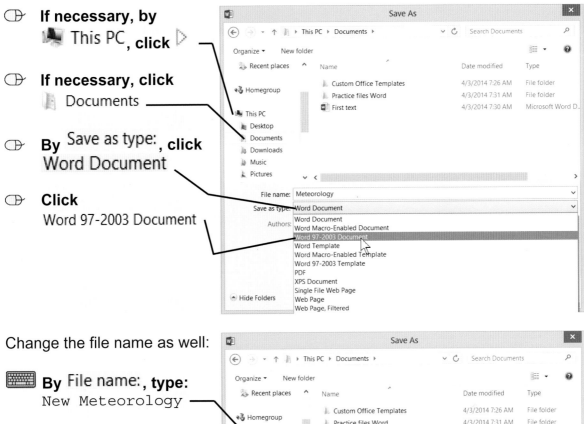

Change the file name as well:

⌨ **By** File name: **, type:** New Meteorology

☞ **Click** [Save]

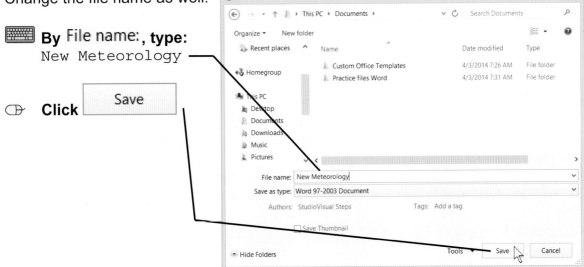

Close *Word*:

☞ **Close *Word*** 👣2

In the following exercises you can practice what you have just learned.

2.13 Exercises

Have you forgotten how to do something? Use the number beside the footsteps to look it up in the appendix *How Do I Do That Again?* at the end of the book.

Exercise 1: Inserting Symbols

In this exercise you will be inserting symbols.

☞ Open *Word*. 🦶¹

☞ Open the document called *Wind* from the *Practice files Word* folder. 🦶¹⁰

☞ If necessary, enable editing. 🦶⁸²

☞ Insert the ® symbol after the title. 🦶¹²

Exercise 2: Hyphenation

In this exercise you will practice hyphenating words in the *Wind* document.

☞ Start the manual hyphenation function. 🦶¹³

☞ Add a hyphen after 'parti' in 'particles'. 🦶¹⁴

☞ Do not add a hyphen to 'differential'. 🦶¹⁴

☞ Stop the hyphenation function. 🦶¹⁴

Exercise 3: Save As

☞ Save the *Wind* document as a Word 97-2003 document in the *(My) Documents* folder. 🦶¹⁶

☞ Close *Word*. 🦶²

2.14 Background Information

Dictionary

AutoCorrect	A function that tries to correct typing errors right away using the words from the program's built-in dictionary.
Automatic spell checker	A function that immediately checks the text you have typed for spelling errors, by using the program's built-in checklist.
Ctrl key	CTRL is short for Control. A key that is often used in combination with other keys, in order to carry out certain commands or functions.
Fixed hyphen	The type of hyphen that is not considered a hyphen. This type of hyphen prevents a word such as 'e-mail' from being split.
Fixed space	A space you use if you absolutely want to keep two words together.
Hard hyphen	A hard hyphen always remains visible in the text, even if the word fits on the same line.
Save	Command for saving a document.
Save as	Command for saving an existing document using a different name.
Shift key	With this key you can type capital letters and symbols that appear on the key above a letter. Is often used in combination with another key.
Synonym	A word that has the same meaning.
Temporary hyphen	A hyphen added by *Word*; it disappears automatically after edits in the text cause the whole word to fit on the same line again.
Typographical elements	Symbols, such as © and ®.

Source: Word 2013, Word 2010 and Windows Help and Support

New file format for Word 2013, 2010 and 2007

If you are familiar with previous *Word* versions, you will know that *Word* files could be identified by their .DOC extension, for example, *Myfile.doc*. In *Word 2013* (and also in *Word 2010* and *2007*) the extension .DOC is no longer used. The extension now used is called .DOCX. According to *Microsoft*, the manufacturer of *Word*, the new file format has several advantages.

For instance, the files are automatically compressed, which means they take up less storage space on your computer (or other storage medium). When you open a file, it is extracted. When you save a file, it is automatically compressed again. Because various parts of a file are stored separately, DOCX files can easily be repaired.

Saving a file in the new format is automatic:

File name:		∨
Save as type:	Word Document	∨

But it is still possible to save a file in the file format used by older versions of *Word*. This is useful when you want to send a *Word* file to someone who does not yet use *Word 2013, 2010* or *2007*.

Save as an older Word 97-2003-document:

File name:		∨
Save as type:	Word Document	∨
Authors:	Word Document	
	Word Macro-Enabled Document	
	Word 97-2003 Document	

The other way round, it is also possible to open documents that have been created in an older version of *Word* or other text editing programs in *Word 2013, 2010* and *2007*. You can open, edit and save these files in the older file format. When you open the file, *Word 2013, 2010* or *2007* will switch to compatibility mode: [Compatibility Mode] - Word. Compatible means 'suitable for use'. It is handy that the *Word 2013, 2010* and *2007* versions remain 'downward compatible' and are capable of using older file formats.

If you have used certain functions or options in the file that only exist in *Word 2013, 2010* or *2007*, but not in previous versions of *Word* or other text editing programs, you will see a warning. If you would save these types of files in the older file format you would lose part of the content. You can still decide to save the file in the new format, if you want.

If you want to open a DOCX file on a computer where *Word 2003* is installed, you need to have installed a special plugin program which allows you to open DOCX files. In other text editing programs this might als be the case. You can download this plugin from the Microsoft website: www.microsoft.com

Save DOC files in Word 2013 or Word 2010 as DOCX

When you are working with DOC files you will notice that certain options on the ribbon are not available. For example, the ribbon looks different when you are working with images. In the examples below you can see what the differences are:

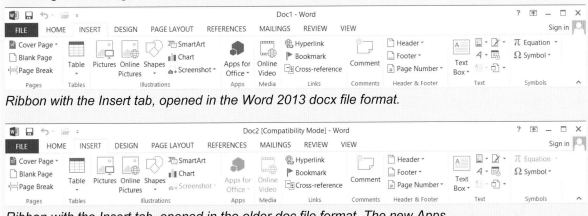

Ribbon with the Insert tab, opened in the Word 2013 docx file format.

Ribbon with the Insert tab, opened in the older doc file format. The new Apps for Office option is not available here, among other items.

Word 2013 or *Word 2010* will automatically display a message if you want to save a file in which you have used certain *Word 2013* or *Word 2010* options, as a DOC *Word* document:

Then you can decide what you want to do with this document.

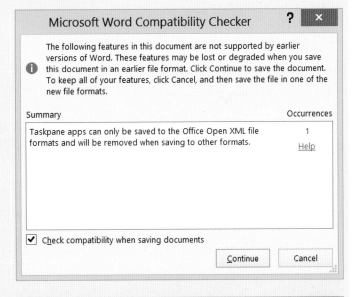

The other way round, you will also see a message when you open, edit, or save a DOC document. Then *Word 2013* or *Word 2010* will ask you if you want to update the document to the most recent file format.

2.15 Tips

  Tip

Spell checker in other languages
In the standard *Word* version, the spelling is checked by default in English. But you can also choose to correct the spelling in French or Spanish, for instance. This is how you set up the French spelling check:

☞ **Click the** REVIEW **tab**

☞ **Click** Language

☞ **Click**
    Set Proofing Language...

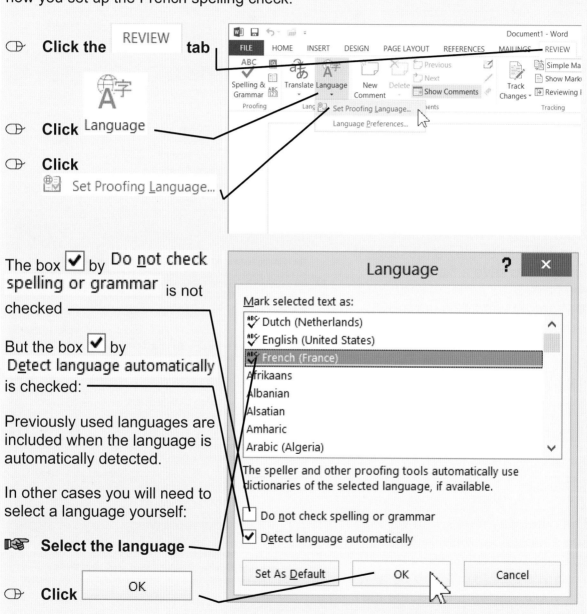

The box ✔ by Do **not** check spelling or grammar is not checked

But the box ✔ by Detect language automatically is checked:

Previously used languages are included when the language is automatically detected.

In other cases you will need to select a language yourself:

☞ **Select the language**

☞ **Click** OK

- Continue on the next page -

 **Type a French text**

While you are typing, the text will automatically be checked in the French language:

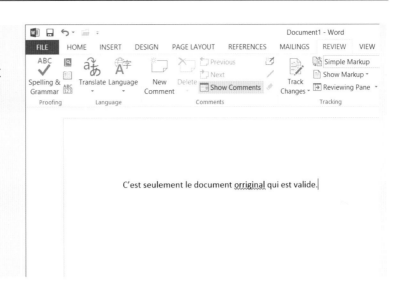

💡 **Tip**
Display hyphens and fixed spaces

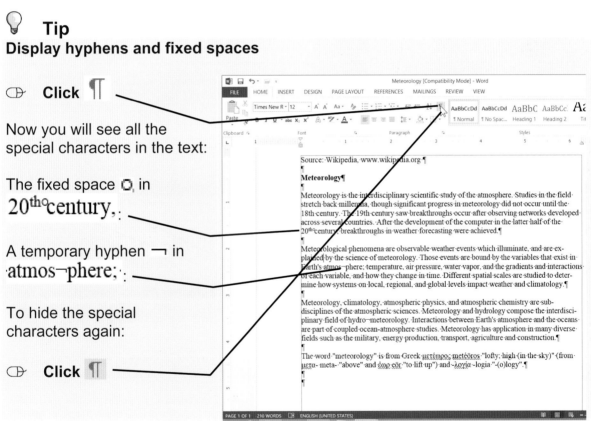

☞ **Click** ¶

Now you will see all the special characters in the text:

The fixed space ⬚ in
20ᵗʰ century,

A temporary hyphen ¬ in
atmos¬phere;

To hide the special characters again:

☞ **Click** ¶

Tip

Open previous versions

While you are working on a file, the AutoRecover function will automatically save copies of your document(s). *Word* saves a copy of the document at regular, set intervals. You can only recover this version while you are still editing the document. Afterwards you cannot recover these AutoRecovery documents in this way.

☞ **Click the** FILE **tab**

☞ **If necessary, click** Info

☞ **By** Versions, **click the desired version**

The previous version of the document is opened:

Now you can Compare the documents to each other,

or Restore the previous version:

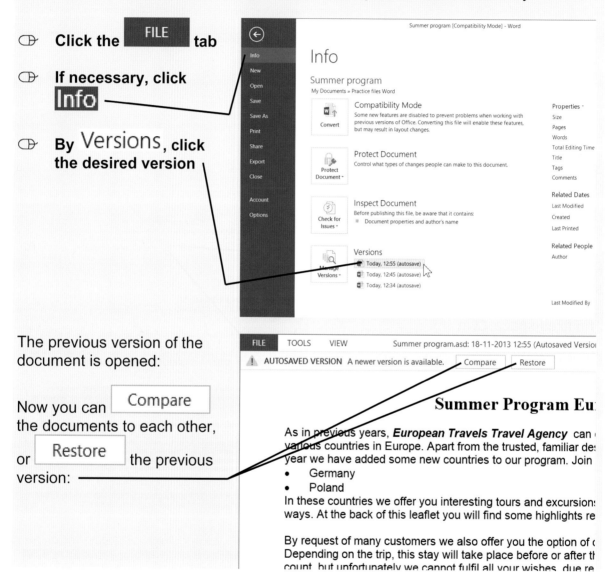

Tip

Open unsaved documents

In *Word* you can even retrieve documents you have not saved. You do that like this:

☞ **Click the** FILE **tab**

☞ **Click** Info

☞ **Click** Manage Versions ▾

☞ **Click** Recover Unsaved Docu... Browse recent unsaved

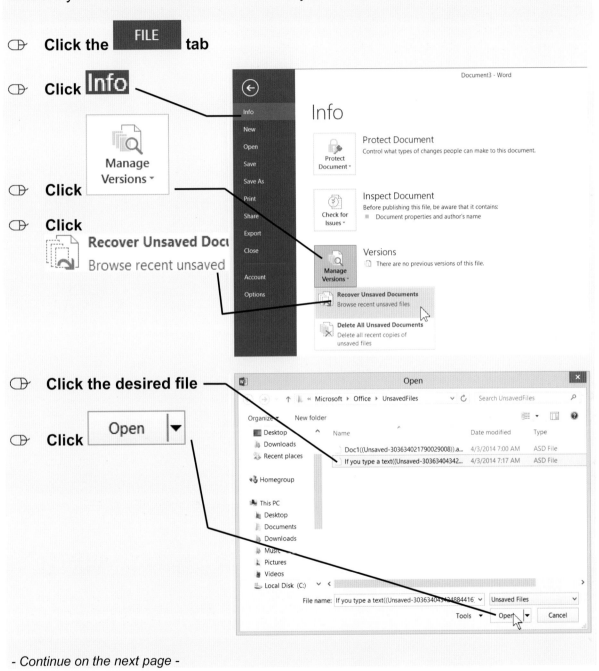

☞ **Click the desired file**

☞ **Click** Open ▾

- Continue on the next page -

You will see the document:

Now you can save the
document by clicking

Save As :

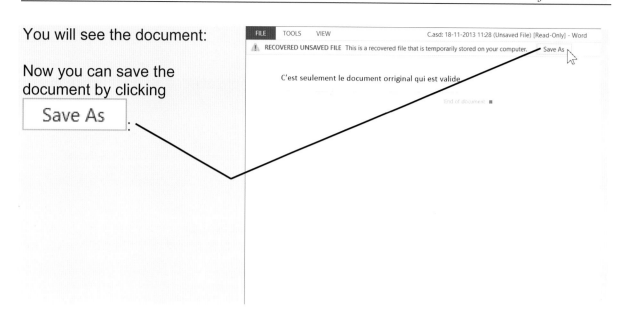

3. Formatting Documents

The document *format* is the (highest) level of formatting for a *Word* document. It is important to select an attractive font and arrange the text in a balanced manner. A good page *layout* will ensure that your documents are easy and pleasant to read.

When you create a document you will sometimes want to emphasize a particular text or phrase by indenting it or using a list. You can achieve this type of formatting easily in *Word* using tabs and bullets. You can also align these elements in several different ways.

Another important element to consider in page layout is deciding how the text and white space will be distributed across the page. Margins, for example will determine the amount of blank space between the border of the paper and the text. Margins not only make the text look good on paper, but are also important if you want to bind the pages.

To make it easier to read larger documents, you can add page numbers, headers and footers.
These are just a few of the formatting options available in *Word* that can be modified and adjusted as you create and edit your own documents.

In this chapter you will learn how to:

- align text with tab stops;
- move tab stops;
- create lists;
- insert text files;
- set page breaks;
- set the page orientation to portrait or landscape;
- select the paper size;
- set margins;
- add a cover page;
- add headers and footers;
- insert page numbers;
- use styles;
- copy formatting.

3.1 Aligning Text with Tabs

To format a summary or list in a document, you can use the **Tab** key on your keyboard. With this key you can place the text on a fixed spot on the line. Where the tabs are placed depends on the tab stops.

In a regular *Word* document, the default tabs are set every half inch. In *Word 2010* you can see them on the ruler. They are not visible in *Word 2013*.

☞ **Open** *Word* ✐¹

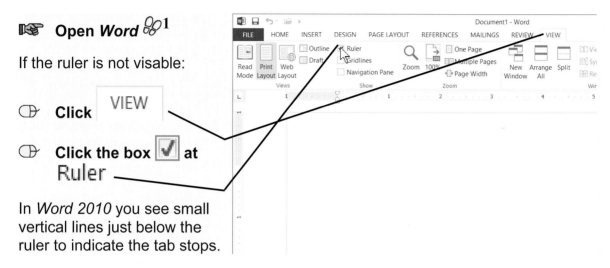

If the ruler is not visable:

🖰   **Click** VIEW

🖰   **Click the box** ☑ **at** Ruler

In *Word 2010* you see small vertical lines just below the ruler to indicate the tab stops.

While you are working through this chapter it is useful to display the text boundaries. You can do that like this:

🖰   **Click the** FILE **tab**

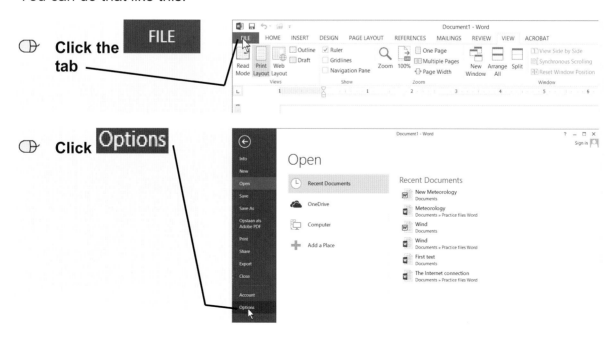

🖰   **Click** Options

You will see the *Options* window for *Word*:

☞ **Click** Advanced

☞ **Drag the scroll box downwards**

By
Show document content :

☞ **Check the box** ☑ **by**
Show te**x**t boundaries

☞ **Click** OK

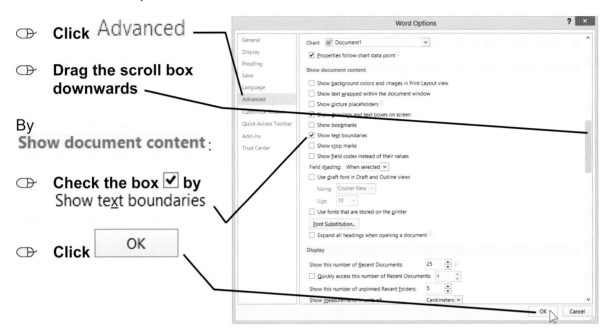

In *Word 2013* you will see a dotted line surrounding the text block. In *Word 2010* a dotted line surrounds the margins.

Now let's take a look at the default tab settings:

☞ **Click the** HOME
tab

☞ **By** Paragraph ,
click 🗗

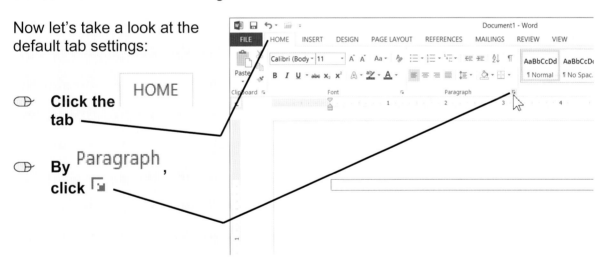

Is the box next to **After:** set to **0 pt**?

Is the line spacing set to **Single**?

If not:

☞ **Set the distance by After: to 0 pt** 👣6

☞ **Set the line spacing to Single** 👣5

To open the *Tabs* window:

☞ **Click** | Tabs... |

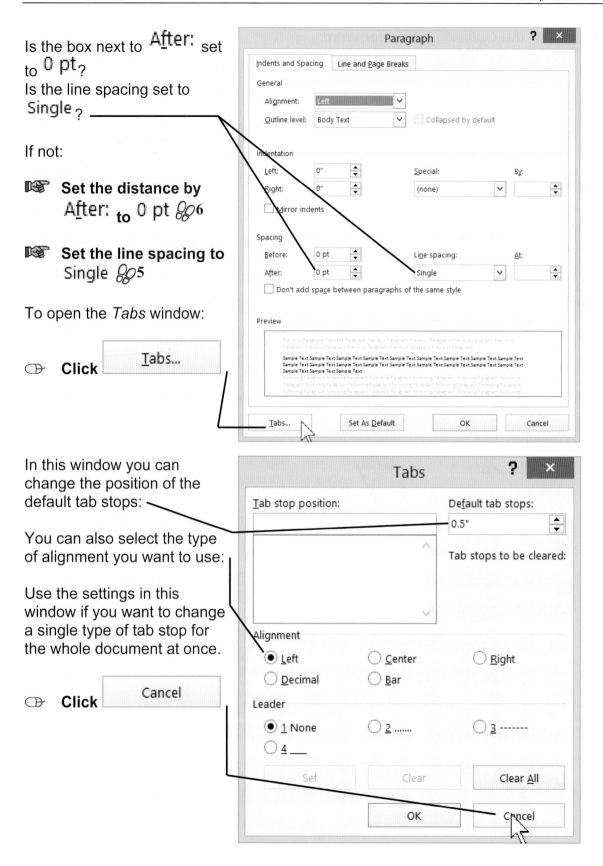

In this window you can change the position of the default tab stops:

You can also select the type of alignment you want to use:

Use the settings in this window if you want to change a single type of tab stop for the whole document at once.

☞ **Click** | Cancel |

Tip
Open the Tabs window
You can also open the *Tabs* window by double-clicking a tab on the ruler.

If you want to apply multiple types of tabs to a paragraph, you need to use a different method of setting the tabs. There are different types of tabs available in *Word*:

- ⌐ *left alignment*: this tab stop is used to position text in columns one below the other, for example, in a list of addresses;

- ⊥ *center tab*: with this tab stop you can put text in the center, above a summary, outline, column, etc.;

- ⌐ *right alignment*: this tab stop is mainly used to align numbers and place them in a straight line below each other;

- ⊥ *decimal tab*: is used to align amounts of money or other numbers that contain a decimal point (dot). It lines up all the decimal points with each other, independent of the number of digits entered;

- I *line tab*: with this tab stop you can place a vertical line within a text line.

Here you can see which type of tab is active: ⸻

Take a look at the other tabs:

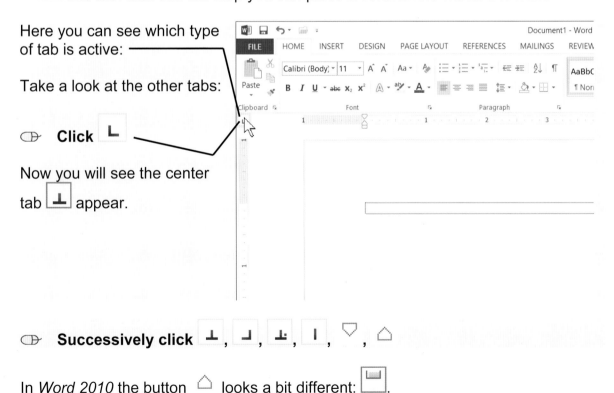

☞ **Click** ⌐

Now you will see the center tab ⊥ appear.

☞ **Successively click** ⊥ , ⌐ , ⊥ , I , ▽ , △

In *Word 2010* the button △ looks a bit different: ⊡ .

With the last two icons in this row you can do the following things:

- ▽ indent the first line of the paragraph;

- △ hanging indent; here, the first line of the paragraph is positioned against the margin, and the next lines are indented.

These options are related to the tab stops and are automatically applied to the lines of a paragraph.

You will see the left tab again. If you want to use tabs you will need to set the tab stop first. This is the place in the document where the text will be aligned. The next exercise will give you some practice setting and using tabs.

Before you start, change the font to *Arial*:

☞ **Set the font to *Arial*** ✂17

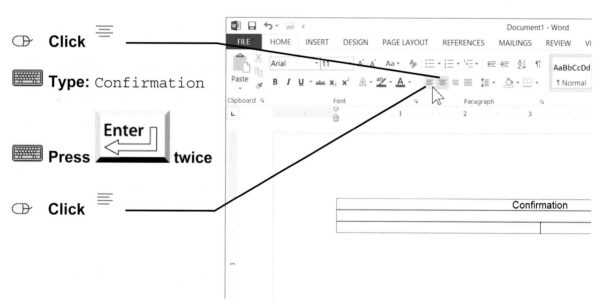

☞ **Click** ≡ ──────

⌨ **Type:** Confirmation

⌨ **Press** ⬅Enter **twice**

☞ **Click** ≡ ──────

In *Word* 2013, the individual lines are displayed in the text block. This is not the case in *Word 2010*.

We will be making a confirmation summary sheet. It needs the following columns:
- name
- first name initials
- age
- price

Start by setting a left aligned tab stop for the names column:

☞ **Click just below** 1

Make sure the pointer looks like this ⇖, while you are clicking:

Now the **L** is placed below the 1:

⌨ **Press** Tab

⌨ **Type:** Fisher

☞ **Click just below** 3

⌨ **Press** Tab

⌨ **Type:** P.

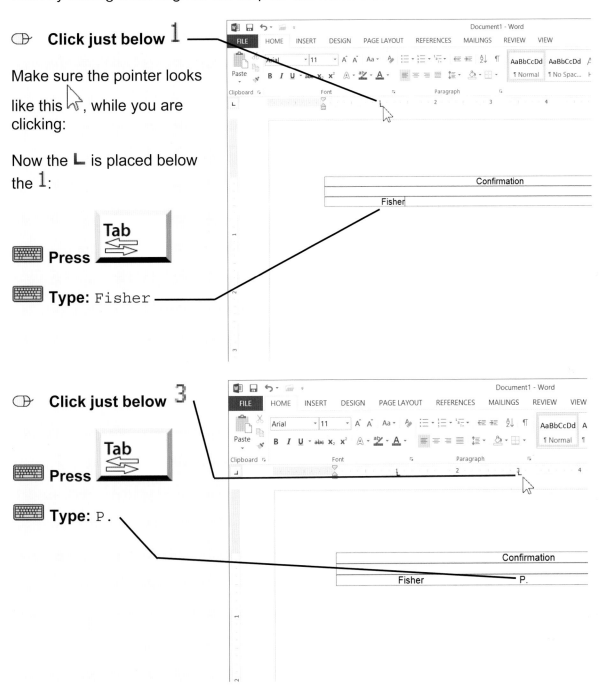

The tabs you have set so far are aligned to the left. In the next column you will be entering the ages. You can set a right aligned tab for this column:

☞ **Click** └ **and** ⊥ **until you see** ⌐

☞ **Click just below** 4

⌨ **Press** Tab

⌨ **Type:** 35

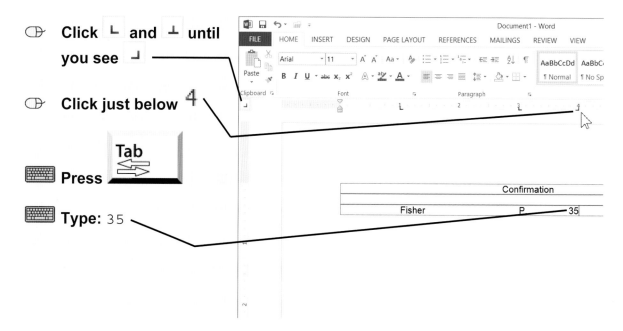

In the last column you will be entering the price. When you use amounts, the decimal points need to be aligned. You can use the decimal tab for this:

☞ **Click** ⌐

Now you see ⊥ :

☞ **Click just below** 5

⌨ **Press** Tab

⌨ **Type:** 194.00

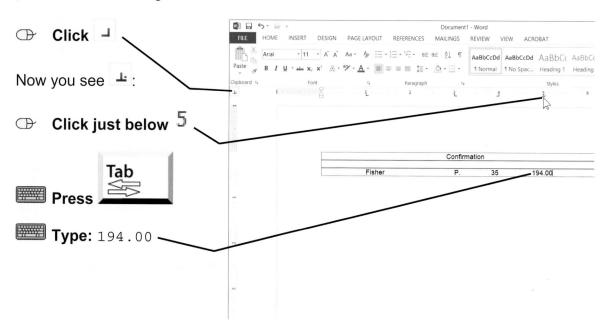

Now you have added specific formatting for the tab stops to the paragraph. All formatting you apply to a paragraph has been saved in the paragraph marker ¶ that is placed at the end of a paragraph. You can display the paragraph markers in the document like this:

⊕ **Click** ¶

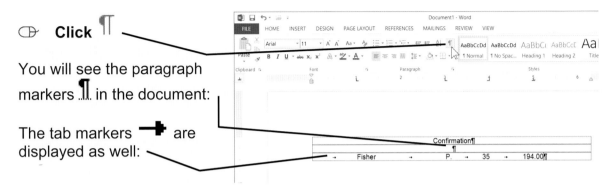

You will see the paragraph markers ¶ in the document:

The tab markers ➔ are displayed as well:

The cursor is currently blinking just before the last paragraph marker. If you press the Enter key now, this paragraph marker, including its formatting, will be transported to the next paragraph (in this case the next line). The same formatting will also apply to the new paragraph.

⌨ **Press** **Enter**

You have just created a new paragraph (in this case a single line).

Here you see that the tab stops will also be applied to this paragraph:

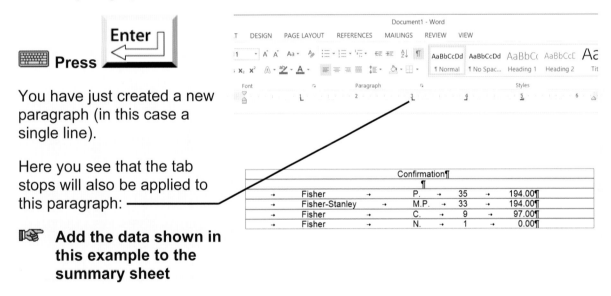

☞ **Add the data shown in this example to the summary sheet**

➜ **Please note:**

To go to the next tab stop, you should only use the Tab key. Do not use the space bar!

The columns will be neatly aligned, even if the text or the numbers are not equal in length. You no longer need to see the paragraph markers:

☞ **Hide the paragraph markers** ✂19

You can use the center tab to insert headings above the columns:

Click the empty line below Confirmation

Click ≡

Now the cursor has been placed at the beginning of the line. This paragraph does not yet have any tab stops:

Click ⊥ five times, until you see ⊥

☞ **Now set tabs under**
1.2
3.2
3.9
5

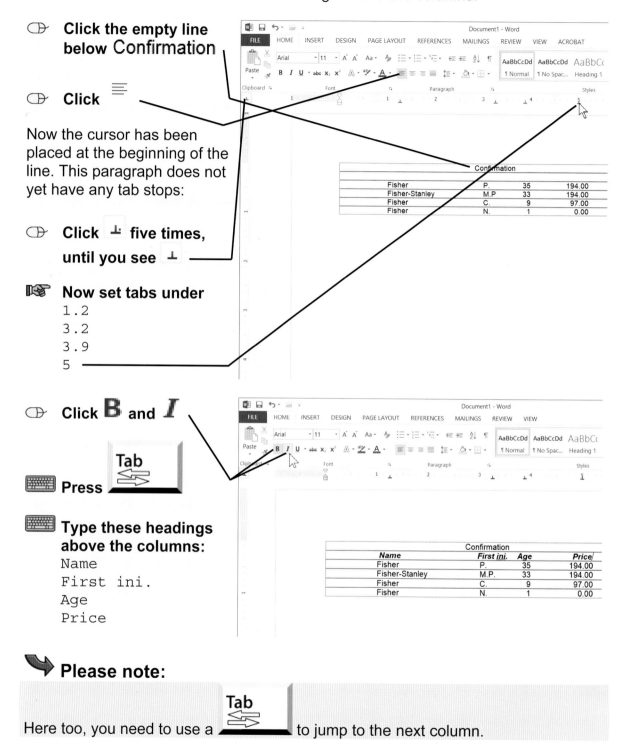

Click B and I

Press Tab

Type these headings above the columns:
Name
First ini.
Age
Price

🖐 **Please note:**

Here too, you need to use a **Tab** to jump to the next column.

Now you have made two different tab settings in the same document. You can make these settings as often as you like: each paragraph can have its own tab settings.

3.2 Moving Tabs

When you place tabs on the ruler, you will need to guess a bit about where to put them. But you can always adjust these tab stops later on. If you want to move the *Price* column a bit further to the left, you can do it like this:

☞ **Click a spot in the paragraph that contains the headings**

☞ **Point at the tab on position 5**

Make sure the pointer looks like this ↖.

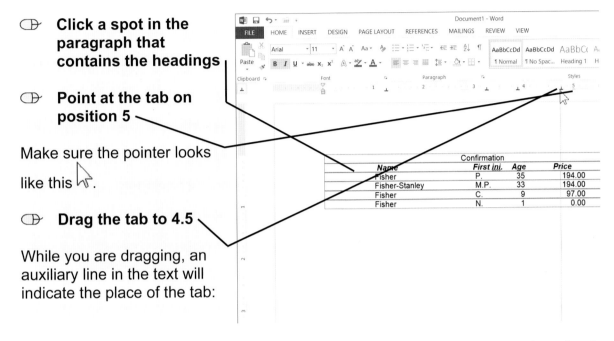

☞ **Drag the tab to 4.5**

While you are dragging, an auxiliary line in the text will indicate the place of the tab:

You will see that only the *Price* heading in the header line has been moved, and not the entire column. This is because the tabs are saved per paragraph. Each line on this sheet constitutes a separate paragraph. By selecting all the paragraphs first, you can adjust the tab settings for multiple paragraphs at once:

☞ **Select the four paragraphs in the summary** 👆20

☞ **Drag the tab from 5 to 4.5**

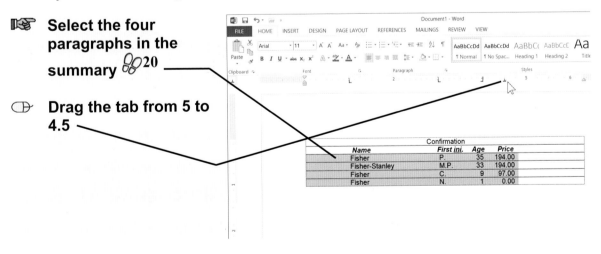

To undo the selection:

 Click somewhere in the text ——

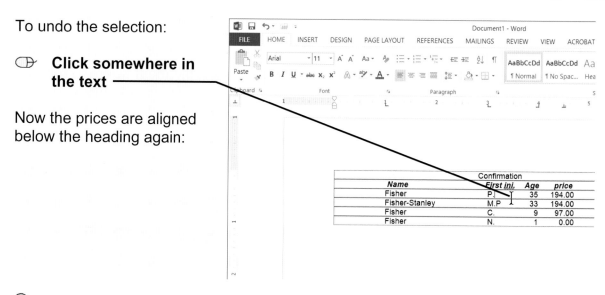

Now the prices are aligned below the heading again:

💡 **Tip**

Save at regular intervals

Save your document at regular intervals while you work. Use the 🖫 button on the *Quick Access* toolbar or click the **FILE** tab, and then **Save** or **Save As**.

3.3 Creating Lists

Some functions cause *Word* to insert its own tabs. For instance, when you use bullets and numbered lists. You can always move these tabs later on. Here is how you do that:

 Click the right-hand side of 0.00 ——

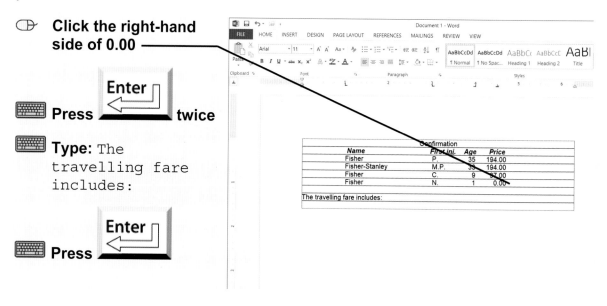

⌨ **Press** ⏎ **twice**

⌨ **Type:** The travelling fare includes:

⌨ **Press** ⏎

Click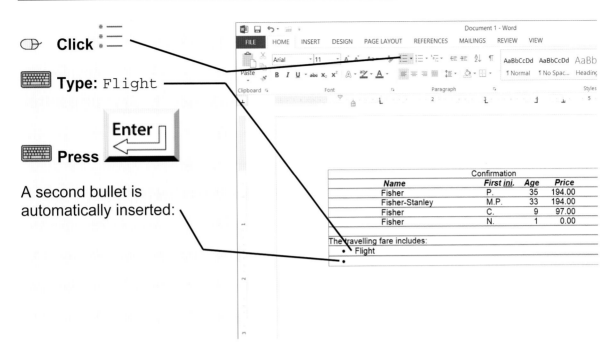

Type: `Flight`

Press Enter

A second bullet is automatically inserted:

HELP! I see a different type of bullet.

Depending on the settings in *Word*, you may see a different type of bullet, or the bullet is aligned on a different position. This will not affect the actions you be practicing.

☞ **Just go on reading**

Type this below:
```
Hotel
Meals
```

After ' Meals', press Enter **twice**

The list will end and the cursor returns to the beginning of the line:

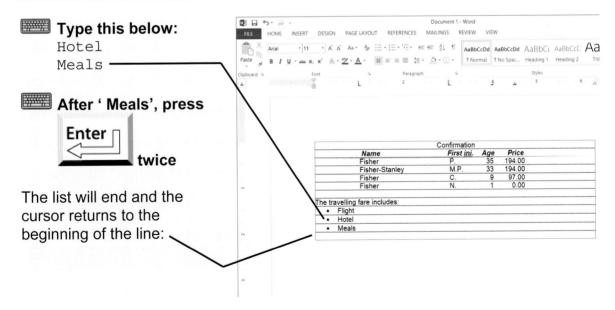

When you make a list, *Word* always uses the most recently used type of bullet. You can change this as well as the indentation. Here is how you do that:

☞ **Select all the lines in the list** 𝄞²⁰

👆 **By** ⊞, **click** ▾

You will see various other options:

To select a different symbol:

👆 **Click** Define New Bullet...

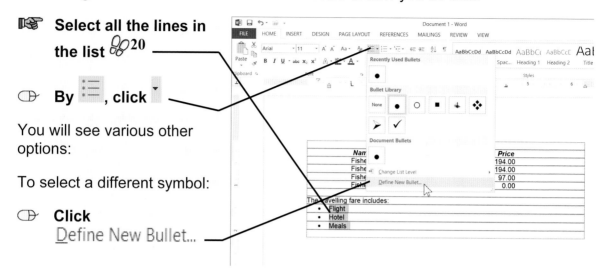

You will see the 'Define New Bullet' window with additional options. You can select another symbol from the *Windows* character set, even if it was not displayed in the previous window. For example, you can select a pointing finger for a bullet:

👆 **Click** Symbol...

☞ **By** Font:, **select** Wingdings :

Please note: you might see other symbols than the symbols in the example.

👆 **If necessary, drag the scroll box up or down**

👆 **Click** ☞

👆 **Click** OK

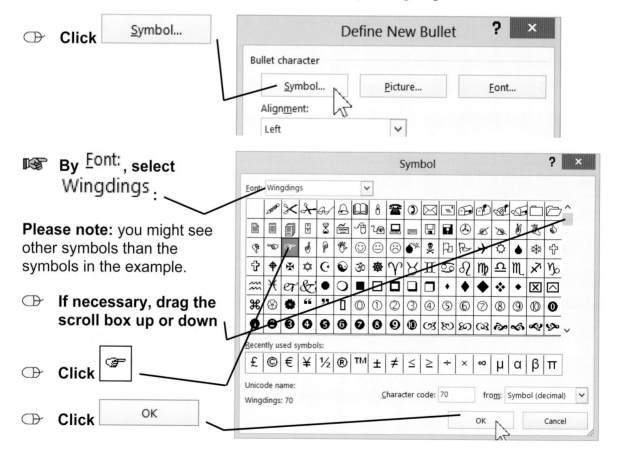

The round bullets have been replaced by ☞ :

Click OK

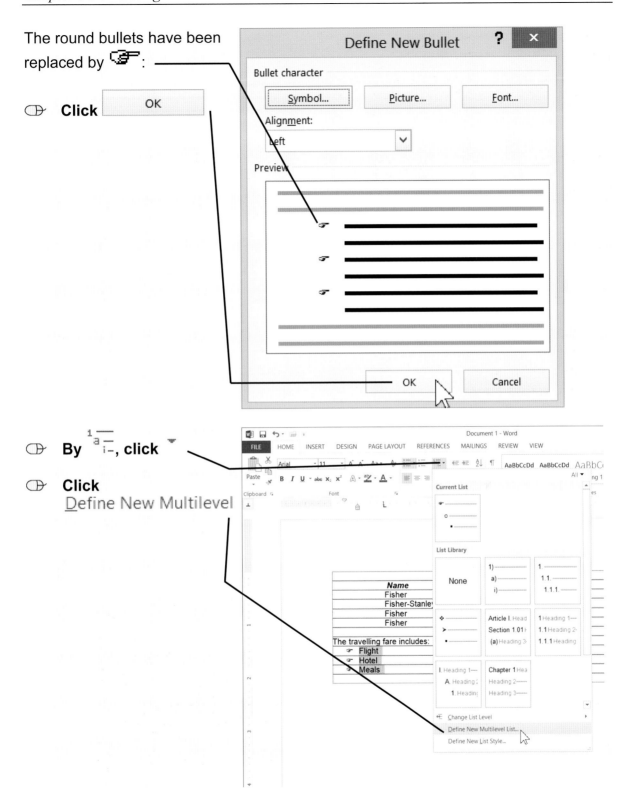

By ₁ₐᵢ-, click ▾

Click Define New Multilevel

By default, the position of the first bullet in this example is set to 0.25".

The position of the text is set to 0.5".

You are going to change this:

By Aligned at:, **type:** 0

By Text indent at:, **type:** 1

☞ **Click** OK

Now the text has been indented to 1 inch and the bullets are aligned along the margin of the page:

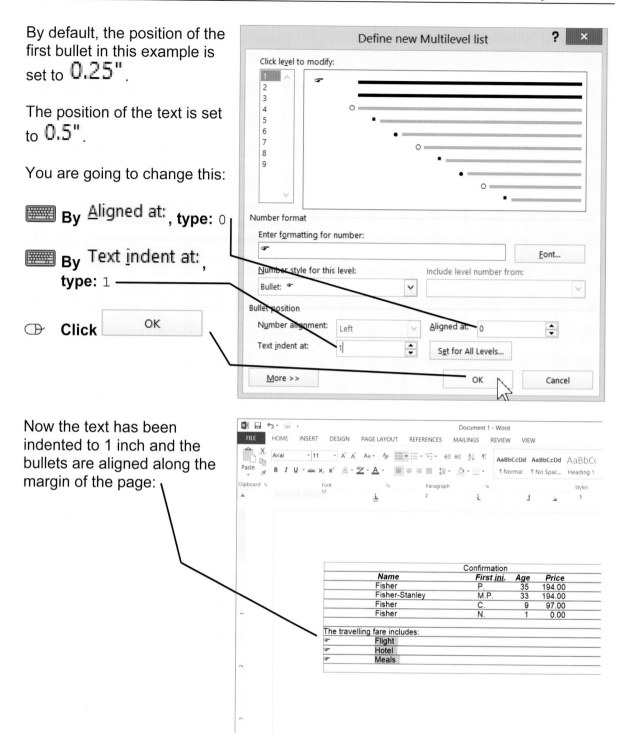

3.4 Multilevel Numbering

Instead of bullets you can also use numbers:

 Click

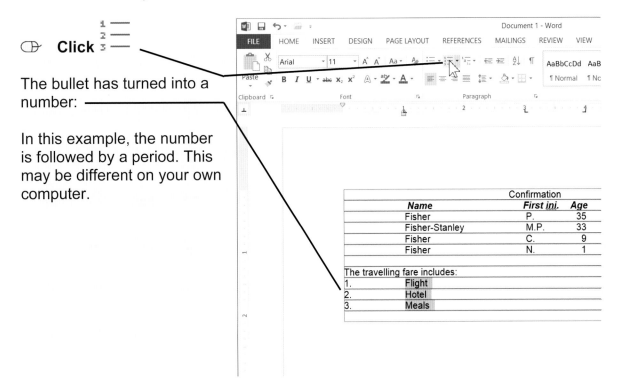

The bullet has turned into a number: ———

In this example, the number is followed by a period. This may be different on your own computer.

Please note:

Before you can change the bullets and replace them by numbers, the lines in the list need to be selected first. If necessary, select the lines once more. &&**20**.

HELP! I see a different number format.

Depending on your default numbers, or in the most recently used method of numbering, you may see a different format for the numbers. You can change this in the same way as you changed the bullets.

Besides these standard numbering methods, you can also create multilevel numbering in *Word*. This can look like this, for example:

1. Flight
2. Hotel
   a) double room
   b) child's crib
3. Meals
   a) breakfast

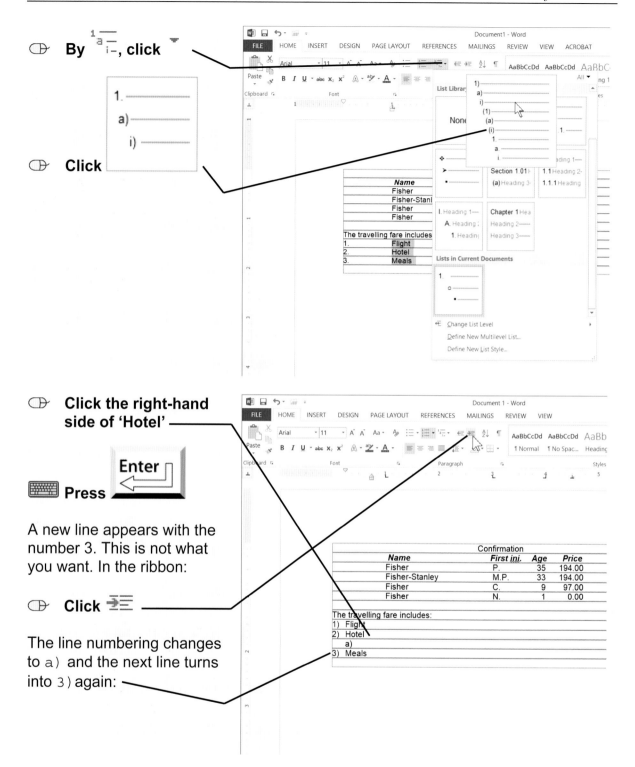

By ¹_a_i-, click

Click

Click the right-hand side of 'Hotel'

Press Enter

A new line appears with the number 3. This is not what you want. In the ribbon:

Click

The line numbering changes to a) and the next line turns into 3) again:

	Confirmation		
Name	*First ini.*	*Age*	*Price*
Fisher	P.	35	194.00
Fisher-Stanley	M.P.	33	194.00
Fisher	C.	9	97.00
Fisher	N.	1	0.00

The travelling fare includes:
1) Flight
2) Hotel
   a)
3) Meals

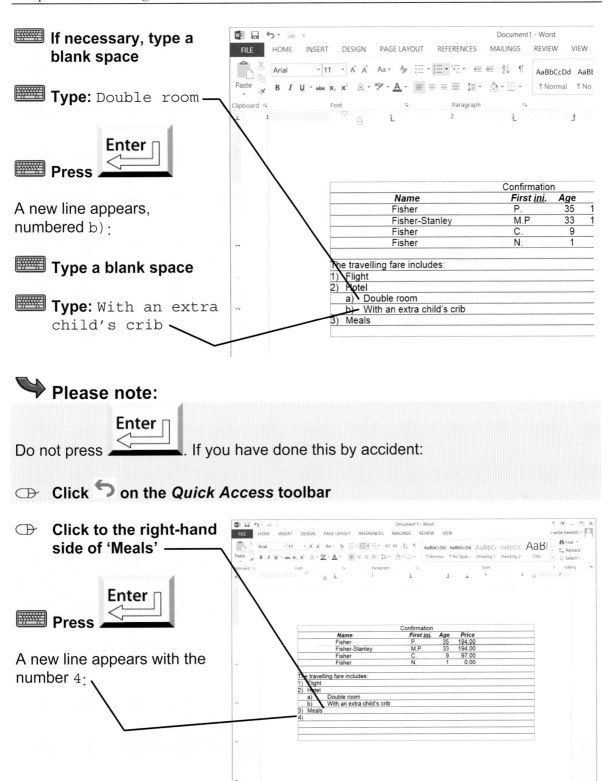

If necessary, type a blank space

Type: Double room

Press Enter

A new line appears, numbered b):

Type a blank space

Type: With an extra child's crib

Please note:

Do not press Enter. If you have done this by accident:

☞ **Click** ↶ **on the *Quick Access* toolbar**

☞ **Click to the right-hand side of 'Meals'**

Press Enter

A new line appears with the number 4:

👉 **Click**

The line number changes to
`a)`:

⌨ **Type:**
`Breakfast`
`Dinner`

Please note: if necessary, add a blank space before each word.

⌨ **Press** Enter

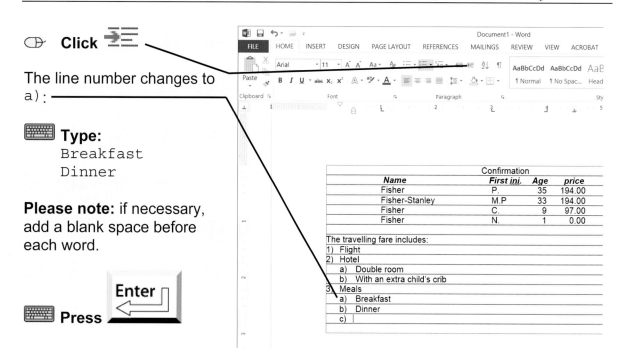

Now you see a line with `c)`. If you want to enter a fourth number, you will need to go up to the previous level. You do that like this:

👉 **Click**

The numbering changes from `c)` to `4)`:

⌨ **Type:** `Transfers`

⌨ **Press** Enter

A new line appears, with number `5)`.

👉 **Click**

Now the numbering will be disabled.

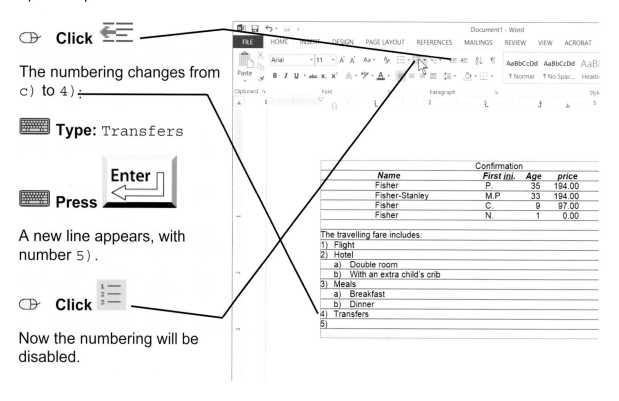

3.5 Inserting Text Files

A previously saved document can be inserted into a new *Word* document. The document is inserted on the spot where you place the cursor.

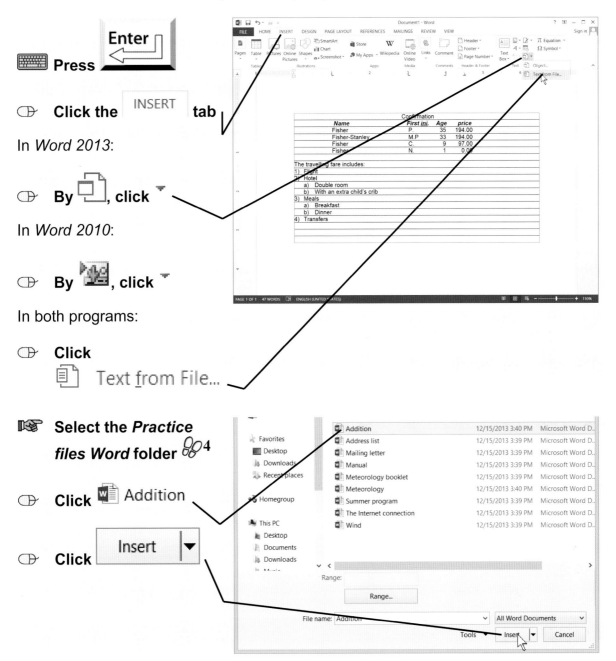

Press Enter

☞ **Click the** INSERT **tab**

In *Word 2013*:

☞ **By** , **click**

In *Word 2010*:

☞ **By** , **click**

In both programs:

☞ **Click** Text from File...

☞ **Select the *Practice files Word* folder** 🐾4

☞ **Click** Addition

☞ **Click** Insert

Now the text from the Addition document has been inserted at the bottom.

The font of the inserted text depends on the *Style* you have used. At the end of this chapter you can find additional information about *Styles*.

☞ **Select the inserted text** 🐾[20]

☞ **Set the font to *Arial*** 🐾[17]

☞ **If necessary, set the line spacing to *Single* 🐾[5] and the paragraph spacing after to *0 points* 🐾[6]**

☞ **Go to the beginning of the text** 🐾[21]

3.6 Page Breaks

You can allow a page to end at a certain spot. The next paragraph will then begin on the following page. This is called a *page-break*. An (invisible) marker is inserted that tells the program to move the rest of the text to the next page.

👆 **Click the**

    PAGE LAYOUT   **tab**

👆 **Set the cursor on the left side of 'Summer program'**

👆 **Click** ⊞ Breaks ▾

You will see a menu with various types of breaks:

👆 **Click**

    Page
    Mark the point at which
    and the next page begin

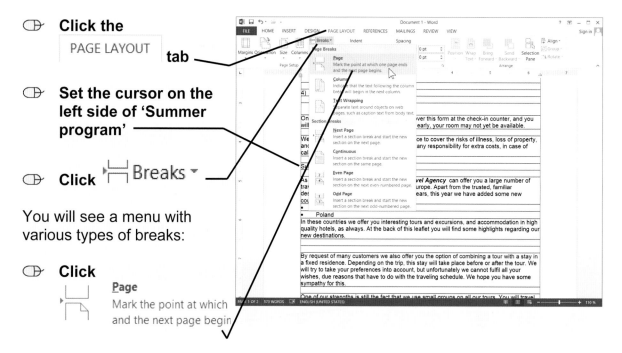

You see that the remaining text has been moved to the next page:

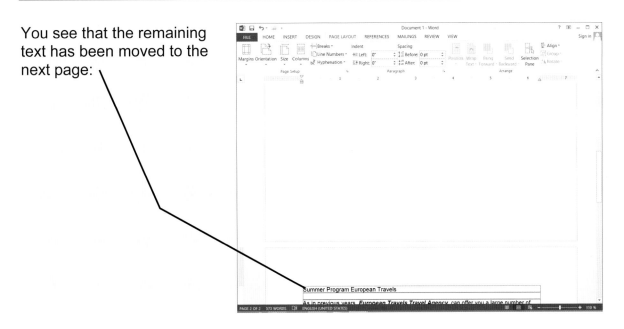

💡 Tip

Delete a page break

You can easily delete a page break:

⌨ **Press** Backspace ⟸ **twice**

💡 Tip

Use the keyboard to insert a page break

You can also use the keyboard to insert a page break. Use the key combination of the **Ctrl** and **Enter** keys:

⌨ **Press and hold Ctrl down**

⌨ **Press Enter**

A page break will be inserted into the text in exactly the same way.

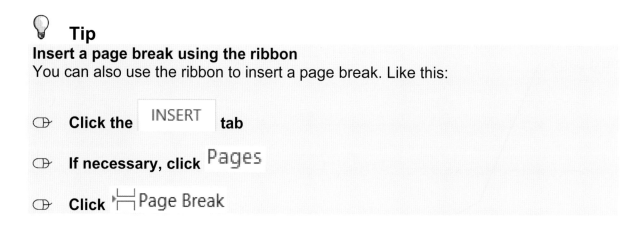

Tip

Insert a page break using the ribbon

You can also use the ribbon to insert a page break. Like this:

☞ **Click the** INSERT **tab**

☞ **If necessary, click** Pages

☞ **Click** Page Break

3.7 Set Page Orientation to Portrait or Landscape

The text of this practice file is displayed in portrait mode. To display the page in landscape mode:

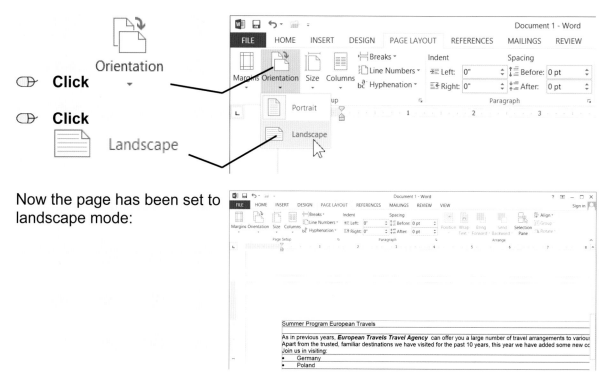

☞ **Click** Orientation

☞ **Click** Landscape

Now the page has been set to landscape mode:

Return to portrait mode again:

☞ **Click** Orientation , Portrait

3.8 The Margins

The white borders around the pages are called the margins. This is how you set the margins:

Margins

☞ **Click** ▼

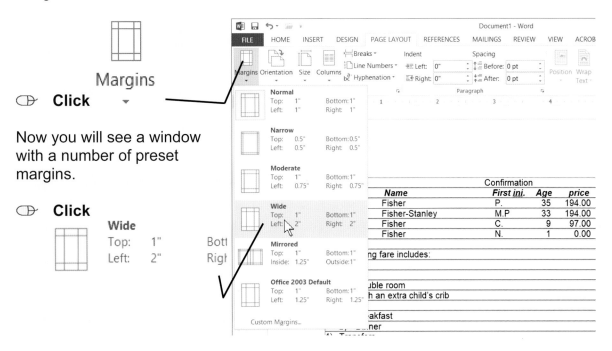

Now you will see a window with a number of preset margins.

☞ **Click**

Wide
Top: 1"   Bott
Left: 2"   Rig

You will see more white space to the left and right side of the page. And you will also see that you need to move the tab stops in order to fit the text within the margins.

To restore the original margins:

☞ **Click** ↶

You can also set the margins manually:

Margins

☞ **Click** ▼

☞ **Click**
Custom Margins...

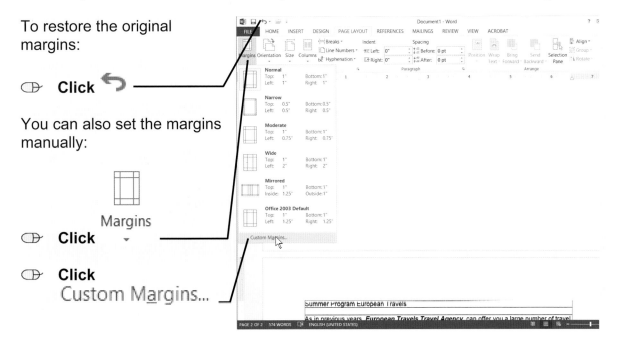

Now you will see a small window in which you can change the page settings:

You can define separate settings for the top, bottom, left and right margins:

To enlarge the top margin:

☞ **By Top:, click ⏶ until you see 1.9"**

☞ **Click OK**

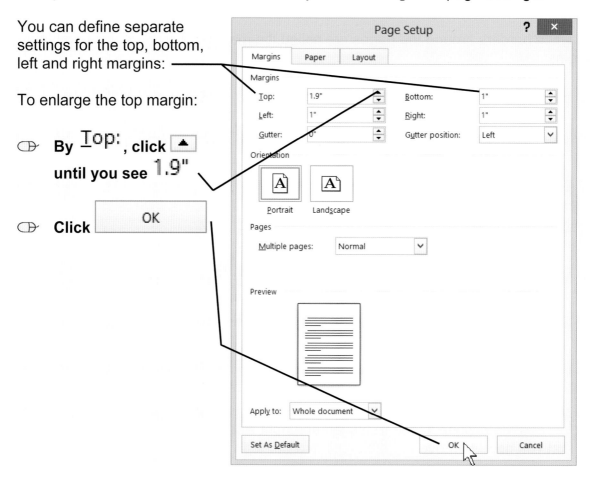

☞ **Go to the beginning of the text** ⌕²¹

You will see that the white space at the top of the page has increased:

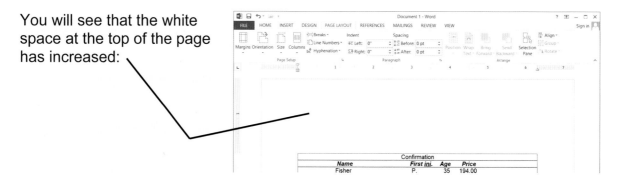

In this way you can also adjust the other margins. The text will automatically fit within these margins.

Usually, setting the margins is done just once, for the entire document. To decide how large the margins need to be is a matter of taste and may also depend on the size of paper you will be using.

Tip

Gutter margin

Apart from the top, bottom, left and right margins, *Word* knows another type of margin: the *gutter*.

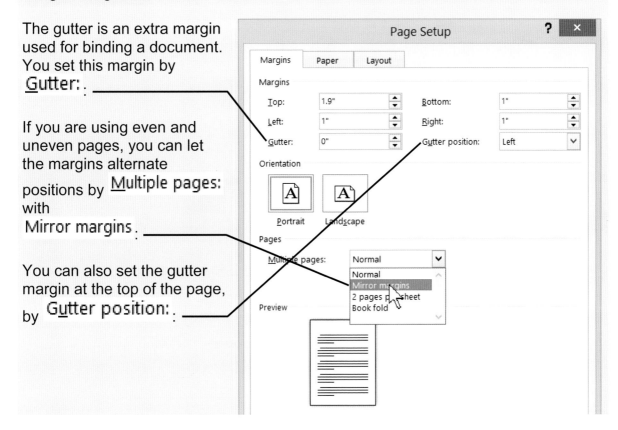

The gutter is an extra margin used for binding a document. You set this margin by Gutter:.

If you are using even and uneven pages, you can let the margins alternate positions by Multiple pages: with Mirror margins.

You can also set the gutter margin at the top of the page, by Gutter position:.

 Tip

Minimum margins

Almost every printer has a non-printable area. This is a border on the paper that cannot be printed. With some inkjet printers, this border can be quite wide. Laser printers usually have a narrow border.

If you set the paper margins too narrow, you will see a warning message, like the one in this example:

⊕ **Click** Fix

Word will fix the document. But you can also enlarge the margins yourself.

3.9 Adding a Cover Page

If you are writing a report or creating a booklet, you may want to add a cover page. You do that like this:

☞ **Click the** | INSERT | **tab**

☞ **If necessary, click**

Pages

☞ **Click** 🎑 Cover Page ▾

☞ **If neccesary, drag the scroll box down**

☞ **Click** Motion

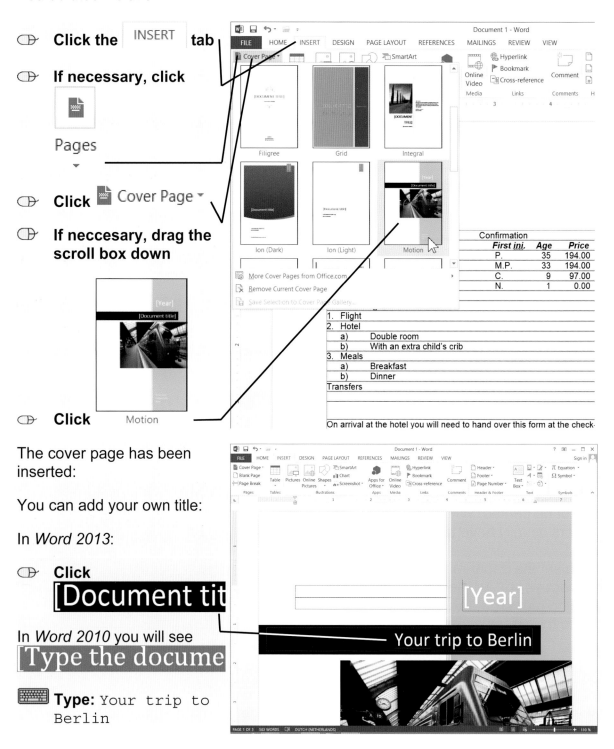

The cover page has been inserted:

You can add your own title:

In *Word 2013*:

☞ **Click**
[Document tit

In *Word 2010* you will see
Type the docume

⌨ **Type:** Your trip to Berlin

In this case you do not need to enter the rest of the information. You can delete the other fields:

☞ **Double-click** **[Year]**

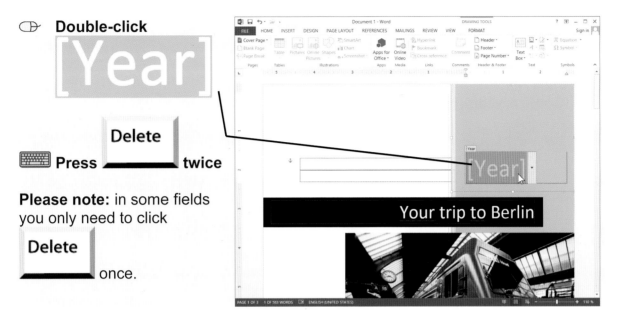

⌨ **Press** ⌷Delete⌷ **twice**

Please note: in some fields you only need to click ⌷Delete⌷ once.

👉 **Delete the fields at the bottom of the cover page as well**

If you wish you can also change the picture. In *Chapter 4 Pictures* you will learn how to work with pictures.

3.10 Headers and Footers

Headers and footers can help to make your documents look more professional and make them easier to read. A header is a line at the top of the page, usually containing the title of the document or chapter and possibly the page number.

Many longer documents will also have a footer. This is a similar line at the bottom of the page. Some documents will only display the page number in the footer, but other information can be included here as well. You do not need to type a header or footer separately for every page. You just need to set them up once. *Word* will automatically print the headers or footers on every page regardless of the number of pages in the document. You can also edit the header and footer as often as you need.

The header and footer sections appear in the top or bottom margin of a page. Here is how you insert a header or a footer:

☞ **Go to the second page**
&⅞21

☞ **Click the word 'Confirmation'**

☞ **Click — 📄 Header ▾**

You will see a menu with pre-defined headers:

☞ **Click the**
Blank

[Type here]

header

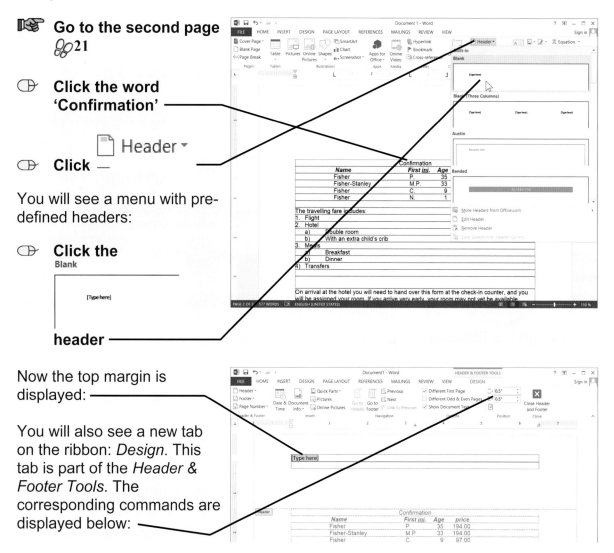

Now the top margin is displayed: ────

You will also see a new tab on the ribbon: *Design*. This tab is part of the *Header & Footer Tools*. The corresponding commands are displayed below: ──

With this new tab you can set a large number of preferences for the headers and footers:

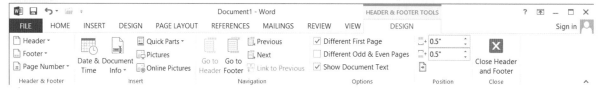

You can also skip to the footer with these options:

Go to

👉 **Click** Footer

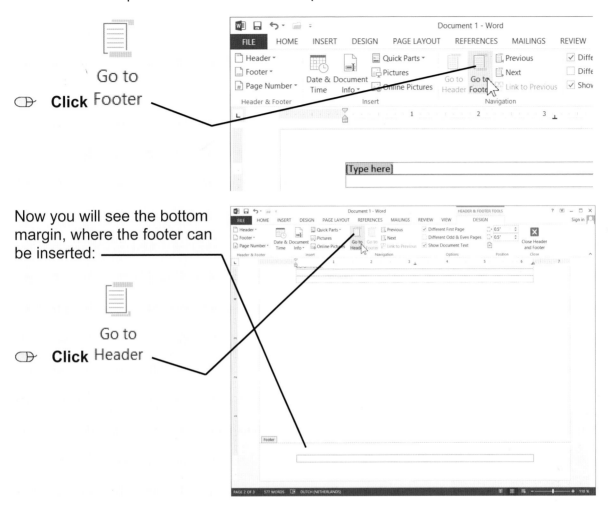

Now you will see the bottom margin, where the footer can be inserted: ———

Go to

👉 **Click** Header

Now you see the location for the header again. You can enter a header:

👉 **Click** [Type here] (*Word 2013*) or [Type·text]¶ (*Word 2010*)

⌨ **Type:** Your trip to Berlin

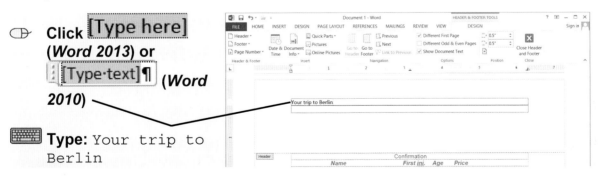

A header or a footer can be edited just like any other text. If the box ☑ by Different First Page is checked, on the DESIGN tab, no header or footer will be inserted on the cover page if you do not enter text on the cover page.

If you would like to display different text in the headers or footers on odd and even pages, check the box ☑ by Different Odd & Even Pages, on the DESIGN tab.

3.11 Page Numbers

Headers often display the page numbers as well. You can insert them like this:

☞ **Click** 🔲 Page Number ▾

☞ **Click** 🔲 Top of Page

You will see a menu with various pre-defined methods for inserting page numbers:

☞ **Click**
Plain Number 2

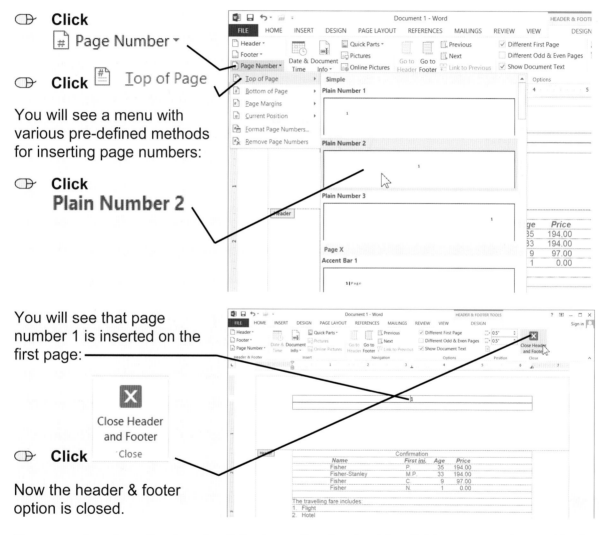

You will see that page number 1 is inserted on the first page:

☞ **Click** ⊠ Close Header and Footer / Close

Now the header & footer option is closed.

You can also close the header & footer option by double-clicking an empty spot in the document.

Word can also display the total amount of pages. You can apply this option in important documents, where not a single page should be missing. For example, you can insert *page 1 of 4* as a header.

Please note:

There is a disadvantage to the use of pre-defined headers and page numbers: each new selection automatically replaces the previous selection. For example, you have seen that the text *Your trip to Berlin* disappeared as soon as you inserted page numbers into the header. However, there is a simple solution to this problem. Just insert the page numbers, and afterwards you can carry on typing in the box where the header or footer is displayed. In this way your header or footer can contain both text and page numbers.

3.12 Using Styles

Sometimes it can be handy to apply the same style to certain types of documents. Companies or clubs, for instance, will want to maintain a uniform style in all their reports or letters; that is they will want to use the same font and layout. But you may also want to use a specific style for your own letters or texts.

Word has a useful built-in option for this called *styles*. A style is a type of layout in which several text characteristics have been defined. For example, a style can define all these aspects at once:

- the font;
- the font size;
- the line spacing;
- the indentation;
- the color.

By selecting a style you select a certain way of formatting the text. You can apply styles to the entire text, or use them for just a single element, word or phrase.

For example, you can apply the *Title* style to the word 'Confirmation':

☞ **If neccesary, click the word 'Confirmation'**

In the *Styles* group you see

that the ¶ Normal style is selected:

☞ **Click**

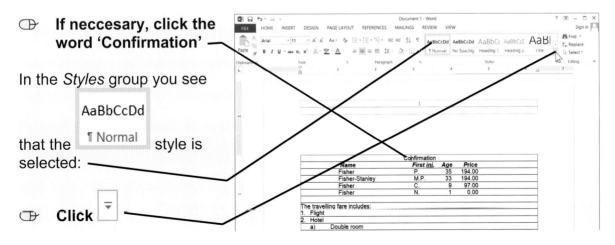

Please note:

A paragraph style always applies to the entire paragraph. If you want to apply a specific style to a paragraph, you do not need to select the whole paragraph first. Just place the cursor in the paragraph you want to edit.

Now you will see a window with various styles:

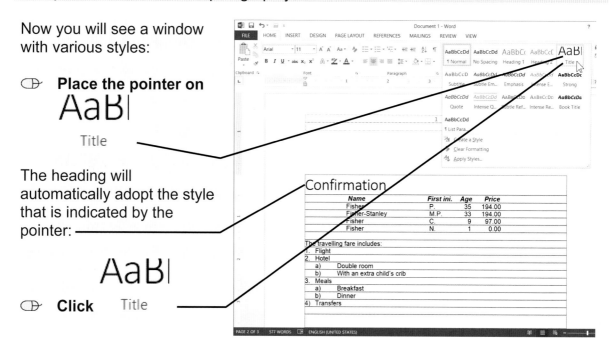

☞ **Place the pointer on**

$$\mathsf{AaB}|$$

Title

The heading will automatically adopt the style that is indicated by the pointer: ──────

$$\mathsf{AaB}|$$

☞ **Click**   Title

Now the heading has taken on the formatting characteristics of the *Title* style. Styles are often used to standardize headings and titles. For instance, for a company you can decide to always use *Heading 1* for the main heading of an article, and to use *Heading 2* for sub-headings, etc.

 Tip

View styles without clicking

Instead of clicking right away, you can just move the pointer 🐭 over the styles in the options window. The paragraph automatically takes on the style to which you point. This way, you can quickly view the results before choosing the style you want to use.

3.13 Copying Styles

Word has a very useful function for copying and pasting formatting styles. For example, let's say you have just created this paragraph title:

Paragraph 1.1

Normally you would need to set the font, font size, and alignment for each subsequent paragraph, over and over again. This is a lot of work, and you would need to remember or look up the settings quite a few times. In such a case you can also use the *format painter*.

With the 🖌 button you do not copy the style, but only the formatting. It takes three steps:

- Click the text that contains the formatting you want to copy (the example);
- Click 🖌 ;
- Drag the pointer across the text that should be formatted in the same way.

Just try it for yourself.

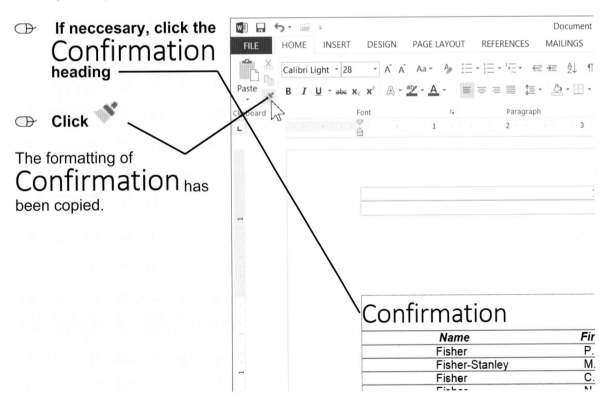

👉 **If neccesary, click the** Confirmation **heading**

👉 **Click** 🖌

The formatting of Confirmation has been copied.

Now you can apply this style to another section of the text:

☞ **Go to the next page** ✍*21*

👉 **Drag the pointer** across
Summer Program E

Note that the pointer has changed shape while you were dragging it :

After you release the mouse, the formatting will change:

👉 **Click beside the text**

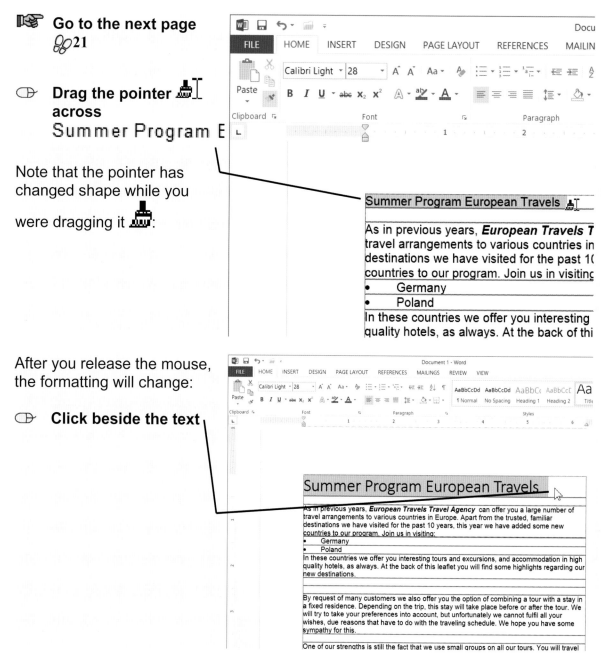

☞ **Close *Word* and do not save the changes** ✍*2*

In the next couple of exercises you can practice the actions we have discussed.

3.14 Exercises

Have you forgotten how to do something? Use the number beside the footsteps to look it up in the appendix *How Do I Do That Again?* at the end of the book.

Exercise 1: Tabs and Bullets

☞ Open *Word*. ◐◑**1**

☞ Insert a left tab stop by 1, 3, 4 and 5. ◐◑**22**

☞ Fill in the summary sheet with the items you see below:

	Game 1	Game 2	Game 3
Anne	10	20	10
Joyce	20	30	20
Mary	10	20	30

☞ Enter a blank line. ◐◑ **23**

☞ Drag the first tab stop to 0. ◐◑**24**

☞ Enter this numbered list: ◐◑**25**

Games:

1. Solitaire
2. Poker
3. Blackjack

☞ Insert a second level for *Solitaire*. ◐◑**26**

☞ Add these items to the list:

Games:

1) Solitaire
    a) 1 card
    b) 3 cards
2) Poker
3) Blackjack

☞ Close the document and do not save the changes. 🦶**3**

Exercise 2: Page Layout

In this exercise you will be changing the layout of a page.

☞ Go to the *Practice files Word* folder and open the document named *The Internet connection.* 🦶**10**

☞ Set the top margin for the page to 1.5 inches (or 4 cm). 🦶**27**

☞ Insert a page break before the fifth paragraph (starting with *When it comes to the disadvantages*). 🦶**28**

☞ Add a header and insert the text *exercise.* 🦶**29**

☞ Add a footer with a page number. 🦶**30**

☞ Close *Word* and do not save the changes. 🦶**2**

3.15 Background Information

Dictionary

Bullet	A symbol that precedes each item in a list.
Footer	A line found at the bottom of the page. May contain the title of the book or chapter, date, page numbers, etc.
Header	A line found at the top of the page. May contain the title of the book or chapter, date, page numbers and more.
Line spacing	The distance between two lines of text.
Margins	The amount of white space between the border of the paper and the text.
Numbering	The numbers preceding each item in a list.
Page break marker	An invisible marker that indicate where the page ends. Also called a 'hard' marker.
Paragraph	A paragraph is a part of a text. A paragraph always begins on a new line and ends at the spot where you press the Enter key.
Paragraph marker	A symbol that indicates the end of a paragraph ¶.
Space	A blank space between words.
Style	A group of settings that determine the formatting of the text.
Tab key	A key with which you move the cursor to the next tab stop.
Tab stop	A pre-set spot on the horizontal ruler.

Source: Word 2013, Word 2010 and Windows Help and Support

Themes

A theme is a set of formatting options. It consists of three elements: a set of theme colors, a set of theme fonts (among which are the fonts for headers and footers), and a set of theme effects (among which are lines and fill effects).

Every document you create with *Word* has a theme, even new, blank documents. The default theme is the *Office* theme. For example, when you apply the *Metropolitan* theme, the group of styles will change into bright colors. All the contents in a document are linked to the theme; when you change the theme, the layout of the document automatically changes too, unless you change the layout yourself.

You can select a different theme in *Word 2013* by clicking the DESIGN tab. Then click . In *Word 2010* you first click the Page Layout tab, and then Themes.

You can see right away how your document will look by allowing the pointer to hover over the various pre-set themes in the Themes window.

Paper size

There are various standards that determine the size of a sheet of paper. Most of the world uses the widespread international ISO standard. A different standard, ANSI, is used in North America (adopted by the American National Standards Institute).

Current paper sizes used in North America are:

Letter	8.5" x 11"
Legal	8.5" x 14"
Tabloid/Ledger	11" x 17"

The most frequently used paper size in Europe is A4. A sheet of A4 paper is 297 mm (8.27") by 210 mm (11.69"). A sheet of A5 paper is exactly half the size of an A4 sheet and an A3 sheet is twice the size of an A4 sheet. The main paper sizes are:

A3	420 x 297 mm (11.69" x 16.5")
A4	297 x 210 mm (8.27" x 11.69")
A5	210 x 148 mm (5.83" x 8.27")

Make sure you select the correct paper size. If you select a different size from the paper you have in your printer, the text will not be printed correctly.

- Continue on the next page -

To change the paper size:

Click the tab
PAGE LAYOUT

Click ▾

Click the desired page size

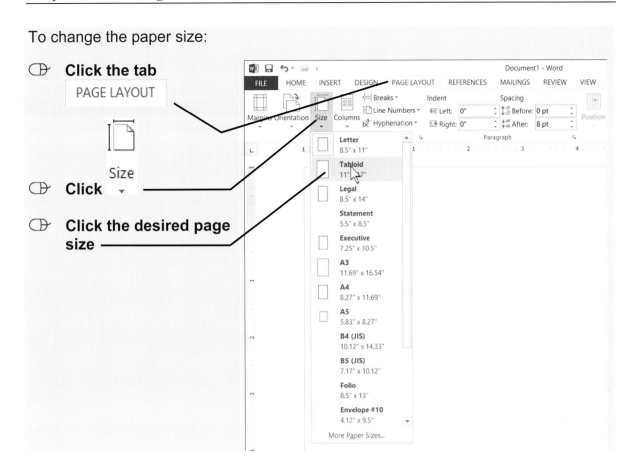

3.16 Tips

 Tip

Delete a tab

If you want to delete a tab you have placed on the ruler, you can just drag it away from the ruler:

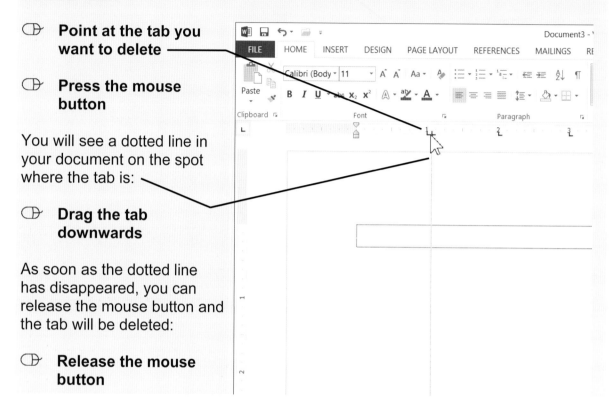

☞ **Point at the tab you want to delete**

☞ **Press the mouse button**

You will see a dotted line in your document on the spot where the tab is:

☞ **Drag the tab downwards**

As soon as the dotted line has disappeared, you can release the mouse button and the tab will be deleted:

☞ **Release the mouse button**

 Tip

Move the margin for an individual paragraph

If you want to move the left margin of a single paragraph, you can also use the

Decrease indent or *Increase indent* buttons in the *Paragraph* section. The margin of the paragraph where the cursor is placed (or of the selected paragraphs) will be placed on the next tab position.

Decrease indent:

Increase indent:

Tip

Position of bullets and text

Not only can you change the symbol used in a bulleted list, you can also change the position of the indent or the distance between the bullet and the text. Take at look at the following list examples:

- line 1
- line 2

Or:

> • line 1
> • line 2

You can change these settings in the window called *Define new Multilevel list*. There you can define two positions:

Click ⅓☰▾, Define New Multilevel List...

The position of the bullet:

The position of the text directly next to the bullet:

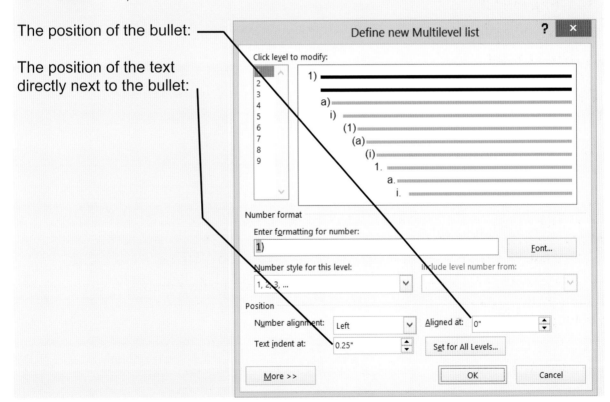

💡 Tip

Formatting page numbers
You can select different types of numbering, such as *I, II, III* or a, b, c.

☞ **Click the** INSERT **tab, and then** ⊞ Page Number ▾,
 ⊞ Format Page Numbers...

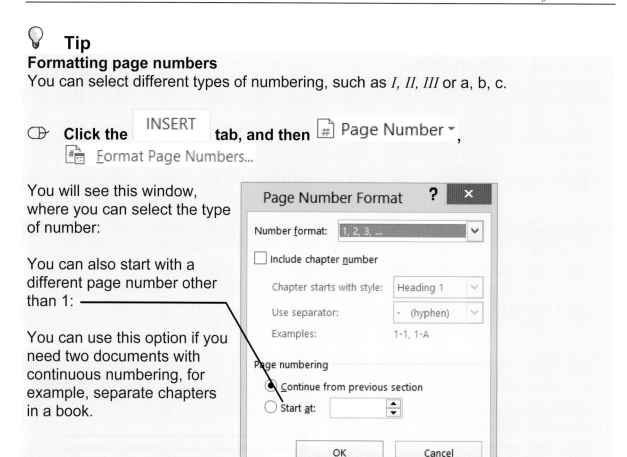

You will see this window, where you can select the type of number:

You can also start with a different page number other than 1:

You can use this option if you need two documents with continuous numbering, for example, separate chapters in a book.

💡 Tip

Position of the header
The header is usually placed in the top margin. The position of this header is set by indicating the distance to the border of the paper. Naturally, this distance cannot be bigger than the top margin.

☞ **Click the** INSERT **tab, and then** ▯ Header ▾, ▯ Edit Header

On the *Design* tab you will see the *Position* group.

Here you can set the distance:

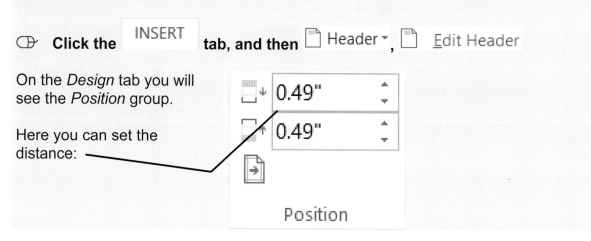

Tip

Print a single page of a document in landscape mode

You can print a single page, such as a diagram, with *Landscape* orientation while the rest of the document remains in *Portrait* mode, like this:

☞ **Place the cursor at the end of the page that precedes the landscape page**

☞ **Open the *Page Setup* window** ◊◊**31**

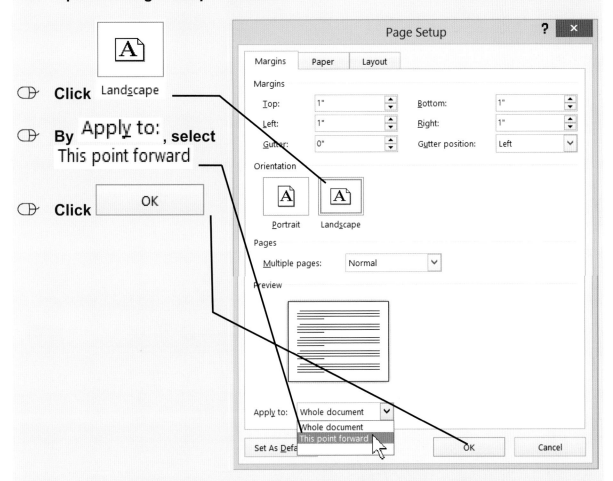

Now the rest of the document will be printed in landscape mode after the spot where the cursor has been placed.

If you want to print the rest of the document in *Portrait* mode, except for this single landscape page, then do the following:

☞ **Place the cursor at the end of the landscape page**

☞ **Open the *Page Setup* window** ◊◊**31**

- Continue on the next page -

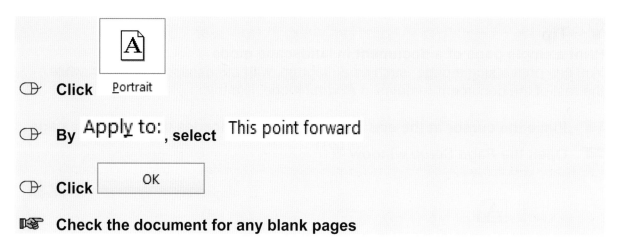

☞ **Click**   Portrait

☞ **By** Apply to: **, select**   This point forward

☞ **Click** [OK   ]

☞ **Check the document for any blank pages**

💡 **Tip**

Page breaks and paragraphs

If you want to place a specific paragraph at the top of a new page, you can add the page break marker to the paragraph itself. There may also be times when you want to prevent the lines of a paragraph from being distributed over multiple pages. Here is how you change the settings to accomplish this:

☞ **Click the** PAGE LAYOUT **tab**

☞ **By** Paragraph **, click** 🔲

☞ **If necessary, click the** [Line and Page Breaks] **tab**

Place at least two lines of a paragraph at the top or bottom of the page:

Prevent page breaks between paragraphs:

Prevent page breaks within a paragraph:

Insert a fixed page break before a paragraph:

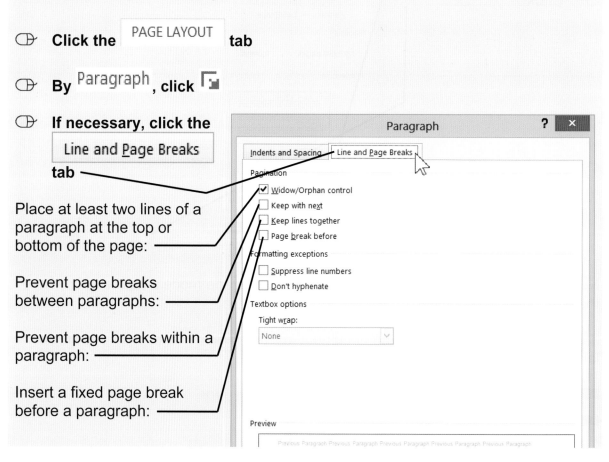

💡 Tip

Pasting text

In *Word* you can copy and paste text in different ways. Pasted text does not have to come from a text editing program. It can be copied from a web page, for example.

To copy a text:

👉 **Select the text** 👣**20**

👉 **Click** 📋

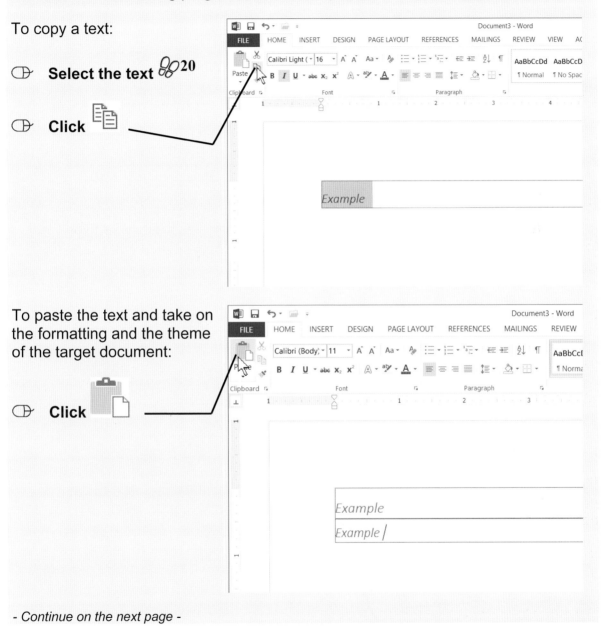

To paste the text and take on the formatting and the theme of the target document:

👉 **Click** 📋📄

- Continue on the next page -

To paste the text and keep the formatting of the source document:

Click ▼

Click

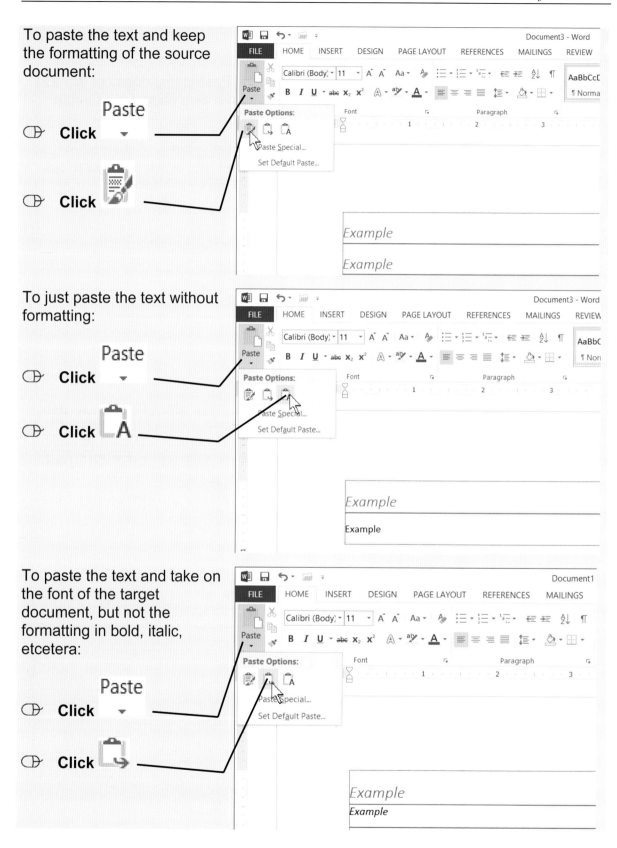

To just paste the text without formatting:

Click ▼

Click A

To paste the text and take on the font of the target document, but not the formatting in bold, italic, etcetera:

Click ▼

Click

Tip

Create and change styles

If you have your own standard way of formatting specific texts, you can create your own style with these settings. The easiest way of defining a new style, is to format the text first:

⌨ **Type a text**

☞ **Select the font** 👣17
and the font size 👣18

☞ **Select the text** 👣20

🖱 **By** *Styles*, **click** ▾

In *Word 2013*:

🖱 **Click** 🅰 Create a Style

In *Word 2010*:

🖱 **Click**
Save Selection as
a New Quick Style...

⌨ **Type a name for the style**

🖱 **Click** OK

Now the style will be applied to this document.

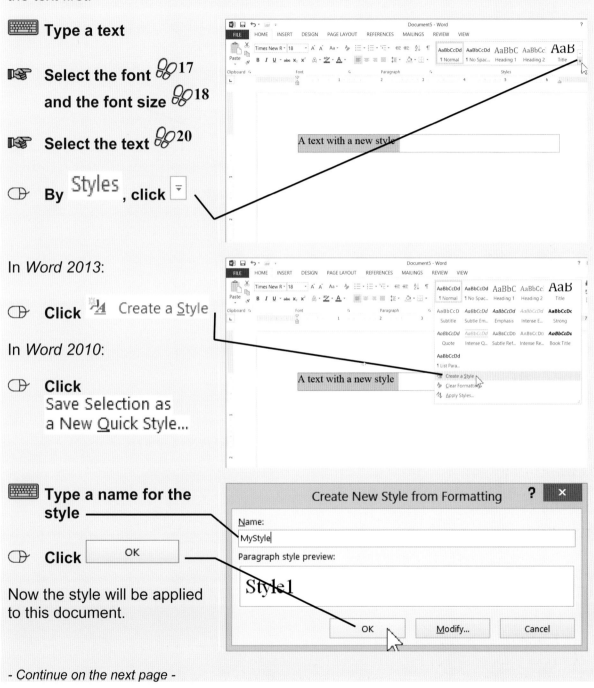

- Continue on the next page -

If you want to apply this style to all documents:

☞ **Click** | Modify... |

☞ **Click the radio button** ⦿ **by** New documents based on this template

You can also change an existing style. You do that like this:

☞ **Select the text** 👣²⁰

☞ **Right-click the style**

☞ **Click**
Update Normal to Match S‹

4 Pictures

'A picture is worth a thousand words' is a well-known phrase. A photo or an illustration in your text can help to make your content easier to understand. It can also help to make the text look more attractive, professional and polished.

You can easily add photos, illustrations and drawings to a text in *Word*. You can edit an image later on to fit the text in the best possible manner. By changing the size, color and position of the image you can match the styles used with other images in the document so that they reflect the theme of your document as a whole.

In this chapter you will learn how to:

- insert a picture;
- open the *Picture Tools Format* tab;
- move a picture;
- change the size of a picture;
- restore the original picture and size settings;
- crop a picture;
- remove the background of a picture;
- adjust the brightness and contrast of a photo;
- restore the initial settings of a photo;
- change colors;
- add artistic effects;
- create a watermark;
- delete a picture;
- use SmartArt.

4.1 Inserting a Picture

In *Word,* the general name 'picture' is used for various types of images. An image can be an illustration (line drawing), a drawing (bitmap) or a photo.

☞ **Open** *Word* ⌇⌇^{1}

☞ **Open the document named** *Wind* **in the** *Practice files Word* **folder** ⌇⌇^{10}

You see the text. Now you are going to practice inserting a photo into this text. The first step is to move the cursor to the spot where you want the photo inserted. Later, you will see that you can insert the photo in any random position in the text.

⊕ **Click the second blank line**

⊕ **Click the** INSERT **tab**

⊕ **Click** Pictures

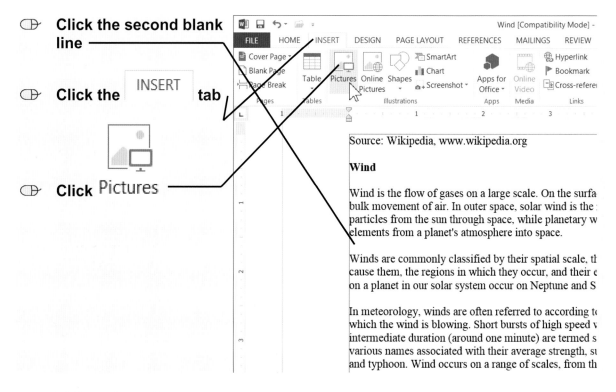

☞ **Open the** *Practice files Word* **folder** ⌇⌇^{4}

You will see several pictures:

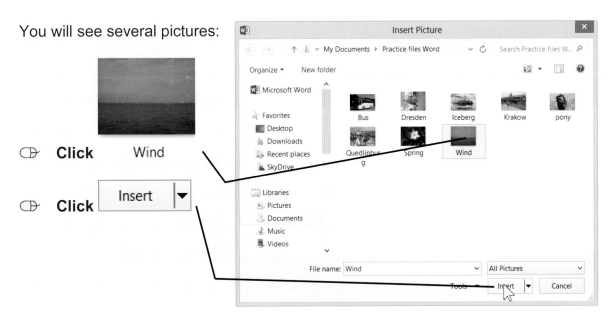

 Click   Wind

 Click | Insert | ▼ |

 HELP! The window looks a bit different.

Your window may look a little different, but this will not affect the following actions you need to perform.

The photo of the lake with the boat and windmills in the background will be inserted.

4.2 The Picture Tools

When you start working with a photo, *Word* automatically opens the PICTURE TOOLS :

The FORMAT tab with its corresponding commands has already been opened:

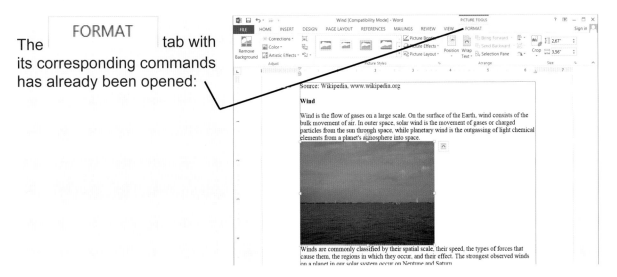

☞ **Click an area next to the photo** ——

Now the *Format* tab has disappeared:

☞ **Click the photo**

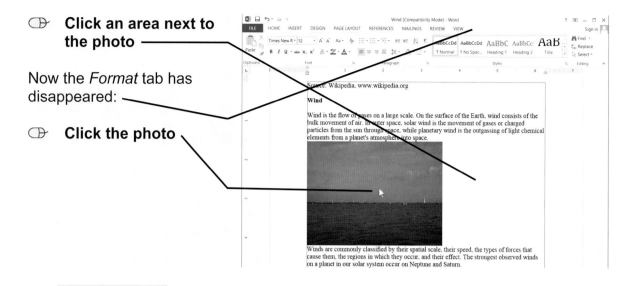

The ┌─── FORMAT ───┐ tab is displayed again. You will see this tab appear when you have selected the picture. When you click an area next to the photo, the *Format* tab will disappear.

4.3 Moving a Picture

There are several ways of inserting the photo into the text. You can also choose different methods for wrapping the text around the picture:

The photo is still selected. This means you can see the *Format* tab:

☞ **If necessary, click the** FORMAT **tab**

☞ **Click** Wrap Text ▾ ——

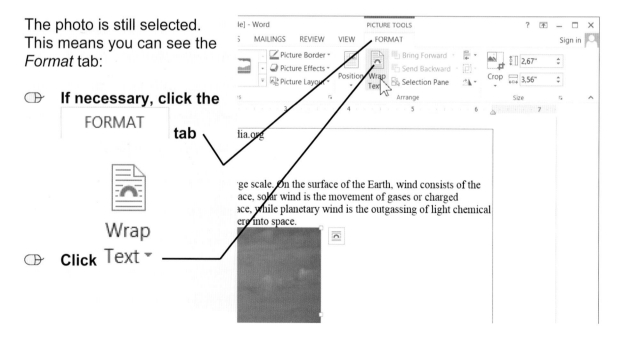

You will see the various ways in which the picture can be inserted into the text. The default setting is for the picture to be inserted on a line in the text. You can try this out and see how it looks when you want to wrap the text around the picture:

☞ **Place the pointer on**

Square

You will see an example of what the page will look like right away:

☞ **Click** **Square**

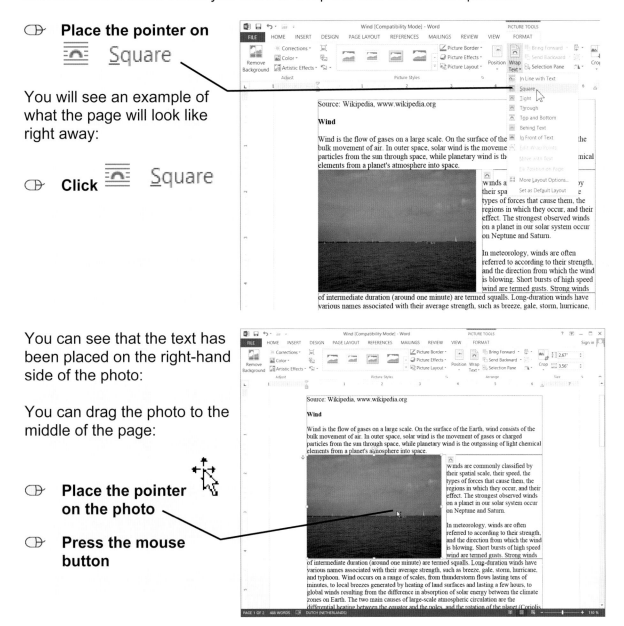

You can see that the text has been placed on the right-hand side of the photo:

You can drag the photo to the middle of the page:

☞ **Place the pointer on the photo**

☞ **Press the mouse button**

☞ **Drag the photo to the middle**

☞ **Release the mouse button**

Now you see that the text has been wrapped around the photo on both the left and right sides:

This makes the text a little less easy to read as the lines of the text continue right across the photo.

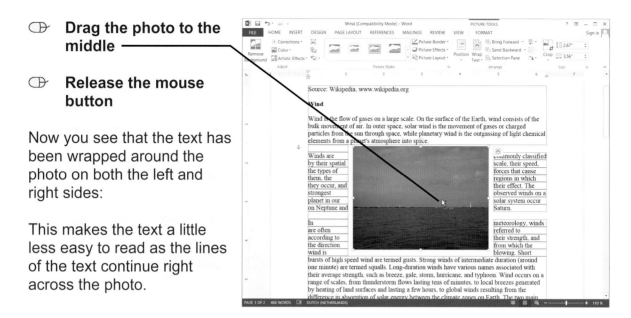

There are several more settings that *Word* offers for positioning a photo. Just take a look at some of these options:

The photo is still selected.

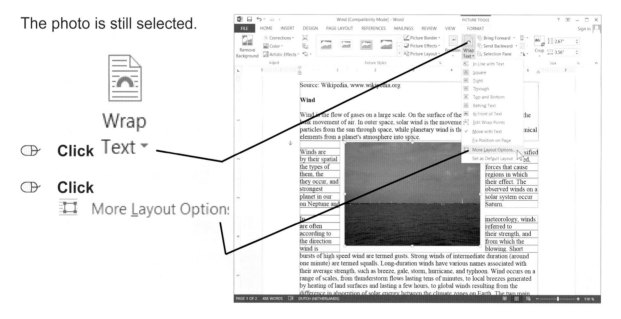

☞ **Click** Wrap Text ▾

☞ **Click**
⊞ More Layout Options

You see additional options for positioning the text:

The text is placed on both sides of the photo. You can also place the text on the right-hand side only.

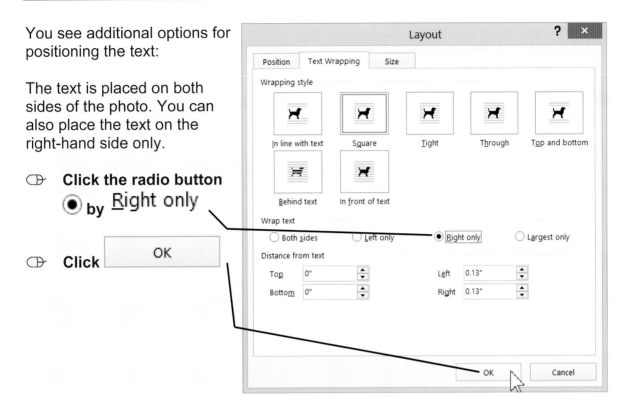

 Click the radio button **by** Right only

 Click OK

The text is now placed on the right-hand side of the photo.

Tip
Other ways of wrapping the text
There are even more ways of wrapping text around a picture. We will discuss these methods a little later on in this book.

Please note:

If you have selected the In line with text method of wrapping text, you will not be able to move the picture. The photo will remain positioned on the line.

4.4 Shrinking or Enlarging a Picture

You can make a photo smaller or larger by scaling it. This is easily done with the mouse:

The photo is still selected:

If you look at the edges of the photo, you will notice small rectangles or circles. These are the so-called *handles*:

If you drag the handles on the corners with the mouse, you can enlarge or shrink the photo.

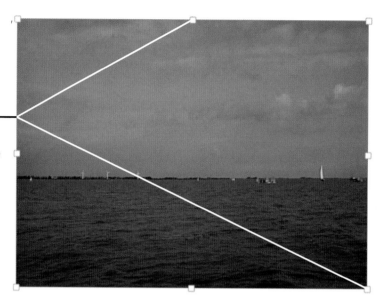

☞ **Place the pointer on the handle in the bottom right corner**

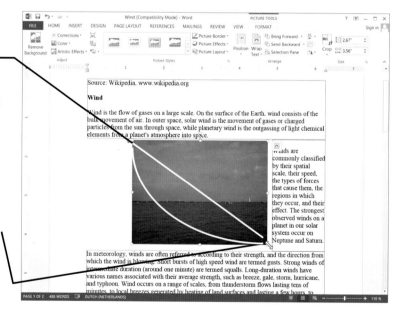

The handle will turn into ⬉:

☞ **Press the mouse button and hold it down**

☞ **Drag the corner handle to the top left**

☞ **Release the mouse button**

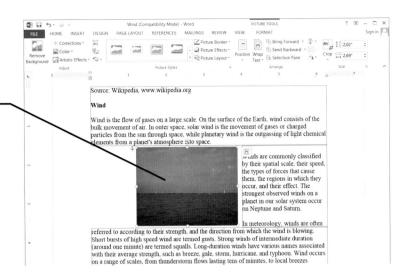

You will see that the photo has become smaller: ———

Enlarging a photo works in the same way, but then you drag the corner handle outwards:

☞ **Enlarge the photo**
35

Now you will see that the photo has become larger:

The text will adapt to the photo each time you change the size.

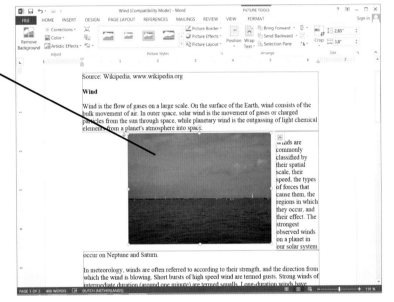

🖑 **Please note:**

If you drag one of the handles in the middle or on the sides, instead of a corner handle, the photo will be 'distorted'. The photo will lose its correct height and width ratio and will look stretched out or squished in a strange way.

You can 'flatten' a photo, for example, like this:

4.5 Restoring the Original Picture and Picture Size

If you have changed anything regarding the size of a picture, you can restore the original settings like this:

The photo is still selected and the FORMAT tab is still open:

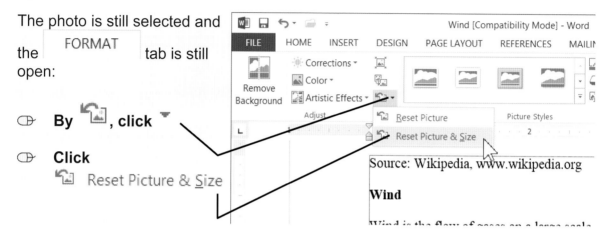

☞ **By** 🖼, **click** ▼

☞ **Click** 🖼 Reset Picture & Size

Now you see that the photo is reset to its original size.

4.6 Cropping a Picture

You can also crop part of a picture if you do not want to use it. In the sample photo, for example, you might want to crop some of the water away in order to emphasize the sky a bit more. You can use the mouse again to practice this method, but first you need to select the cropping tool.

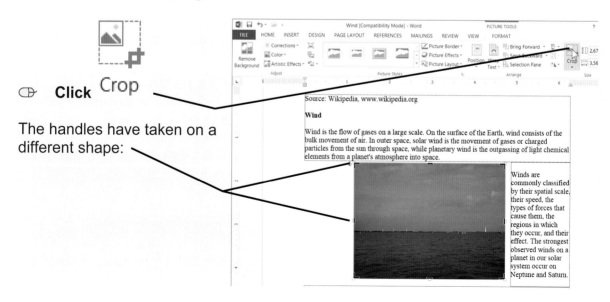

☞ **Click** Crop

The handles have taken on a different shape:

Now you can crop the bottom of the photo, for example:

☞ **Place the pointer on the lowest handle**

Please note: the pointer should take on the shape of a **T**.

☞ **Press the left mouse button and drag the handle upwards**

☞ **Release the mouse button**

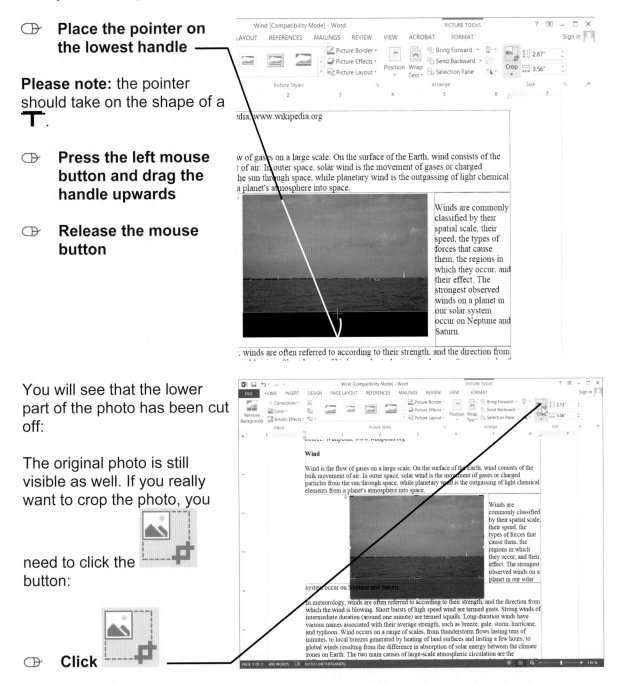

You will see that the lower part of the photo has been cut off:

The original photo is still visible as well. If you really want to crop the photo, you need to click the

button:

☞ **Click**

Now the photo has been cropped.

💡 **Tip**

Crop a picture to a specific shape

You can also crop a picture so that it conforms to a specific shape:

☞ **Click** ▼

☞ **Click**
   ⬭ Crop to Shape

☞ **Click the desired shape**

The picture is cropped.

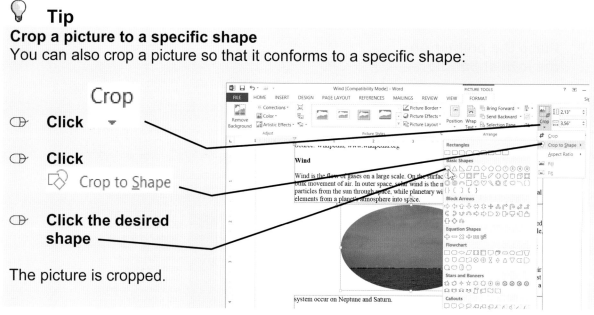

💡 **Tip**

Crop with an aspect ratio

If you want to crop a picture to its specific height/width aspect ratio:

☞ **Click** ▼

☞ **Click** Aspect Ratio

☞ **Click the desired ratio**

☞ **Click**

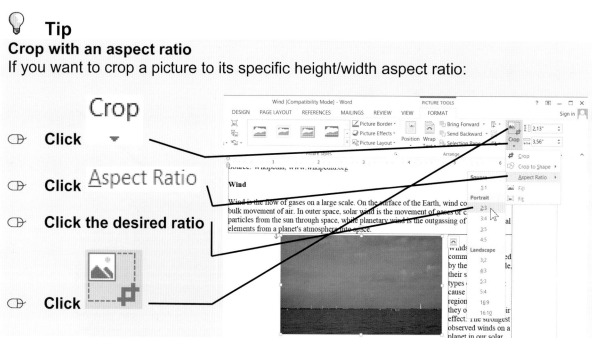

4.7 Automatically Remove the Background

You can also remove the background from a photo. You can practice doing this with the sample photo named *pony* in the *Practice files Word* folder:

☞ **Click the blank line under the *Wind* photo**

☞ **Insert the *pony* photo from the *Practice files Word* folder** ✂³⁹

The picture is selected:

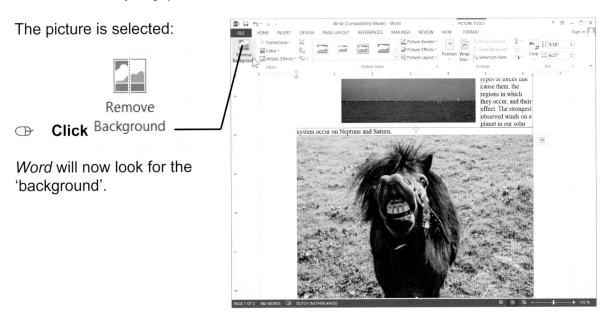

☞ **Click** Remove Background

Word will now look for the 'background'.

You will see that not all the areas have been correctly marked, such as the pony's neck. You can mark the areas you want to keep:

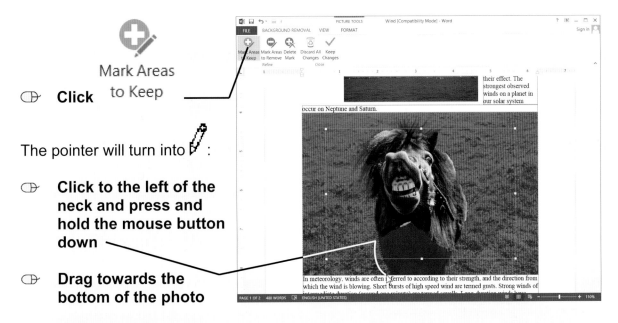

☞ **Click** Mark Areas to Keep

The pointer will turn into ✐ :

☞ **Click to the left of the neck and press and hold the mouse button down**

☞ **Drag towards the bottom of the photo**

☞ **Release the mouse button**

To apply the changes:

Keep

☞ **Click** Changes

The background of the photo has been removed:

You no longer need this photo, so you can delete it. The photo is still selected:

Press

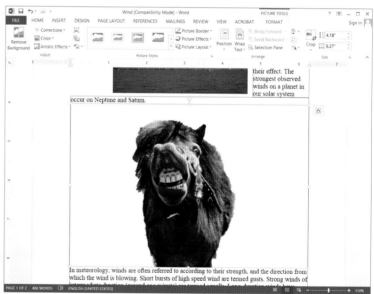

It is not always easy to remove the background from a photo. Removing the background from a photo with a lot of scenery, for instance, may not work very well.

4.8 Editing a Photo

Word has a number of tools with which you can edit photos. For example, you can edit the following items:

- the brightness;
- the contrast.

And you can also:

- change the color of a photo to greyscale;
- change a photo into a black-and-white photo;
- select different colors;
- apply a watermark.

These effects are located in the Adjust group on the FORMAT tab. You can change the brightness and contrast of a photo, for example:

☞ **Click the *Wind* photo**

☞ **Click the** FORMAT **tab**

☞ **Click** ☀ Corrections ▾

☞ **Move the pointer over the options**

You will see that *Word* displays the effect, even before you have clicked it.

☞ **Click** [Brightness: +20% Contrast: +20%]

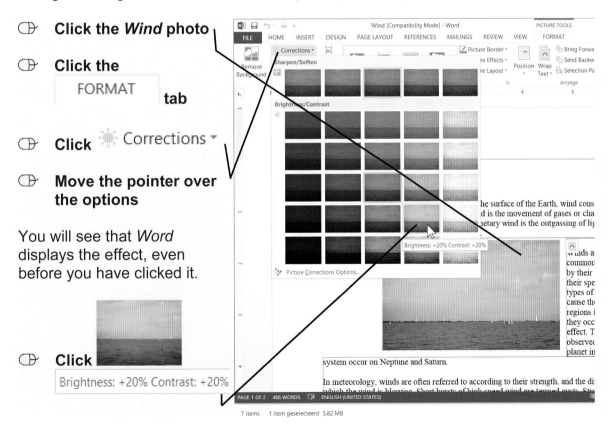

The photo has become lighter.

4.9 Resetting a Picture

You can reset the photo. This means that all the edits you have applied and the portions you have cropped away will be removed and the photo will be restored to its original state. But if you use the ⬚ button to reset the photo, the size will not be restored:

Click ⬚

The photo is now restored to its original state:

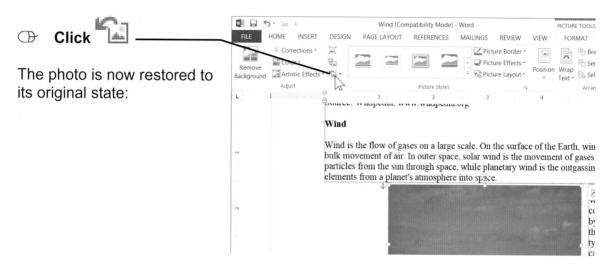

4.10 Changing Colors

You can turn a full color photo to one that has only grey shades. The result resembles a print of a color photo that has been made with a monochrome printer. You can also convert the photo entirely to a black-and-white photo. Just take a look:

Click Color ▾

You will see all the different options:

Click Grayscale

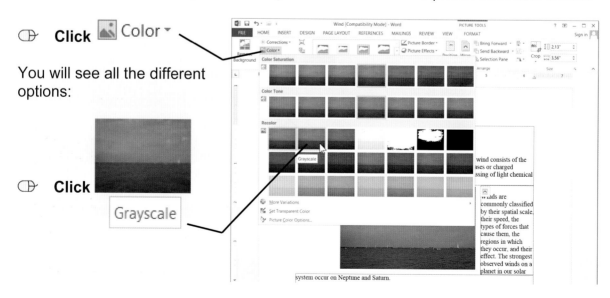

Now the colors have
disappeared:

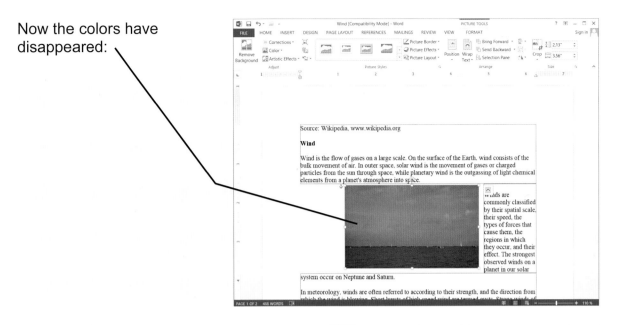

👉 **Try a few of the other options on the** 🖼 Color ▾ **menu**

👉 **Reset the photo to its original state** 🐾34

4.11 Artistic Effects

You can achieve a more unusual effect by applying one or more of the artistic effects:

🖼 **Click**
    🖼 Artistic Effects ▾

Here you see various options:

🖼 **Click**
    Chalk Sketch

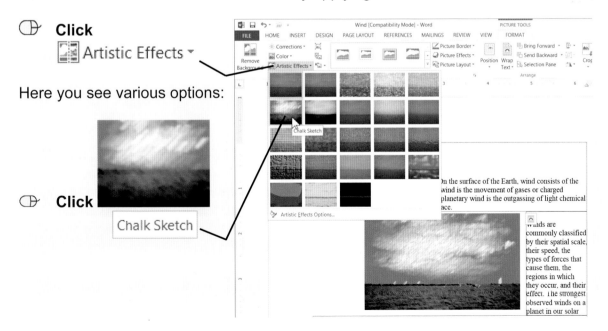

Now the photo looks as though it was sketched over with chalk:

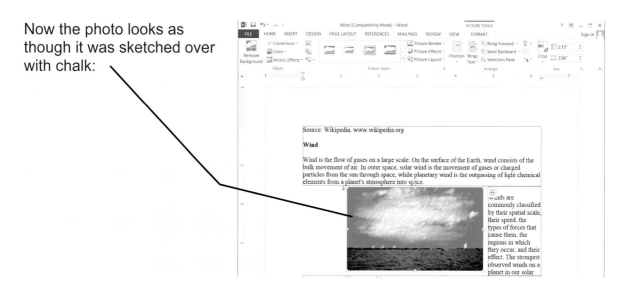

☞ **Try a few of the other options on the** 🔲 Artistic Effects ▾ **menu**

☞ **Reset the photo to its original state** 👣 **34**

4.12 The 'Washout' Effect

Word lets you create a watermark on the page from a photo you select. This is also called a 'washout' effect. Text can also be printed on top of the photo, if you wish.

👆 **Click** 🖼 Color ▾

👆 **Click** Washout

The photo will be 'washed'.

Now practice enlarging the photo to make it as wide as the lines of the text:

☞ **Enlarge the photo**
&°35

☞ **Drag the photo precisely between the left and right margins**

☞ **Drag the photo below the first paragraph**

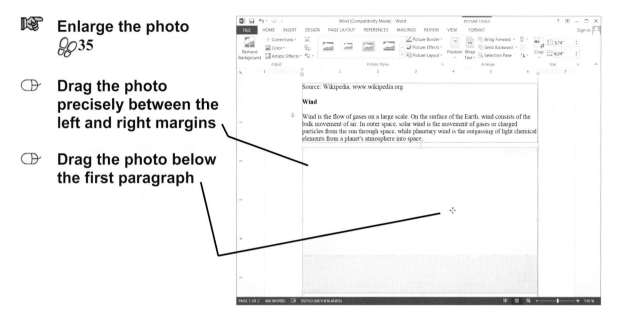

Now you can change the way the text is wrapped around the picture, allowing it to be visible on top of the photo:

☞ **Click** Wrap Text ▾

☞ **Click** Behind Text

The text is now displayed on top of the 'washed out' photo.

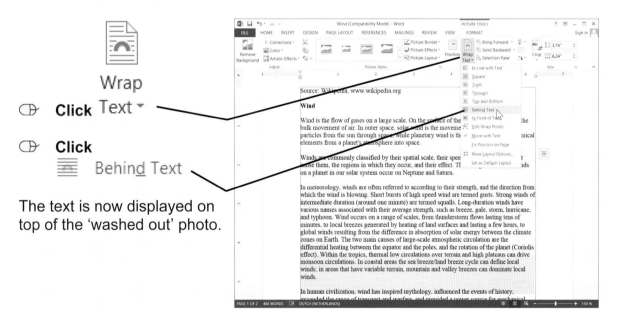

The photo is now being used as a watermark. Watermarks can be used to create artistic writing paper for things such as a diploma or a certificate.

4.13 Deleting a Picture

It is very easy to delete a picture:

First, you need to select the photo.

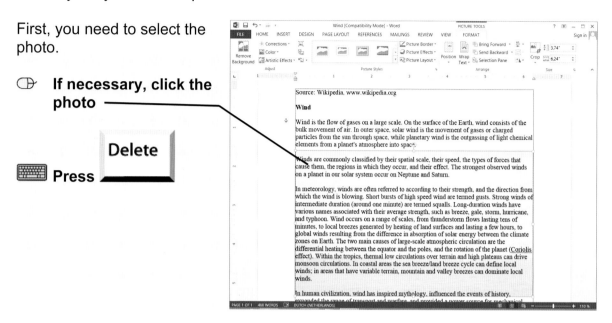

☞ **If necessary, click the photo**

  Press `Delete`

The photo has been deleted.

☞ **Close the document and do not save the changes** &3

💡 **Tip**

Cutting

Instead of deleting a picture, you can also cut it. You can then paste the same picture into another document. You do that like this:

☞ **Right-click the photo**

☞ **Click** ✂ **Cut**

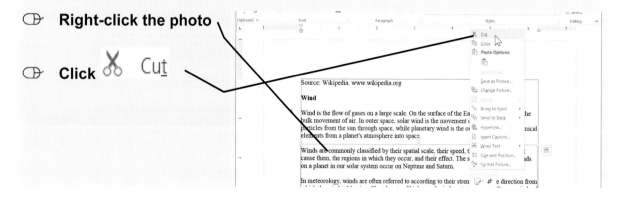

4.14 Working with SmartArt

With SmartArt you can create professional illustrations with just a few mouse-clicks. You can choose from a large number of different shapes and layouts. To see how this works, go ahead and open a new, blank document:

☞ **If necessary, open *Word* ⚐¹**

⊕ **Click the** 〔 **FILE** 〕 **tab, and then** 〔 **New** 〕, Blank document

Only in *Word 2010*:

⊕ **Click** Create

⊕ **Click the** 〔 INSERT 〕 **tab**

⊕ **Click** ◨ SmartArt

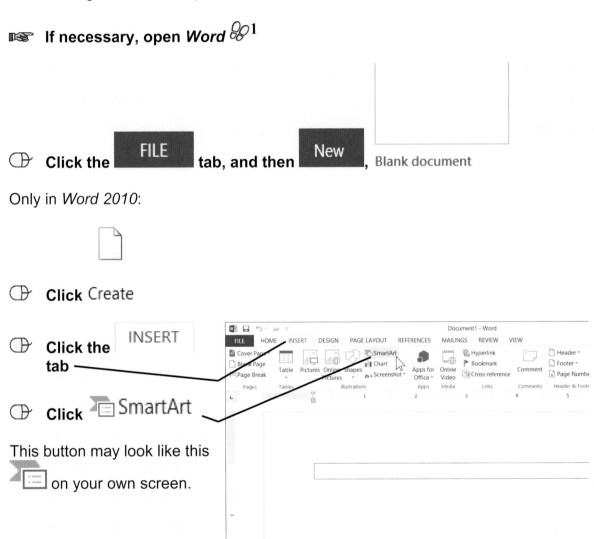

This button may look like this ▰ on your own screen.

You will see the various SmartArt illustrations you can select:

⊕ **Click** 🖼 Picture

⊕ **Click** ⬜

In *Word 2010*, this button

looks like this .

⊕ **Click** OK

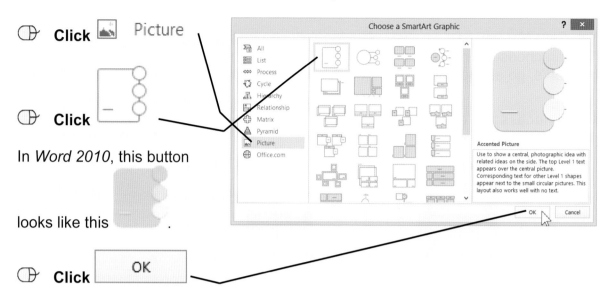

The picture has been inserted into the document. You will see the DESIGN and

FORMAT tabs appear on the ribbon.

Now you can add some text:

⌨ **Type:** By bus to

You will see the text appear inside the picture:

⊕ **If necessary, click** ‹

⊕ **Click** • [Text]

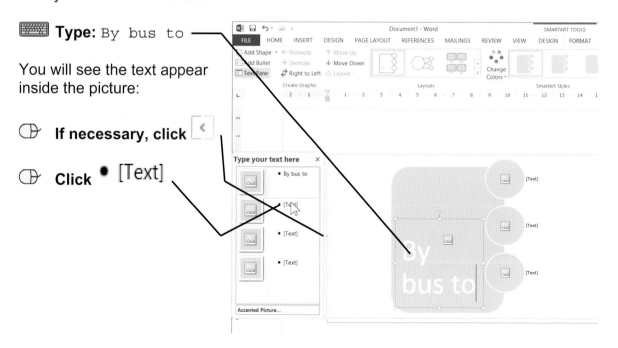

Type: Dresden

☞ **Enter these names in the other two text fields:** Quedlinburg **and** Krakow

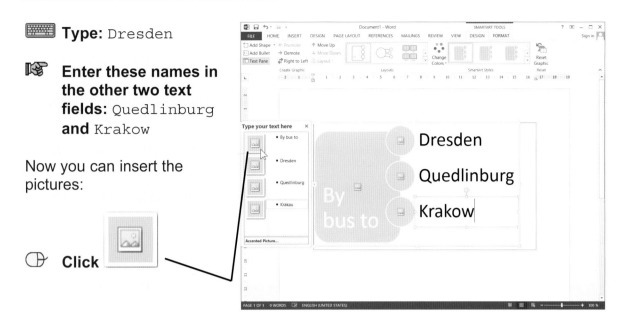

Now you can insert the pictures:

🖱 **Click**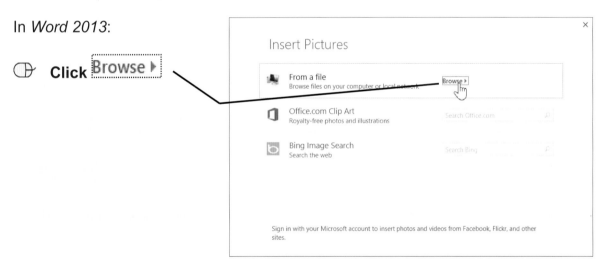

In *Word 2010*:

☞ **Insert the *Bus* picture from the *Practice files Word* folder** 👣**81**

In *Word 2013*:

🖱 **Click** Browse ▶

If necessary, open the *Practice files Word* folder 👣**4**

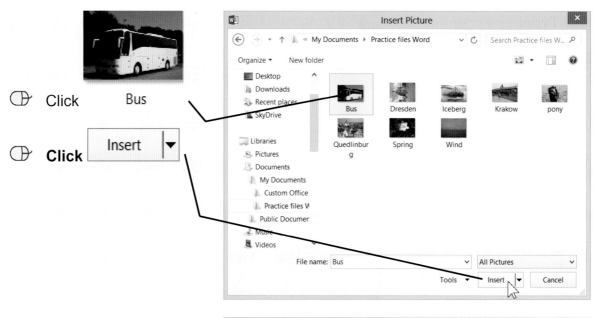

$\oplus$ Click   Bus

$\oplus$ **Click** Insert ▼

The picture has been
inserted:

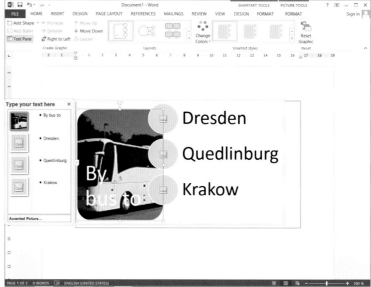

☞ Add the *Dresden* picture to the second item, from the *Practice files Word* folder 𝕏𝕏⁸¹

☞ Add the *Quedlinburg* picture to the third item, from the *Practice files Word* folder 𝕏𝕏⁸¹

☞ Add the *Krakow* picture to the fourth item, from the *Practice files Word* folder 𝕏𝕏⁸¹

The pictures have been added. You can even rotate the *Dresden* picture:

Click the *Dresden* picture

At SMARTART TOOLS :

Click the FORMAT tab

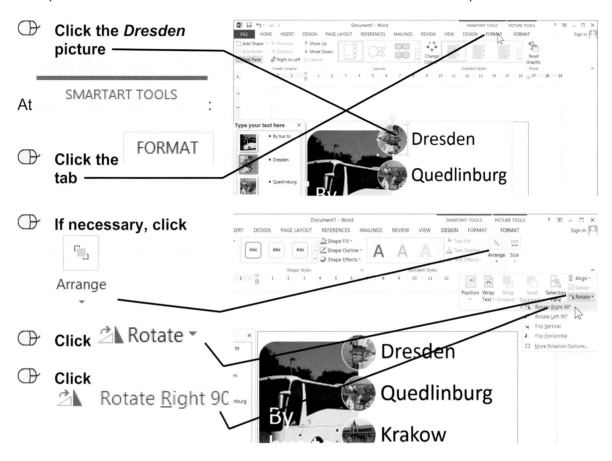

If necessary, click

Arrange

Click ⚞ Rotate ▾

Click ⚞ Rotate Right 90

To add more shapes:

Click the DESIGN tab

By ⬚ Add Shape, click ▾

Click ⬚ Add Shape After

The shape has been added:

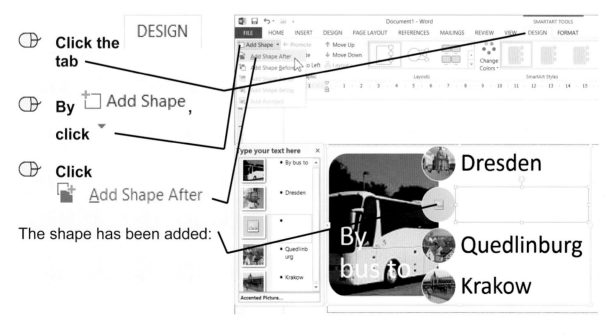

You can also alter the shape of the SmartArt picture:

In the Layouts group:

Click ⬇

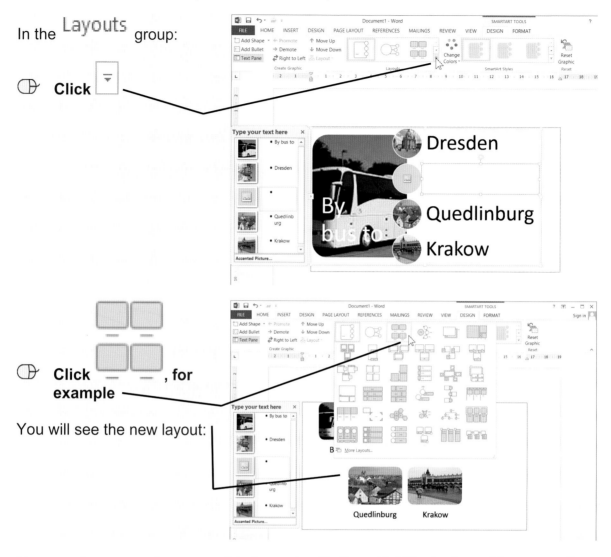

Click ⬛—⬛, for example

You will see the new layout:

Now you have seen how easy it is to work with SmartArt illustrations. You can edit and change the pictures and text as much as you want.

☞ **Close *Word* and do not save the changes** 🦶²

In this chapter you have learned how to insert pictures into a text. In the next couple of exercises you will repeat some of the actions we have discussed.

4.15 Exercises

Have you forgotten how to do something? Use the number beside the footsteps to look it up in the appendix *How Do I Do That Again?* at the end of this book.

Exercise 1: Insert and Edit a Picture

In this exercise you will be inserting and editing a picture in a document.

☞ Open *Word*. 🐾1

☞ Open the *Meteorology* file in the *Practice files Word* folder. 🐾10

☞ Insert the *Iceberg* photo from the *Practice files Word* folder. 🐾34

☞ Wrap the text around the photo with the *Square* option. 🐾36

☞ Place the photo in the middle of the text. 🐾37

☞ Wrap the text to the right-hand side of the photo. 🐾38

☞ Reduce and enlarge the size of the photo. 🐾35

☞ Reset the picture and its size to its original state. 🐾34

☞ Crop the photo. 🐾39

☞ Use the corrections option and select the brightness +20 and contrast 0 option. 🐾40

☞ Change the photo to a black-and-white photo. 🐾41

☞ Turn the photo into a watermark within the text. 🐾42

☞ Delete the photo. 🐾43

☞ Close *Word* and do not save the changes. 🐾2

4.16 Background Information

Dictionary

Brightness	Make a picture lighter or darker.
Contrast	Difference between opposite shades, for instance light-dark.
Crop	Make a photo bigger or smaller by cutting off part of the photo.
Illustration	Picture.
Picture	Collective name for all sorts of pictures, such as illustrations or photos.
Reset picture	Restore a picture to its original state.
Rotation handle	Use this handle to rotate a picture.
Scale	Reduce or enlarge the size of a picture.
Sizing handles	The dots that appear on the borders of a selected picture. You can resize the picture by dragging the handles.
SmartArt	A series of ready-made layouts and shapes.
Text wrap	The way in which the text wraps around the picture.
Washout	Create a very light image of a photo. The result can be used as a watermark that constitutes the background of a text.

Source: Word 2013, Word 2010 and Windows Help and Support

4.17 Tips

💡 Tip
Enlarging and shrinking
If you want to be very precise while enlarging or reducing the size of a picture, you can open the *Layout* window:

👉 **Click the picture**

👉 **Click the** FORMAT **tab**

👉 **By** Size **, click** 🔲

Height and width in inches:

Height and width in percentages:

Lock the ratio of the height and width, so the picture will not distort:

The percentage indicates the size in relation to the picture's original size:

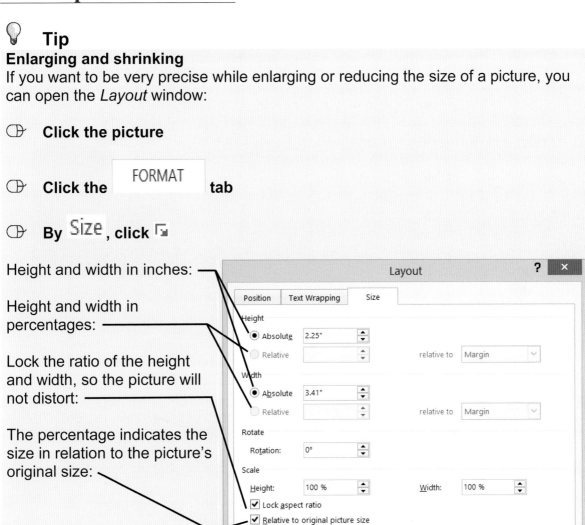

Tip

Rotate a picture

You can move a picture within the text and also rotate it.

In order to do this you need to use the rotation handle (*Word 2013*) (*Word 2010*) on the top border of the frame surrounding the selected picture.

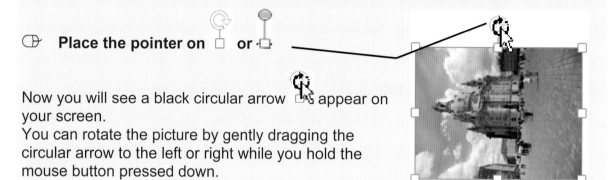

☞ **Place the pointer on** or

Now you will see a black circular arrow appear on your screen.
You can rotate the picture by gently dragging the circular arrow to the left or right while you hold the mouse button pressed down.

 Tip

Quick position

After you have inserted a picture, you can quickly select a certain position on the page. You can do this on the *Format* tab:

☞ **Click the picture**

☞ **Click the** FORMAT **tab**

Position

☞ **Click**

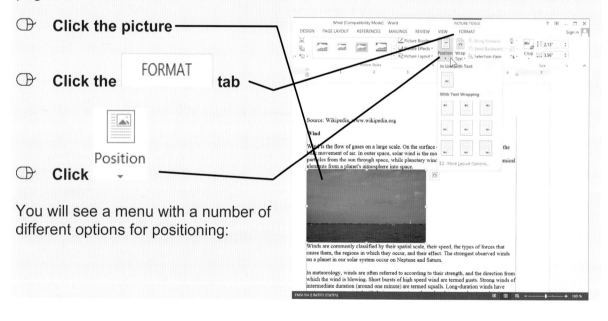

You will see a menu with a number of different options for positioning:

Tip

Picture styles

After you have inserted a picture, you can apply a special style to it. You do this with the *Format* tab:

☞ **Click the picture**

☞ **Click the** FORMAT **tab**

In the Picture Styles group you will see all kinds of effects you can apply to the selected picture.

Frames and borders, for example, but also three-dimensional shapes and shadow effects. As you move the mouse over the various options you can see right away how the effect will look.

Go ahead and try some of these options, for example, in a test document where you have inserted a picture. You may be surprised at the number of different things that can be done with a picture.

 Tip

Move a picture with the text

You can indicate whether you want to move a picture including the text. This will only work if the wrap text option *In line with text* is not selected.

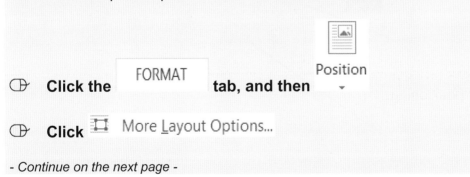

☞ **Click the** FORMAT **tab, and then** Position

☞ **Click** More Layout Options...

- Continue on the next page -

The picture will move along with the text: ——

Another picture is allowed to cover the picture: ——

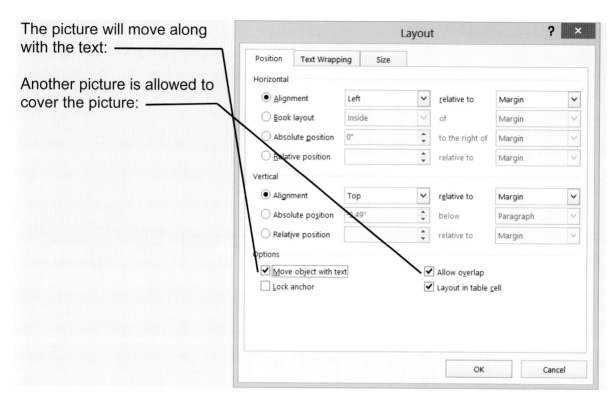

 Tip

Illustrations in *Word 2013*

In *Word 2013* you can insert illustrations that have been saved from the Internet into your documents. You can choose if you want to use the copyright-free *Office* illustrations or the illustrations you have found on the Internet with the *Bing* search engine:

↻ **Click the** `INSERT` **tab** ——

↻ **Click** **Online Pictures**

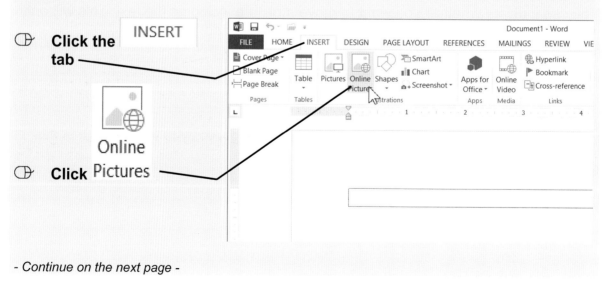

- Continue on the next page -

To view the *Office* illustrations:

Type a keyword in the text box by

Office.com Clip Art
Royalty-free photos and illust

Click

To view illustrations with *Bing:*

Type a keyword in the text box by

Bing Image Search
Search the web

Click

You will see the available illustrations:

Click an illustration

Click Insert

The illustration is inserted into the document right away.

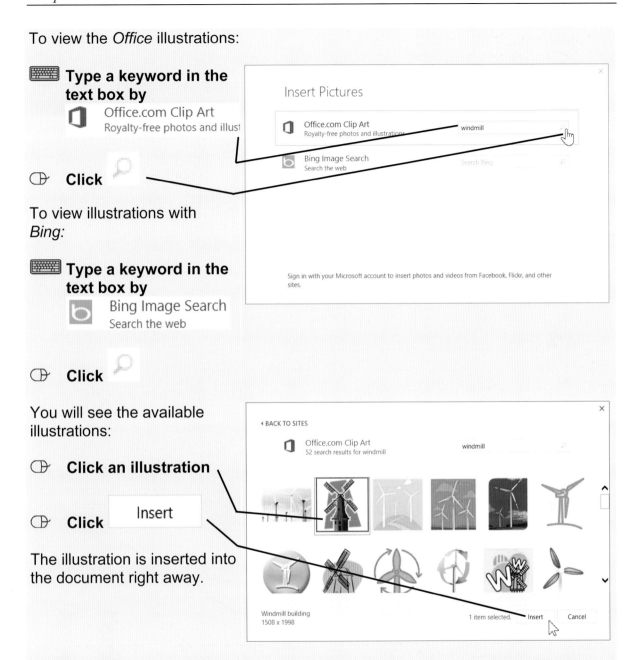

An illustration can be edited in the same way as the photos you worked with in this chapter.

Tip

Illustrations in *Word 2010*

Word 2010 contains a large number of illustrations for you to use. Depending on the installation of the *Word 2010* program you will have a larger or smaller number of illustrations at your disposal. Here is how to display the available illustrations:

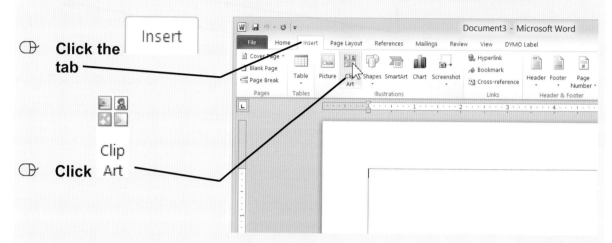

☞ **Click the** Insert **tab**

☞ **Click** Clip **Art**

On the right-hand side you will see the *Illustrations* window. Here you can look for illustrations.

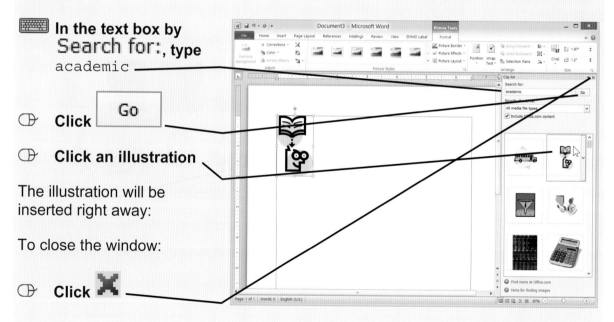

⌨ **In the text box by** **Search for:**, **type** `academic`

☞ **Click** Go

☞ **Click an illustration**

The illustration will be inserted right away:

To close the window:

☞ **Click** ✖

An illustration can be edited in the same way as the photos you worked with in this chapter.

5. Tables

Tables are often used to format text. A table consists of horizontal *rows* and vertical *columns*. The individual squares generated in this way are called *cells*.

In this chapter you will take a look at some of the many options *Word* offers for formatting a table. You can add borders and shades, for example. You can format the text or numbers in the cells in a variety of different ways: you can even display text vertically. If you create a table containing numbers, *Word* can also perform simple calculations with the data.

Once you have mastered the creation of tables you will have another useful tool on hand to present your text in a neat and orderly fashion.

In this chapter you will learn how to:

- create a new table;
- insert rows and columns;
- adjust the width of the columns;
- adjust the height of the rows;
- automatically adjust the columns and rows;
- add borders and shading to a table;
- use ready-made formatting;
- place the text in a cell;
- change the direction of the text;
- add up numbers in columns;
- neatly align monetary values one below the other;
- compute with bookmarks;
- merge and split cells;
- delete a table.

5.1 Creating a New Table

Word makes it very easy to add a table to your document.

	January	February
	5	6

Table

You use the ▾ button on the INSERT tab to add a table. Once you have added a table, you will notice two new tabs, called *Design* and *Layout*:

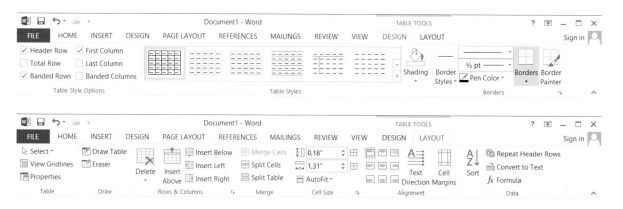

☞ **Open *Word* ⬦¹**

☞ **Set the font to *Times New Roman* ⬦¹⁷**

☞ **Set the font size to *12 points* ⬦ ¹⁸**

☞ **Set the line spacing to *Single* ⬦⁵**

☞ **Set the paragraph spacing after to *0 points* ⬦⁶**

In this exercise we will be creating a table consisting of two rows and three columns.

☞ **Click the** **INSERT** **tab**

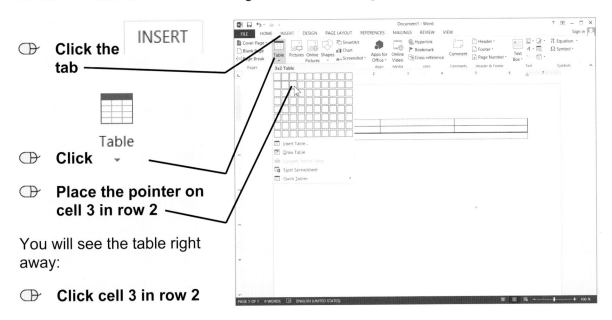

☞ **Click** **Table** ▾

☞ **Place the pointer on cell 3 in row 2**

You will see the table right away:

☞ **Click cell 3 in row 2**

The table has been inserted. You can enter text in the individual squares or boxes. These squares are called *cells*. You place the cursor in a cell by clicking inside it:

☞ **Click the second cell in the first row**

⌨ **Type:** Rilana

You can move the cursor to the next cell by pressing the Tab key:

⌨ **Press** **Tab**

⌨ **Type:** Mara

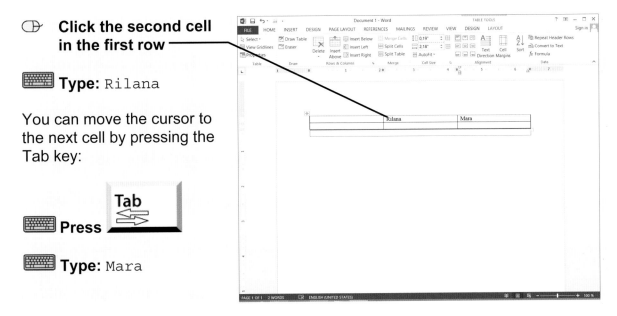

➦ **Please note:**

In *Word 2013*, the row below the table is the text box. This row is shown because Show text boundaries is still marked in the *Options* window.

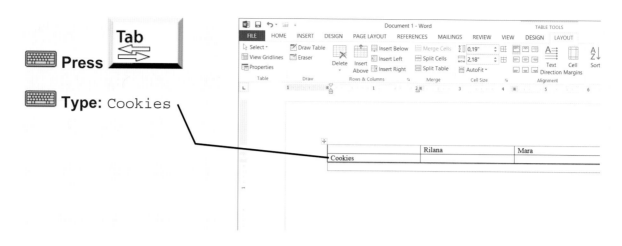

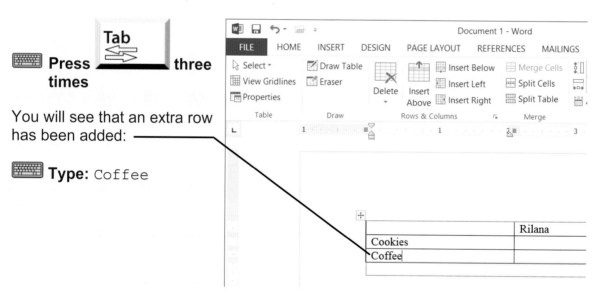

5.2 Adding a Row

It is very easy to add an extra row to a table. This will happen automatically when you press the Tab key. Just try it:

Word often has more than one way of doing things. There is also another way of adding rows or columns to a table.

5.3 Inserting Columns

If you want to insert a new column on the right-hand side of the table, you need to first place the cursor in the last column on the right:

☞ **Click in the cell with the name 'Mara'**

☞ **Click the** LAYOUT **tab**

☞ **Click** Insert Right

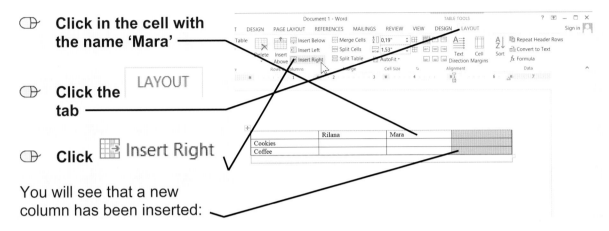

You will see that a new column has been inserted:

5.4 Adjusting the Width of the Columns

You can use the mouse to set the width of the columns yourself. Like this:

☞ **Place the pointer on the line between column 1 and 2**

The pointer ⌶ turns into ╬:

☞ **Drag the line to the left**

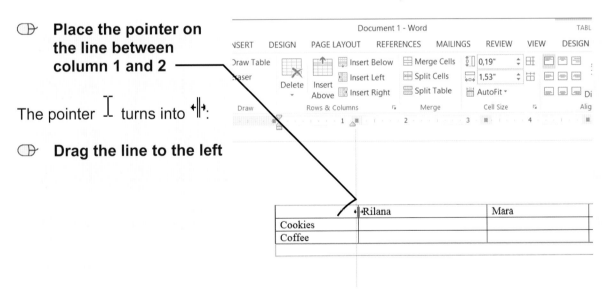

You will see that the second column with the name 'Rilana' has become wider.

5.5 Adjusting the Height of the Rows

You can also adjust the height of a row.

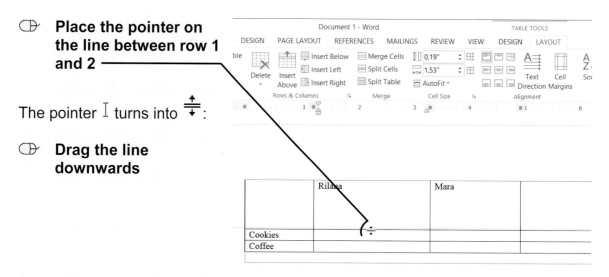

☞ **Place the pointer on the line between row 1 and 2**

The pointer I turns into ÷ :

☞ **Drag the line downwards**

The row has become higher.

5.6 Automatic Adjustment

Now you have a table with rows that are uneven in height. Also, some columns are wider than others. You can try to adjust these differences with the mouse, but you cannot be very precise. Fortunately, *Word* has a command to help you. First you need to select the whole table:

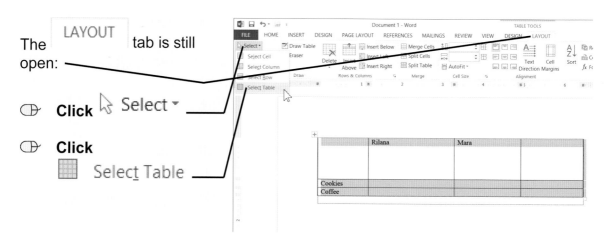

The LAYOUT tab is still open:

☞ **Click ☒ Select ▾**

☞ **Click ☒ Select Table**

Now the whole table has been selected:

By Cell Size, click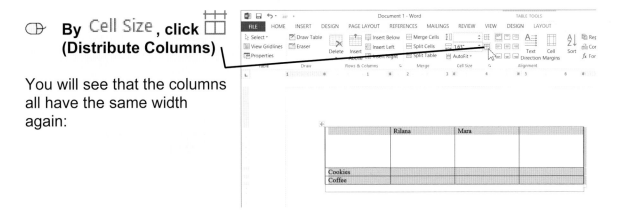
(Distribute Columns)

You will see that the columns
all have the same width
again:

In the same way you can make all the rows even in height:

By Cell Size, click
(Distribute Rows)

Now the rows are all exactly
the same height too:

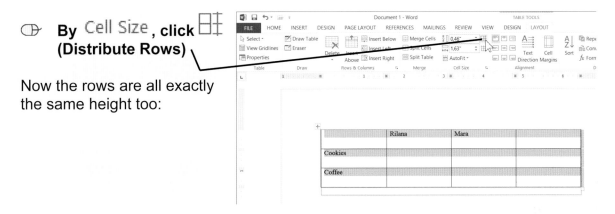

5.7 Borders

Word will automatically put a thin border around the cells. You can change this border for an each individual cell, column, or row. For example, you can make the borders thicker, or give them a color. But first you will need to select the section of the table that you want to change.

 Please note:
Select first... then choose a border.

For instance, you could adjust only the top row and give it a different type of border. You will need to select the row first. You do that as follows:

👆 **Click a spot in the top row**

The LAYOUT tab is still open:

👆 **Click** Select ▾

👆 **Click** Select Row

Now the top row is selected and you can change the border:

👆 **Click the** DESIGN **tab**

👆 **By** _____,

click ▾

You will see a menu with various types of borders:

👆 **Click** ═══

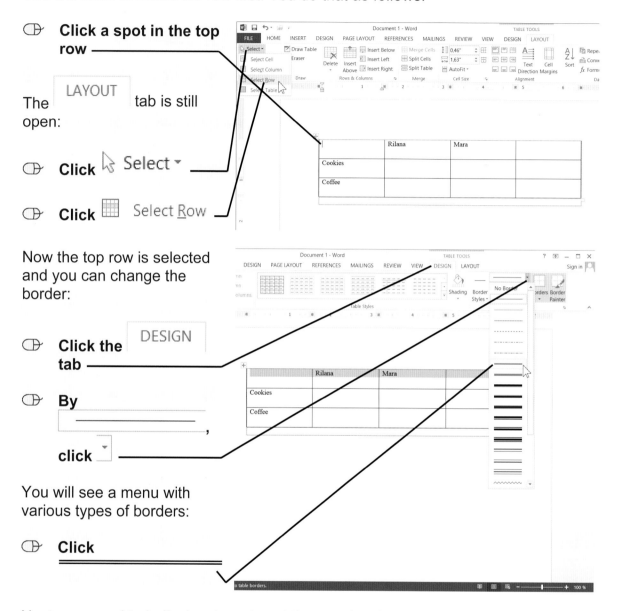

Next, you need to indicate where to put the new border. This could be above, below, or around the entire row, for example.

In *Word 2013*:

☞ **Click** Borders

In *Word 2010*:

☞ **By** ▦ Borders,
    click ▾

Now you can choose where
you want to put the border,
for example, all around the
row, like a frame:

☞ **Click**
    ⊡ Outside Borders

Now the top row is framed
with a double line:

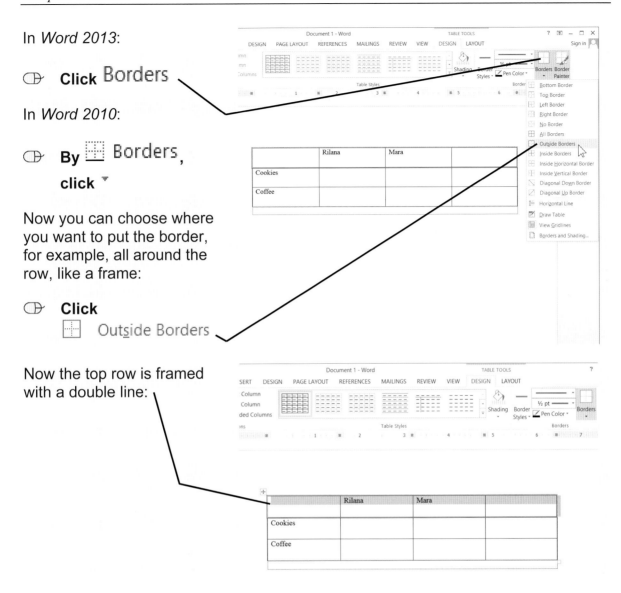

Tip
Applying borders above, below, or to the right

In this menu you can determine how the border will be drawn:

⊞	Bottom Border
⊞	Top Border
⊞	Left Border
⊞	Right Border
⊞	No Border
⊞	All Borders
⊞	Outside Borders
⊞	Inside Borders
⊞	Inside Horizontal Border
⊞	Inside Vertical Border
◩	Diagonal Down Border
◪	Diagonal Up Border
≣	Horizontal Line
▥	Draw Table
▦	View Gridlines
▯	Borders and Shading...

Your choice is applied to the selected part of the table, for instance, a single cell, multiple cells, a row, a column, or the whole table. You can even put one fat line below a single cell, for example, to emphasize something.

5.8 Shading

You can also apply shading or add a background color to a cell, row, or column. You need to select the relevant part of the table first.

Please note:

☞ **Make sure the top row is selected** 44

For example, you can add an background color to this top row.

In *Word 2013*:

⊕ **Click** Shading ▾

In *Word 2010*:

⊕ **By** Shading **click** ▾

You will see a diagram with various colors:

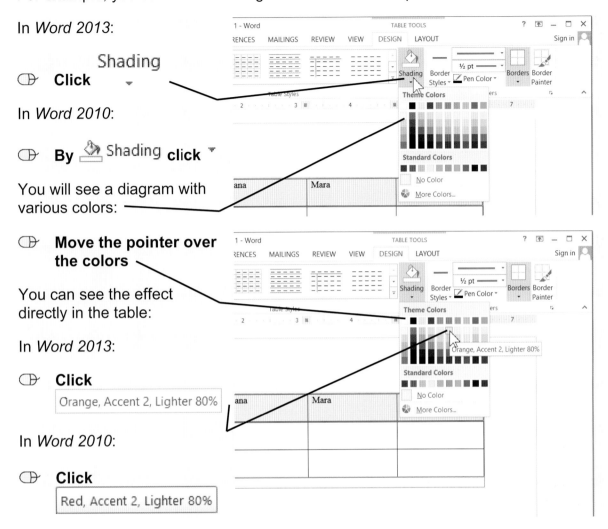

⊕ **Move the pointer over the colors**

You can see the effect directly in the table:

In *Word 2013*:

⊕ **Click**
Orange, Accent 2, Lighter 80%

In *Word 2010*:

⊕ **Click**
Red, Accent 2, Lighter 80%

Now the top row has a background color.

5.9 Ready-To-Use Borders and Shading

Word contains an extensive gallery of templates for various table styles. If you select such a style it will be applied to the whole table at once.

⊕ **Click a spot in the table**

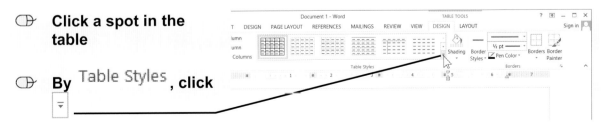

⊕ **By** Table Styles **, click** ▾

HELP! I do not see the Design tab.

Is the DESIGN tab not visible?

☞ **Make sure the cursor is placed within the table: click the table**

In this gallery you can select the style you want to use:

☞ **Click**

Now the table looks very different. You can undo this:

☞ **Click** ↶

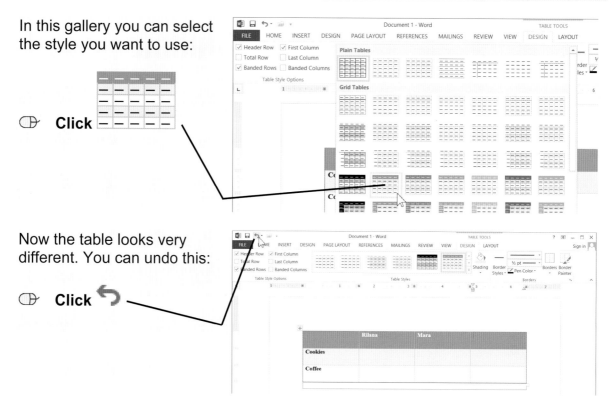

5.10 Inserting Text into a Cell

You can format the text in a cell in various ways. You can render the letters in bold or italics, or give them a color. The text can also be positioned in the cells in different ways:

By default, the text is aligned to the top left corner of the cell. You can change this if you want:

☞ **Click the** LAYOUT **tab**

☞ **Select the top row** ✅44

Now you can select the alignment for the text, for example, to the bottom right corner of the cell:

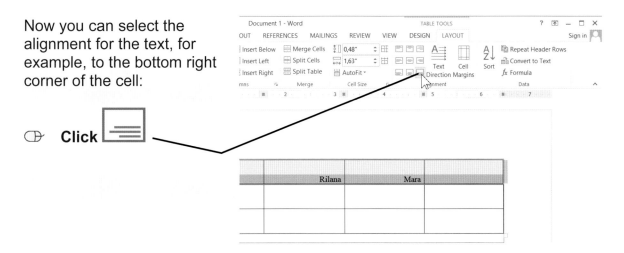

⊕ **Click** [icon]

You will see that the names are now placed in the bottom right corner of the cell.

If you want to center the names horizontally and vertically in the cell:

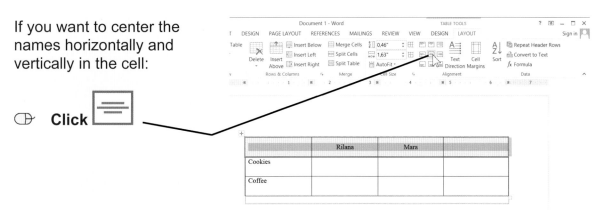

⊕ **Click** [icon]

5.11 The Text Direction

You can change the direction of the text as well. Like this:

⊕ **Click** Direction

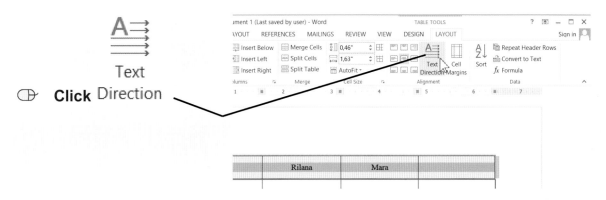

You will see that the names have rotated:

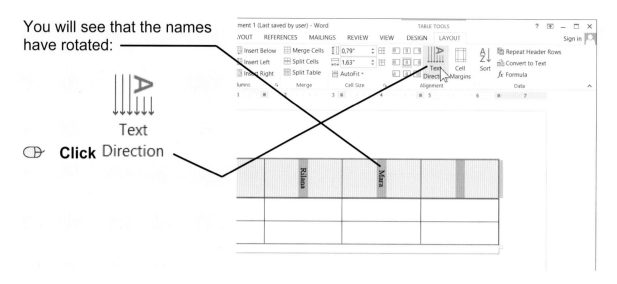

Text

☞ **Click** Direction

The names are rotated again:

Text

☞ **Click** Direction

Notice that the names have been put back to their original position, but the height of the row has increased.

5.12 Calculations in a Table

You can perform simple calculations in *Word*, such as adding numbers. Just try it:

☞ **Enter the figures as shown in this example**

	Rilana	Mara
Cookies	40	30.40
Coffee	50	45.55

Below these figures you will want to create a new row and insert the subtotal of these two numbers in that row. Here is how you add a row below:

⊕ **Click** ⊞ Insert Below **twice**

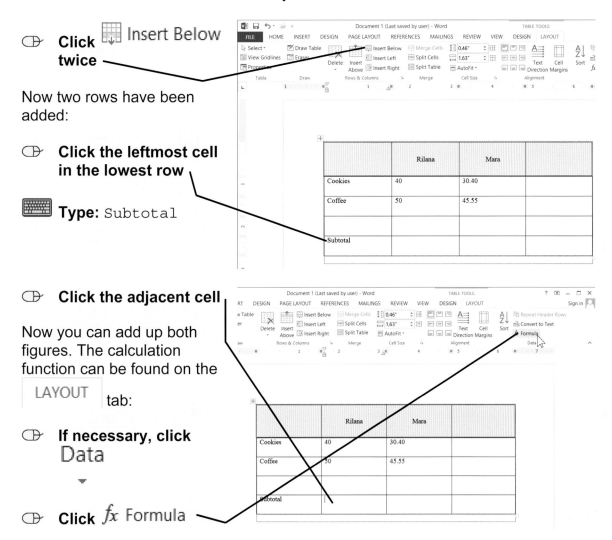

Now two rows have been added:

⊕ **Click the leftmost cell in the lowest row**

⌨ **Type:** Subtotal

⊕ **Click the adjacent cell**

Now you can add up both figures. The calculation function can be found on the LAYOUT tab:

⊕ **If necessary, click**
   Data
   ▾

⊕ **Click** *fx* Formula

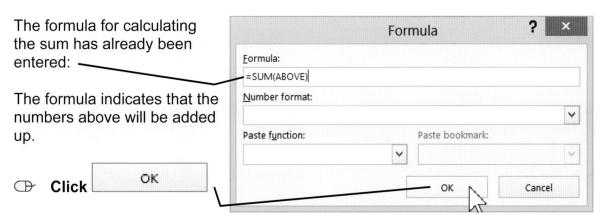

The *Formula* window appears:

The formula for calculating the sum has already been entered:

The formula indicates that the numbers above will be added up.

⊕ **Click** [OK]

Formula ? ✕

Formula:
=SUM(ABOVE)

Number format:
[   ] ▾

Paste function: Paste bookmark:
[   ] ▾   [   ] ▾

                    OK   Cancel

You will see that the total (90) has been computed:

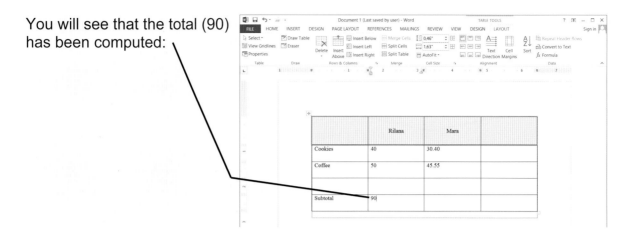

5.13 Align Amounts

You can align the decimal points of the figures in the third column, one below the other, and place them in the center of the column. You can do this by inserting a decimal tab.

Please note:
Select first... then change the tab.

The LAYOUT is already open:

☞ **Click the third column**

☞ **Click** Select ▾

☞ **Click** Select Column

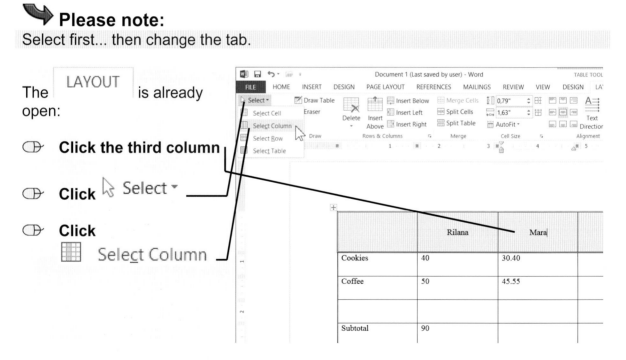

Now the column where the cursor was placed has been selected. If you insert a decimal tab here, it will be applied to all the amounts in this column.

First you need to select the type of tab, in the top left-hand corner of the page:

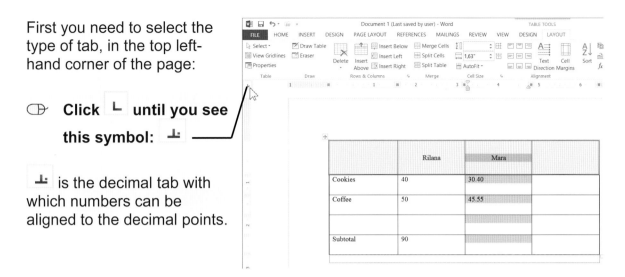

☞ **Click ⌐ until you see this symbol:** ⊥

⊥ is the decimal tab with which numbers can be aligned to the decimal points.

Now you can insert the tab by clicking the ruler:

☞ **Click** 4

You will see that the decimal points in the amounts are neatly aligned in the middle, one below the other:

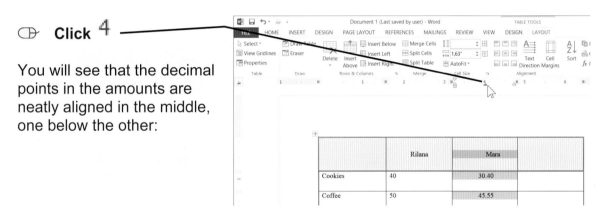

Now you can also add up the amounts in the third column:

☞ **Click the empty cell at the bottom of the third column**

☞ **If necessary, click**
Data
▼

☞ **Click** *fx* Formula

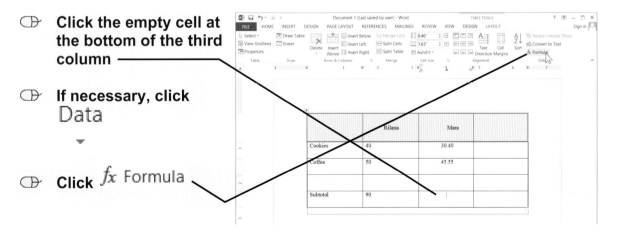

The correct formula is not entered automatically. You can adjust this yourself:

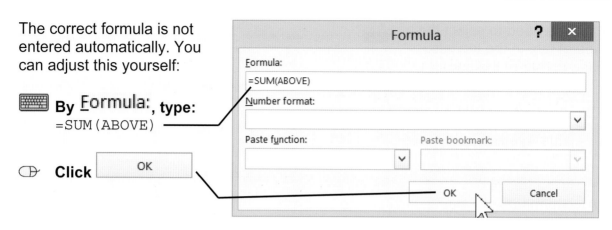

⌨ **By** Formula:, **type:**
=SUM(ABOVE)

🖰 **Click** OK

The subtotal has now been entered, and the decimal point in the amount is neatly aligned with the figures above.

5.14 Calculating with Bookmarks

You can quickly add up a column with numbers by using the formula you previously entered. But you will need to use *bookmarks* for other types of calculations. You can attach a name (bookmark) to the number you want to use for the calculation and in the formula you can refer to this name.

☞ **Add two new rows below the bottom row** 🔖**45**

☞ **Enter the data you see in this example**

	Rilana	Mara	
Cookies	40	30.40	
Coffee	50	45.55	
Subtotal	90	75.95	
Sales tax 5%			
Total			

This is how you can compute the amount of the sales tax:

☞ **Select the subtotal in the second column** ✂20

☞ **Click the** INSERT **tab**

☞ **If necessary, click** Links

☞ **Click** ▶ Bookmark

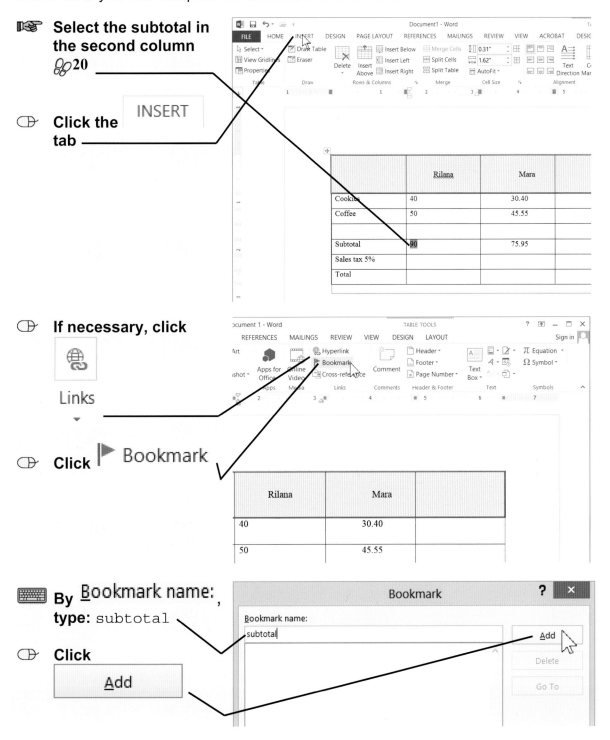

⌨ **By** Bookmark name: **, type:** subtotal

☞ **Click** Add

The amount that has been entered by 'Subtotal' is now associated with the bookmark called *subtotal*.

Next, you need to add another bookmark *tax* for the sales tax percentage:

👉 **Select 5%** 🦶**20**

🖱 **If necessary, click**

Links

🖱 **Click** ⚐ Bookmark

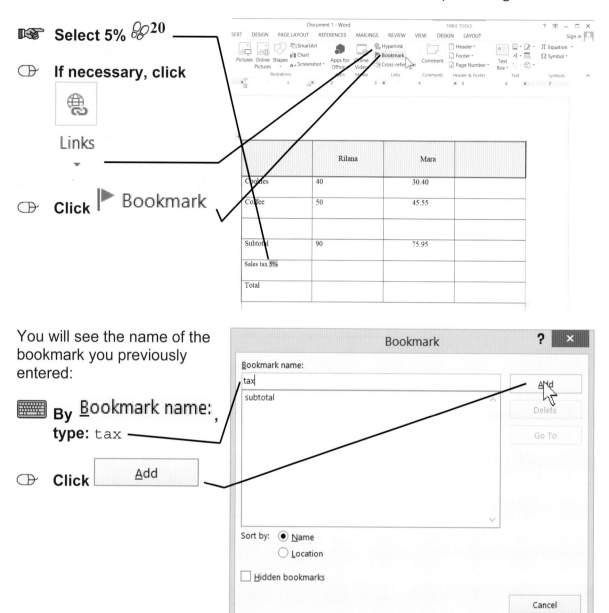

You will see the name of the bookmark you previously entered:

⌨ **By** Bookmark name:, **type:** tax

🖱 **Click** Add

Now you can compute the amount of the sales tax by multiplying the bookmarks called *subtotal* and *tax*:

☞ **Click the cell next to 'Sales tax 5%'** ─────

☞ **Click the** LAYOUT **tab** ─────

☞ **If necessary, click** Data

☞ **Click** *fx* Formula ─────

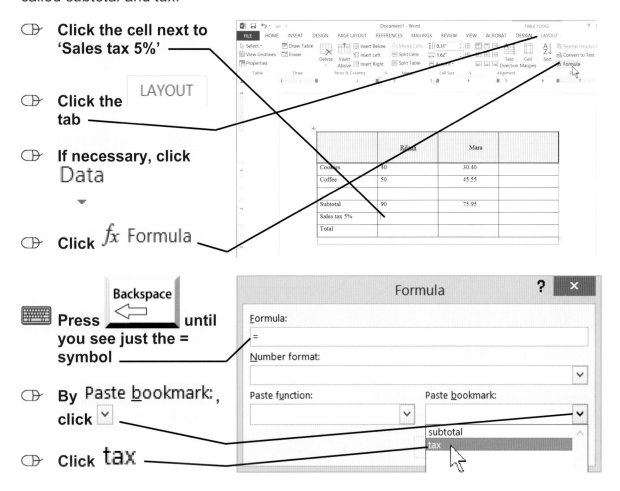

☞ **Press** Backspace **until you see just the = symbol** ─────

☞ **By** Paste bookmark:, **click** ⌄ ─────

☞ **Click** tax ─────

The name of the bookmark is entered and then you can indicate which type of calculation you want to use. In this case, the sales tax percentage needs to be multiplied by the subtotal:

☞ **Press** * ─────

☞ **By** Paste bookmark:, **click** ⌄ ─────

☞ **Click** subtotal ─────

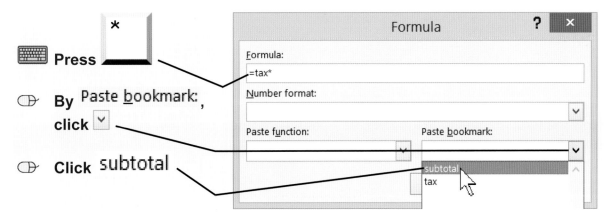

You will see the entire
formula:

☞ **By** Number format: **,
select the** 0.00 **format**

✋ **Click** OK

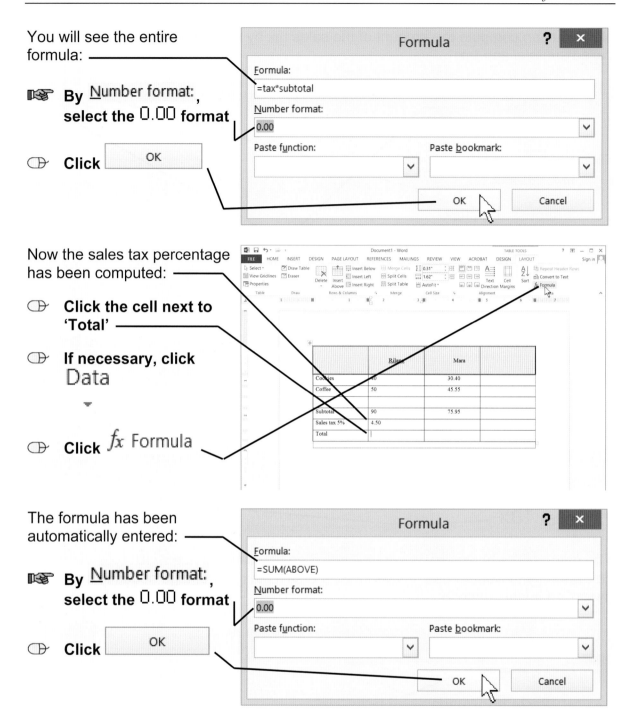

Now the sales tax percentage
has been computed:

✋ **Click the cell next to
'Total'**

✋ **If necessary, click**
Data

✋ **Click** ƒx Formula

The formula has been
automatically entered:

☞ **By** Number format: **,
select the** 0.00 **format**

✋ **Click** OK

Now the total amount of the invoice has been computed. You can compute the sales
tax and the total amount for the other column in the same way. For now this will not
be necessary.

Symbols for doing math

The mathematical symbols used in the computer world may be a little different from the symbols you usually use. The most frequently used symbols are:

+	add
-	subtract
*	multiply
/	divide

On a regular keyboard, the easiest method is to use the keys on the right side of your keyboard (this is called the numeric keypad).

5.15 Merging Cells

You can merge the cells in a table, or split them into multiple cells. Give it a try:

☞ **Select the bottom row**
✂ 44

🖱 **Click** 📑 Merge Cells

The bottom row will merge into a single cell.

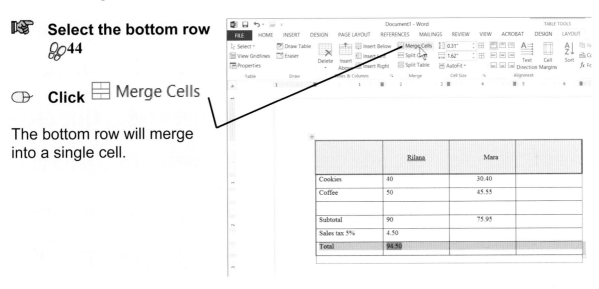

5.16 Splitting a Cell

You can also split a cell into multiple cells. Give it a try:

The bottom row, actually, the bottom cell, is still selected:

Now you can split this cell:

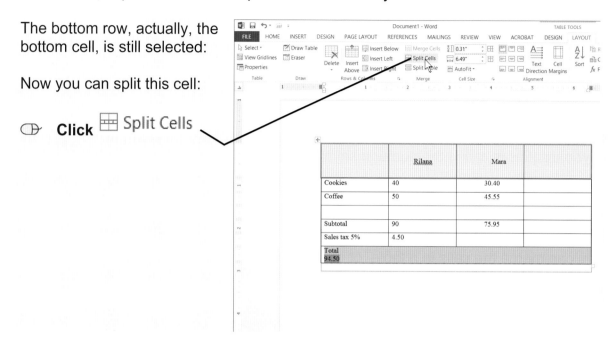

👉 **Click** ⊞ Split Cells

In a small window you can select the number of cells into which you want to split this cell:

By default, it is two cells.
Change that to four cells:

👉 **By** Number of columns:,
    click ▲ **until you see**
    4

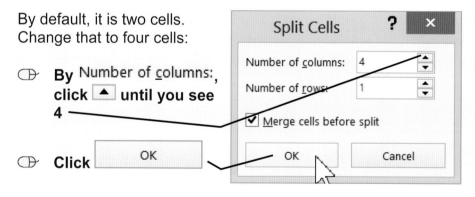

👉 **Click** [OK]

Now the single cell is split back to the original four cells.

5.17 Deleting a Table

This is how you delete a table, or part of a table:

☞ **Select the right-hand** **column** ℰ46

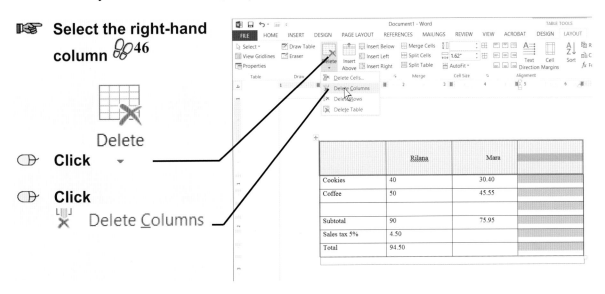

 Click ▾

Click

╳ Delete Columns

Now the right-hand column has been deleted. You will see there is a blank space next to the *Mara* column. In order to fill the whole width of the page, you need to drag the borders of the table in the same way you did earlier in this chapter.

💡 **Tip**
Deleting
In this way you can also delete rows, or even the entire table. In that case you need to select ⊟╳ Delete Rows or ▦╳ Delete Table .

➥ **Please note:**
If you want to use the options in the *Rows&Columns* group, you need to place the cursor in the table. If you do not see the ⬚LAYOUT⬚ tab, then click the table first.

☞ **Close *Word* and do not save the document** ℰ2

In the following exercise you can repeat some of the actions learned in this chapter.

5.18 Exercises

Have you forgotten how to do something? Use the number beside the footsteps to look it up in the appendix *How Do I Do That Again?* at the end of the book.

Exercise 1: Creating a Table

In this exercise you will create a new table, add some data to it, and use a simple calculation.

☞ Open *Word*. 🦶**1**

☞ Set the font to *Times New Roman*. 🦶**17**

☞ Set the font size to *12 points*. 🦶**18**

☞ Create a table with two columns and three rows. 🦶**47**

☞ In column 1, row 2, type: January.

☞ In column 1, row 3: February.

☞ In column 2, row 2, type: 20

☞ In column 2, row 3, type: 30.

☞ Add a row. 🦶**45**

☞ In column 1, row 4, type: Total.

☞ Place the cursor in column 2, row 4.

☞ Let *Word* calculate the total sum in the cell next to *Total*. 🦶**48**

☞ Delete the row with *Total*. 🦶**49**

☞ Close *Word* without saving the document. 🦶**2**

5.19 Background Information

Dictionary

Alignment	The position where the text should begin. The text can be aligned to the left, right or centered.
Column	A vertical series of cells in a table.
Decimal tab	A tab that allows numerical values to be aligned by decimal point.
Merge	Merge two or more cells into one cell.
Row	A horizontal series of cells in a table.
Shading	Background color.
Split	Split a single cell into two or more cells.
Table	A figure consisting of horizontal rows and vertical colums. Tables are often used to format text.

Source: Word 2013, Word 2010 and Windows Help and Support

5.20 Tips

 Tip

Types of tab stops

Word has different types of tab stops. The main types are:

L   *Left tab*: the text is aligned to the left; the text begins at the tab stop.

⊥   *Center tab*: the middle of the text is place below this tab stop.

⅃   *Right tab*: the text is aligned to the right; the text ends at the tab stop.

⊥·   *Decimal tab*: centers the text so the decimal points in numerical values are aligned one below the other.

 Tip

Page layout: portrait or landscape

If your table contains many columns, it can be useful to change the page orientation to 'landscape'. This way, you will have more space available for the table. See *Chapter 3 Formatting Documents* for more information about this topic.

Tip

Sorting

You can order a column with numbers or names, if desired. You do that as follows:

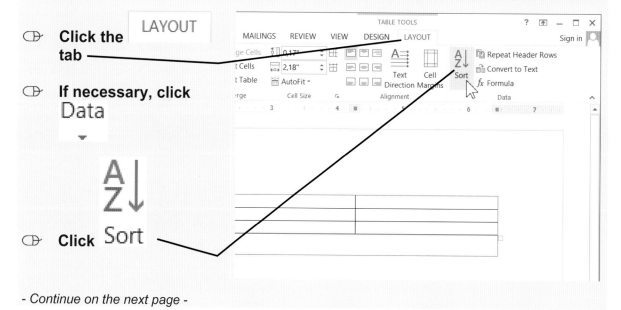

☞ **Click the**   LAYOUT **tab**

☞ **If necessary, click** Data

☞ **Click** Sort

- Continue on the next page -

☞ **By <u>S</u>ort by , select the column you want to order** —————

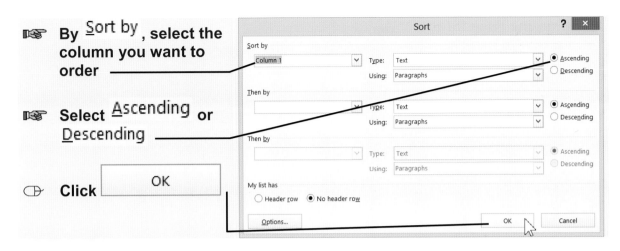

☞ **Select <u>A</u>scending or <u>D</u>escending** —————

☞ **Click** OK

💡 **Tip**

Draw a table

You can also 'draw' a table in *Word* manually, if you like. You start like this:

☞ **Click the INSERT tab** —————

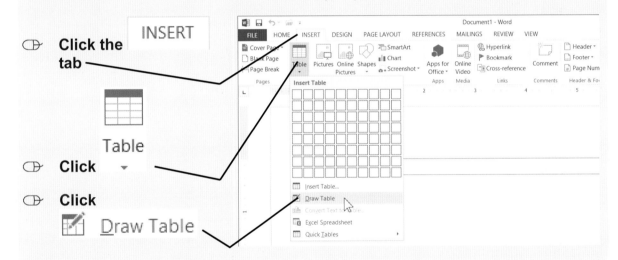

☞ **Click** ▾

☞ **Click** <u>D</u>raw Table

The pointer turns into 🖉. Now you can draw the table by pressing the mouse button and holding it down while you drag the mouse across the page.

☞ **Drag a rectangle**

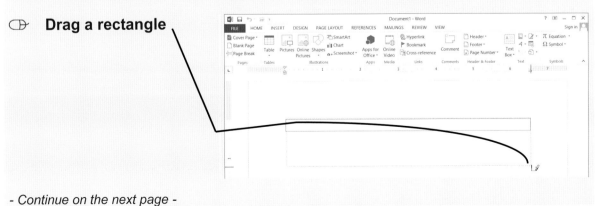

- Continue on the next page -

☞ **Drag the lines for the cells, one by one** ——

After you have finished drawing:

☞ **Click** 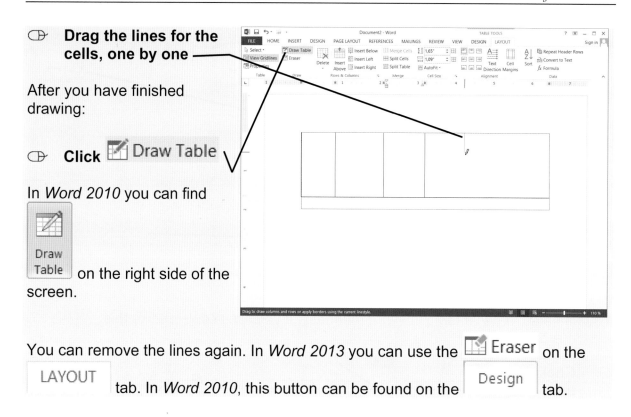 **Draw Table**

In *Word 2010* you can find

Draw Table on the right side of the screen.

You can remove the lines again. In *Word 2013* you can use the ⌨ Eraser on the LAYOUT tab. In *Word 2010*, this button can be found on the Design tab.

6. Creating Professional-quality Documents

Word gives you many options for creating professional-quality documents. Newsletters, leaflets, booklets and other creative documents can be made with little effort. In this chapter you will be creating a simple leaflet, and in the process you will learn how to format text, and work with pictures as well.

In this chapter you will learn how to:

- place text in columns;
- place pictures in columns;
- insert a column break;
- add borders to pages;
- add captions to pictures;
- create new sections;
- embellish text with WordArt;
- insert pictures;
- create and format text boxes;
- combine text boxes with pictures;
- use shapes;
- place text inside shapes;
- create diagrams;
- link text boxes.

6.1 Text in Columns

☞ **Open *Word* 🐾¹**

☞ **Open the *Summer program* document in the *Practice files Word* folder 🐾10**

☞ **If necessary, enable editing 🐾82**

☞ **If necessary, hide paragraph marks and other hidden symbols 🐾19**

In this section you will format the text and divide it over two columns:

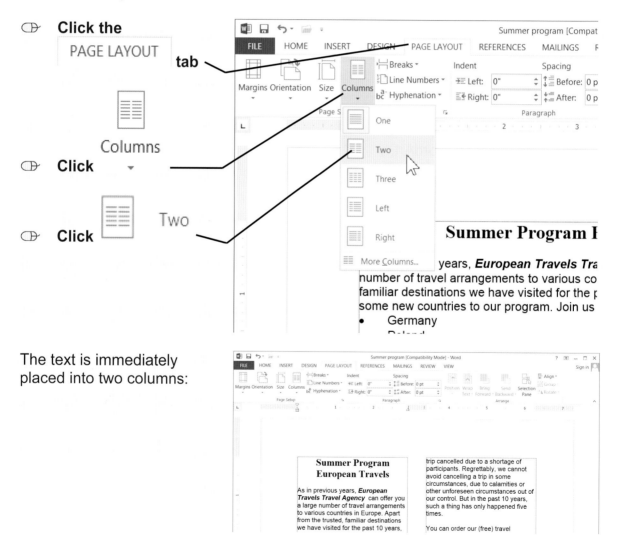

☞ **Click the PAGE LAYOUT tab**

☞ **Click Columns**

☞ **Click Two**

The text is immediately placed into two columns:

At the moment the title appears above the first column only. You can adjust this so that it will appear above both columns:

☞ **Select the title** ✂*20*

Columns

☞ **Click** ▾

☞ **Click** One

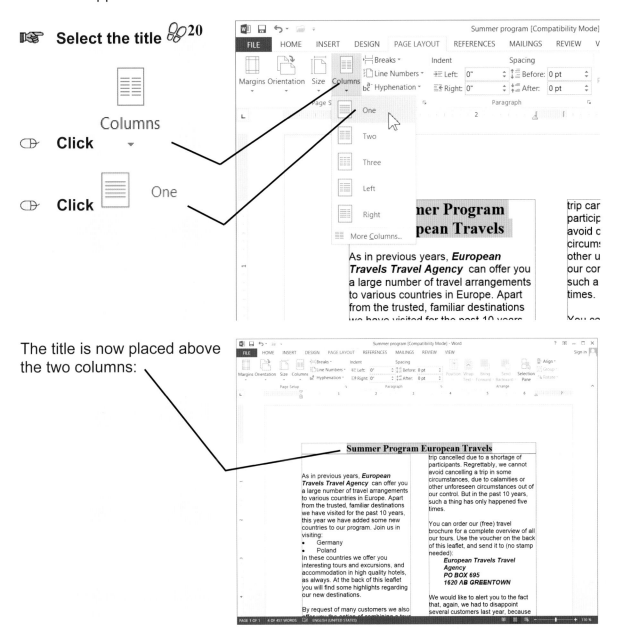

The title is now placed above the two columns:

The formatting is still not quite right yet. The text in both columns should start at the same height, but it is better to correct this later on after you have formatted the rest of the text. First, you can take a look at a print preview of the whole page. This gives you an impression of the layout as it is so far:

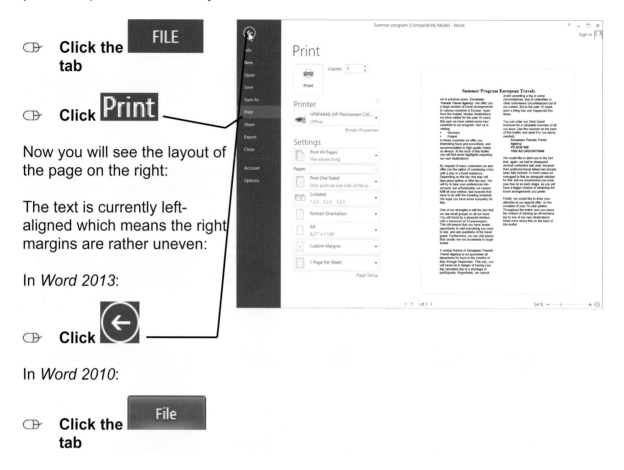

☞ **Click the** FILE **tab**

☞ **Click** Print

Now you will see the layout of the page on the right:

The text is currently left-aligned which means the right margins are rather uneven:

In *Word 2013*:

☞ **Click** ←

In *Word 2010*:

☞ **Click the** File **tab**

You can distribute the text evenly between the columns. This is called 'justifying' the text. It will make the leaflet look a lot neater.

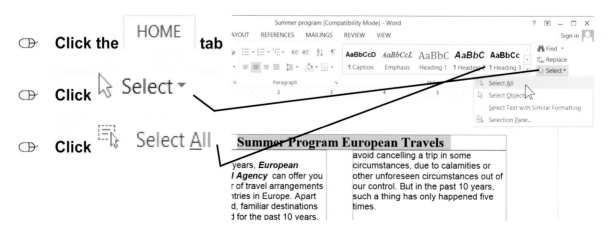

☞ **Click the** HOME **tab**

☞ **Click** Select

☞ **Click** Select All

⊕ **Click** ≡

The text in the columns is now justified. The columns look more consistent:

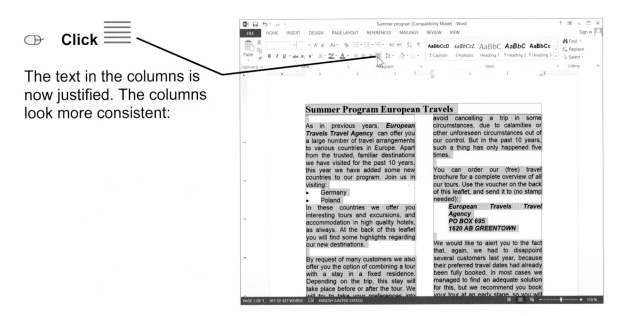

The title is no longer centered. You can easily correct this:

⊕ **Click the title**

⊕ **Click** ≡

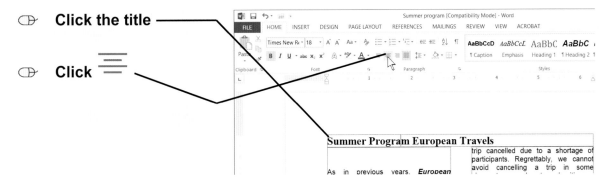

You can see the layout even better if you use the print preview option again.

⊕ **Click the**  **tab, and then** **Print**

☞ **View the result**

In *Word 2013*:

⊕ **Click**

In *Word 2010*:

⊕ **Click the** **File** **tab**

As a result of justifying the text, you may notice an excessive amount of white space between the words. This happens often when you place text in columns. You can limit this by enabling the automatic hyphenation option. You do that as follows:

☞ **Click the**

PAGE LAYOUT **tab**

☞ **Click** bc̲ Hyphenation ▾

☞ **Click**

bc̲ Hyphenation Options.

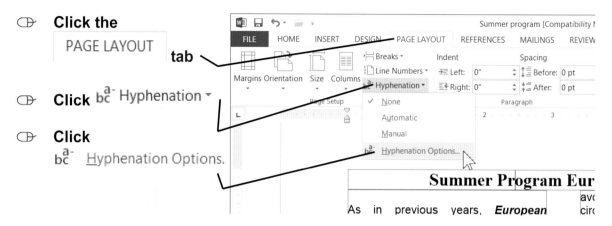

It is better to exclude the words that begin with a capital letter from the automatic hyphenation. It is unusual to hyphenate the names of persons or countries, for instance:

☞ **Check the box ☑ by**
Automatically hyphenat

☞ **Uncheck the box ☑ by**
Hyphenate words in CAI

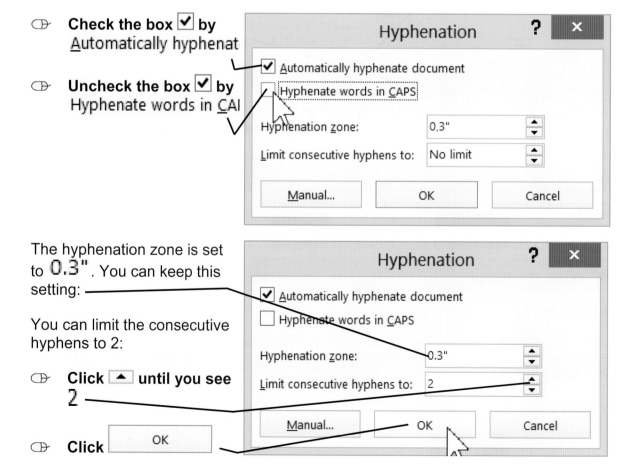

The hyphenation zone is set to 0.3". You can keep this setting: —————

You can limit the consecutive hyphens to 2:

☞ **Click ▲ until you see**
2

☞ **Click** OK

If you want to have full control over the hyphenation, you can click the 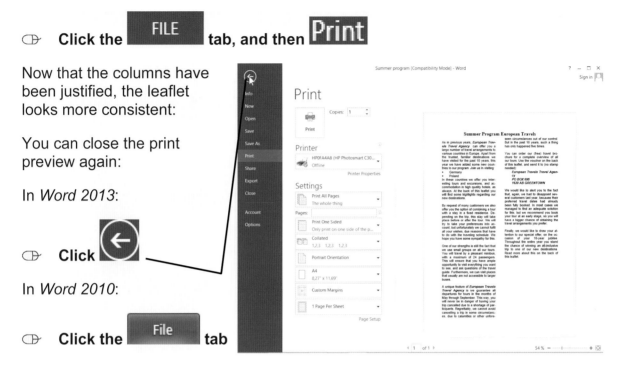Manual option. Then you will be asked to approve each word that is hyphenated. This topic is covered in more detail in *Chapter 2 Entering Text*.

☞ **Click the** FILE **tab, and then** Print

Now that the columns have been justified, the leaflet looks more consistent:

You can close the print preview again:

In *Word 2013*:

☞ **Click**

In *Word 2010*:

☞ **Click the** File **tab**

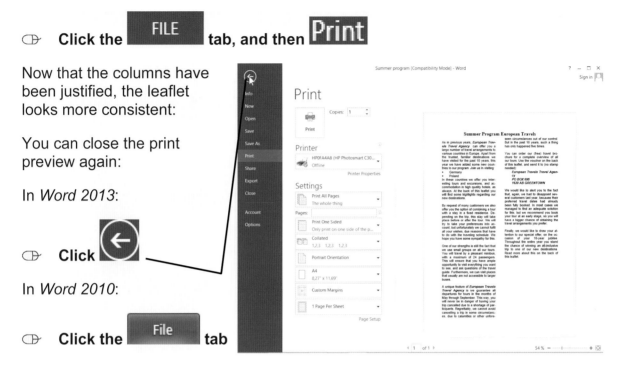

➥ **Please note:**

If you want to set the hyphenation options, you do not need to select the text first. The hyphenation settings will automatically apply to the whole document.

6.2 Pictures in Columns

You can insert pictures into a text that has been formatted into columns in the same way as in a regular document. You can insert them in one column, multiple columns, or even (partly) between columns. In the leaflet, you can start like this:

☞ **Press** Ctrl **+** End

Now the cursor is placed at the end of the text:

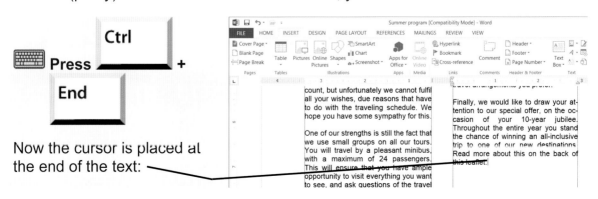

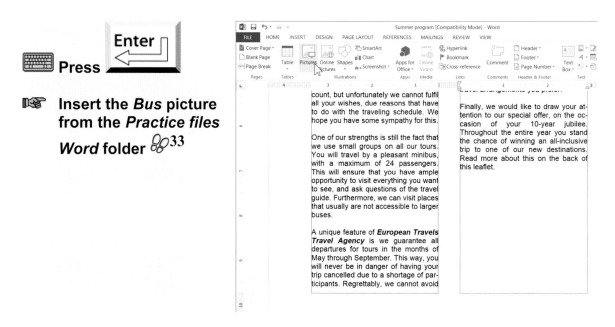

⌨ **Press** **Enter**

☞ **Insert the *Bus* picture from the *Practice files* *Word* folder** 🐾*33*

The picture will be inserted at the spot where the cursor is. You will see the

FORMAT tab with its corresponding commands.

The picture is currently placed in column 2 at the end of the text on a new text line. You can also move the picture to the middle of the page, partly in the first column and partly in the second column. This will make the formatting look a bit less rigid. To do this, you first need to detach the picture from the text:

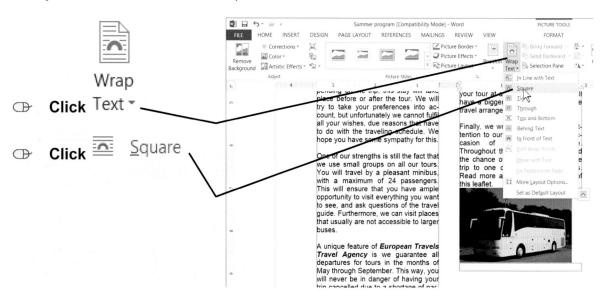

👆 **Click** Wrap Text ▾

👆 **Click** ▣ Square

Now you can freely move the picture around the document. Try to place the picture in the leaflet in such a way that it is just below the address, between both columns:

☞ **Drag the picture to the desired position**

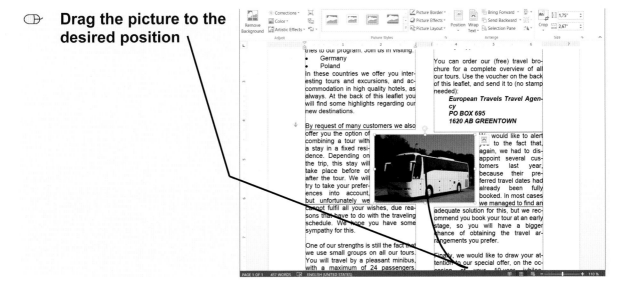

6.3 Inserting Column Breaks

Now that this part of the leaflet is nearly finished, you can complete the formatting of the columns. In this example, the second column begins a bit higher up than the first column. In this case you can let the second column begin at the same height as the first column by inserting a column break below the first column.

At the bottom of the first column:

☞ **Click the blank line below the word 'buses.'** ─────

☞ **Click the**

PAGE LAYOUT **tab** ─

☞ **Click ⊟ Breaks ▾**

☞ **Click**

Column
Indicate that the text fo
break will begin in the

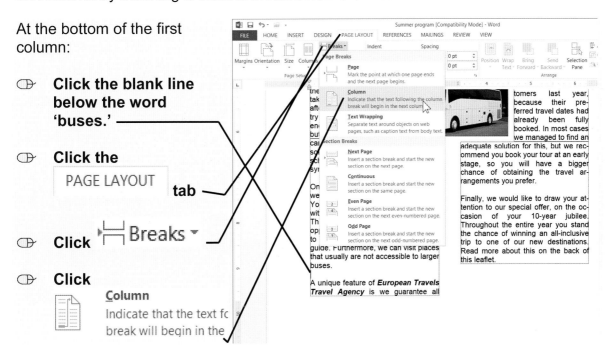

Tip
Column end with the keyboard

You can also use the key combination **Ctrl** + **Shift** + **Enter** to insert a column break. Make sure you place the cursor on the exact spot where you want the column break to be inserted. If it does not go well, then click *Undo insertion*.

Now the text in both columns begins at the same height:

Please note: if the columns do not begin at the same

height, press **Enter** above the second column until it starts at the same height as the first column.

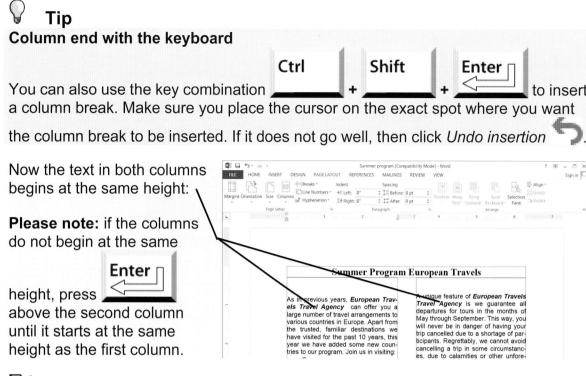

Please note:
Because the formatting has changed, you may need to move the picture again. Look at the print preview at regular intervals, in order to see the effects of the changes you make.

6.4 Page Borders

To frame the leaflet, you can add a border around the page. Here is how to do that:

In *Word 2013*:

☞ **Click somewhere in the text (not on the picture)**

☞ **Click the DESIGN tab**

☞ **Click Page Borders**

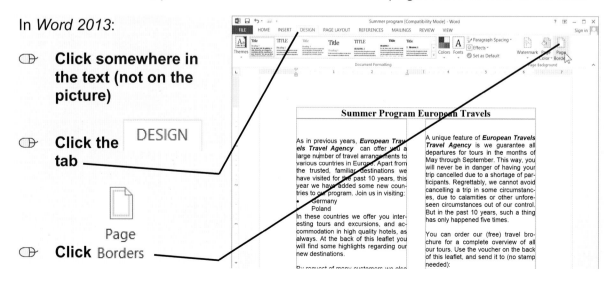

In *Word 2010*:

☞ **Click in the text (not on the picture)**

☞ **Click the** Page Layout **tab**

☞ **Click** 🗔 Page Borders

☞ **By** Style:**, select a border style**

☞ **Select a border color, if you wish**

☞ **Click** OK

Now you can see the layout with the border you selected:

In *Word 2013*:

☞ **Click** ⬅

In *Word 2010*:

☞ **Click** File

☞ **Click the tab** FILE

☞ **Click** Print

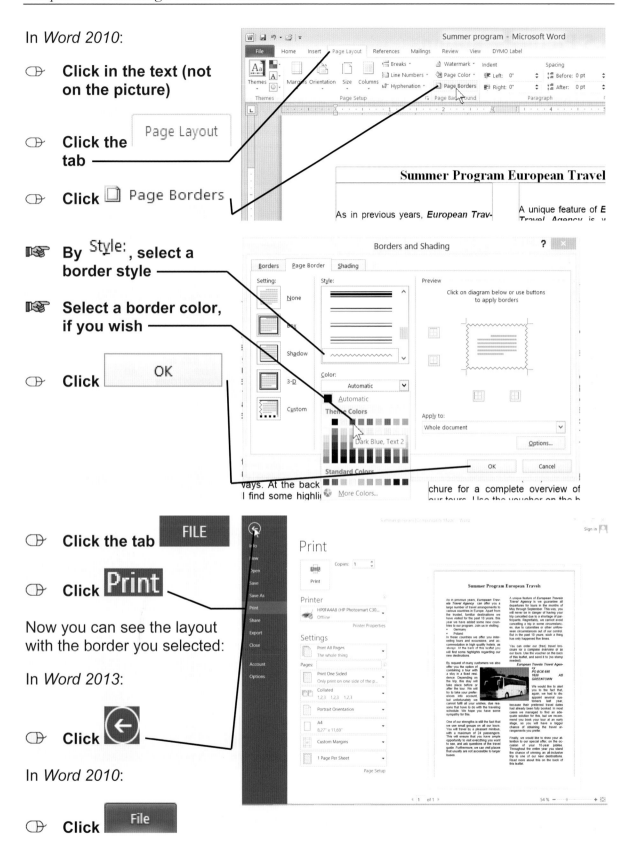

Because you have added a caption, part of the text may have moved to the next page. Here is a way to solve that problem:

☞ **Click the border of the caption** ————

☞ **Drag the caption upwards a bit**

The second page will disappear:

☞ **Click a spot in the text of one of the columns**

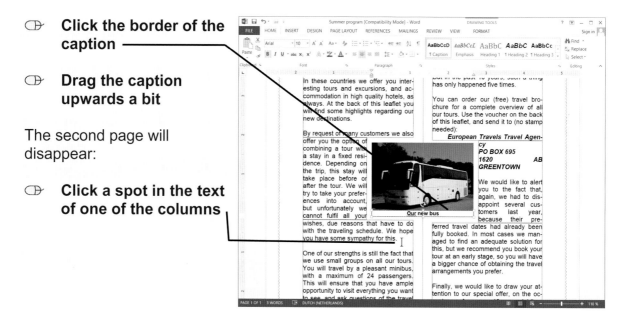

6.6 Sections

In *Word* you can divide documents into sections. Each section can have its own formatting and include one or more of the following settings:
- margins;
- page size;
- page orientation, *Portrait* or *Landscape*;
- column layout.

You can use portrait and landscape oriented pages that alternate each other within a single document, but you will need to create a new section every time you want to change the page orientation. Within the same section you cannot combine horizontal and vertical pages.

Sometimes, sections will be automatically created when you change a certain setting. *Word* can create sections in your document on its own. The status bar can show you in which section the cursor is positioned. But you will need to enable a setting on the status bar first, in order to see this.

 **Press** Ctrl + Home

The cursor is now positioned at the beginning of the document.

☞ **Right-click the status bar** ─────────

☞ **Check the box ✔ by** Se̲ction ─────────

Now you can see **SECTION: 1** in the bottom left corner of the window: ─────────

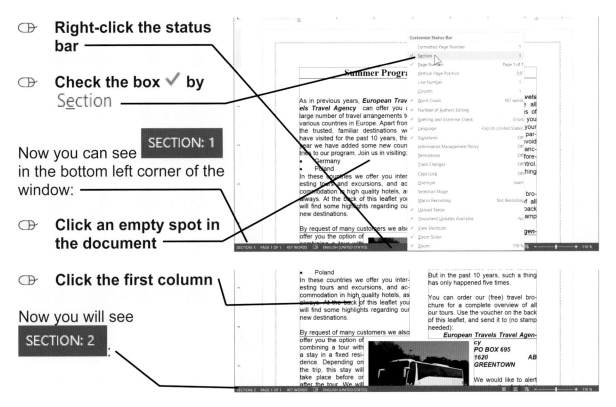

☞ **Click an empty spot in the document** ─────────

☞ **Click the first column**

Now you will see **SECTION: 2** :

Word has created a second section in the document, all by itself. The document consists of:

- *section 1* with one column;
- *section 2* with two columns.

The second section runs right through the document, until the end. You can also set a new section yourself.

⌨ **Press** **Ctrl** + **End**

Now the cursor is placed at the end of the document. If you want to use a single column from this point on, you cannot just go ahead and change the columns. All existing text in this section would be put back into a single column. Just try it:

☞ **Click the** PAGE LAYOUT **tab,** Columns ▾ **,** ▤ One

All the text appears in a single column:

⊕ **Click**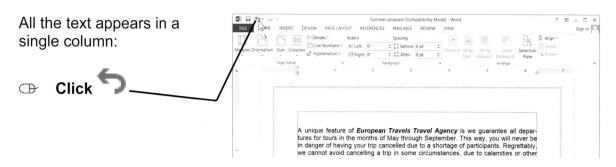

You will see the former two-column layout again. If you want to set the document to have just a single column, starting from the position where the cursor is, you first need to insert a new section:

⊕ **Click** ⊢⊣ Breaks ▾

⊕ **Click**
    Next Page
    Insert a section break
    section on the next pa

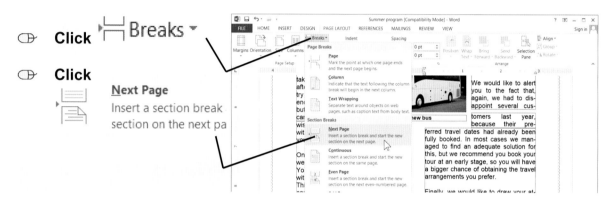

🖐 **Please note:**

Column
Indicate that the text following the column
break will begin in the next column.

Do not select the [ ] **Column** Indicate that the text following the column break will begin in the next column. option in this menu. This option will close the column in which you are working and skip to the next column. In this case you will not be able to change the number of columns.

The cursor is placed on the next page. The new section still has the same column layout as the previous section. Now you can change this without affecting the previous column layouts. The cursor is currently placed in section 3:

⊕ **Click the** PAGE LAYOUT **tab,** Columns ▾ **,**  One

Now the layout for the second page has changed to a single column. The text in the previous section is still spread out over two columns.

💡 Tip

View the column layout by the ruler
You can also view the column layout on the ruler above your document.

In the case of two columns, click one of the columns first. You will see the separation marker between the columns:

Now click the title of the leaflet. Since this is just one column you only see a single long ruler:

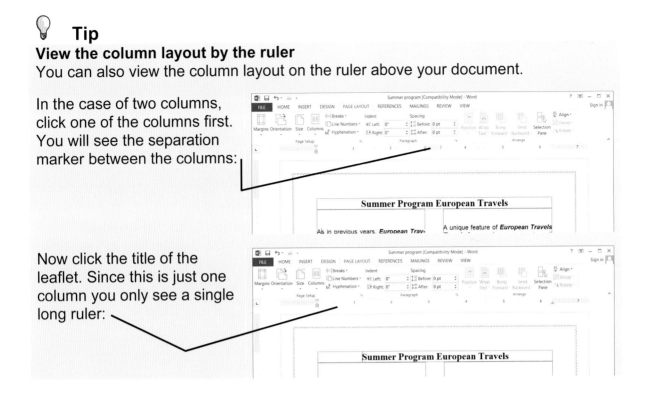

6.7 WordArt

On the new page you want to present a summary of the new destinations that will be offered by your travel agency, by using pictures and text. You can use WordArt to create a nice heading at the top of the page:

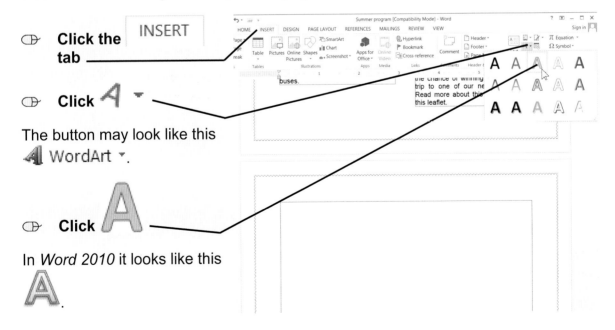

☞ **Click the tab** INSERT

☞ **Click** A ▾

The button may look like this
WordArt ▾.

☞ **Click** A

In *Word 2010* it looks like this
A.

Type:
New Destinations

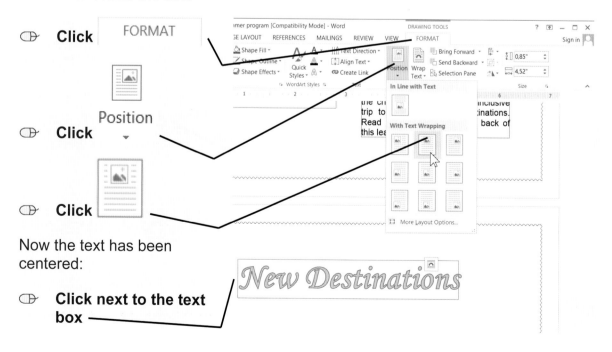 **HELP! The word 'Destinations' is underlined.**

It is possible that your spelling checker will not recognize the word 'Destinations'. You will see a red wavy line below the word in the picture. This wavy line will not be printed, as you can see in the print preview.

☞ **Continue reading**

If you are not happy with this font, you can select a different font:

☞ **Select the 'New Destinations' text** 🦶**20**

☞ **Select the font named *Monotype Corsiva*** 🦶**17**

☞ **Set the font size to *48 points*** 🦶**18**

On the ribbon you will now see the *Format* tab as well. You can use the functions on this tab to center the text:

🖱 **Click**

🖱 **Click**

🖱 **Click**

Now the text has been centered:

🖱 **Click next to the text box**

6.8 Inserting Pictures

Once the title has been placed at the top of the page, you can now add a couple of pictures to the page. Usually, these pictures will have to be resized and moved to the correct position.

 Please note:

In this section, we do not cover in detail the actions necessary for inserting and editing pictures. If you need to review, see *Chapter 4 Pictures* where these topics are fully discussed.

 Please note:

We use the word *picture* in this chapter, even if the picture is actually a photo. This is because the method used is the same for all types of images.

☞ **Insert the *Krakow* picture from the *Practice files Word* folder** ✇³³

The picture is inserted on the left-hand side of the new title. You will want to be able to move the picture freely around the document. To do this, first make sure the picture is still selected:

☞ **Click** Wrap Text ▾, ⌷ Square

☞ **Place the picture below the title on the left-hand side** ✇³⁷

Please note: in *Word 2010* the green line will not appear.

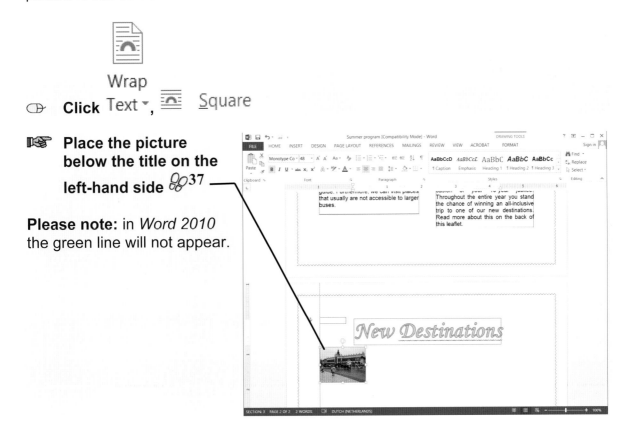

☞ **Enlarge the picture** ✑³⁵

The page looks something like this:

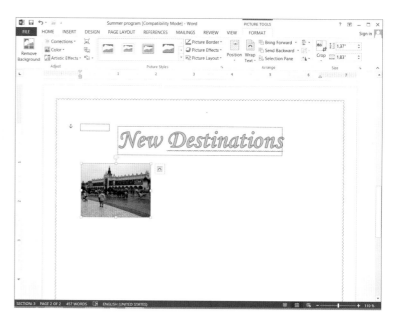

☞ **Insert the *Dresden* picture from the *Practice files Word* folder** ✑³³

👉 **Click** Text ▾, ▣ Square

☞ **Place the picture below the other picture** ✑³⁷

☞ **Rotate the picture 90° to the right** ✑⁵⁰

☞ **Enlarge the picture so that it is the same width as the other picture** ✑⁴¹

At the bottom of the *Dresden* picture you see a large section of the city square. You can remove some of this square:

☞ **Crop the picture, so part of the square is removed** ✑³⁹

The page should now look something like this:

6.9 Text Boxes

Text boxes are used to randomly place text on a page. The difference with regular text is that the text entered in a text box is not restricted to lines and paragraphs. You can place a text box on a page wherever you want.

In the following step, you will be creating a text box with information about a picture. This text will be displayed right on top of the picture.

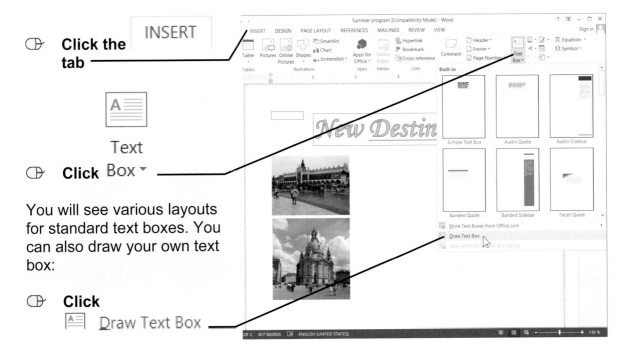

☞ **Click the INSERT tab**

☞ **Click Text Box ▾**

You will see various layouts for standard text boxes. You can also draw your own text box:

☞ **Click Draw Text Box**

Drag a rectangle on the right-hand side of the Krakow picture

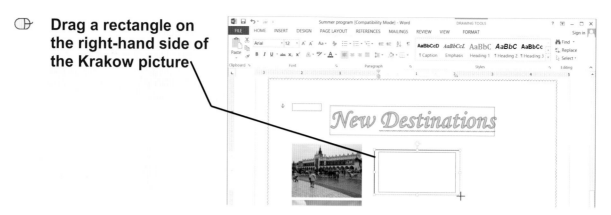

 HELP! The text box does not look right.

If you release the mouse button too quickly, the text box will become too big or too small, or it will be in the wrong spot.

 Just click ↶ **and try again**

You will see a box in which you can enter text:

⌨ **Type:**
`Market in Krakow`

☞ **Make the text bold**
☙**51**

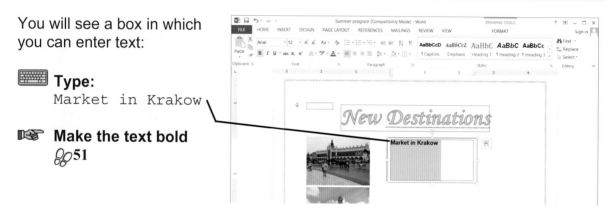

If the text does not fit into the box and you can only see part of the text, you can enlarge the text box. If the text box is much too big for the text you have typed, you can make the box smaller.

Here is how you make the text box fit the text:

In the border around the text box you see various handles:

 Drag a handle, until the text box is the right size

Repeat this until the text box fits the text.

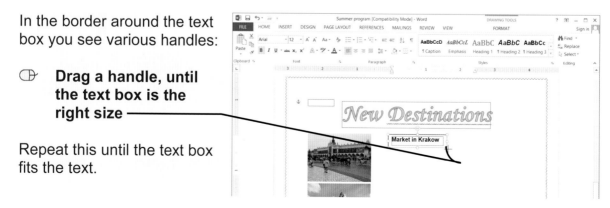

Please note:

You cannot scale the text box to the exact size of the text, because a text box uses a small amount of margin as well. There will be a little space between the border of the text box and the text itself.

Now you can move the text box to the place you want:

☞ **Place the pointer on the top border of the text box (but not on a handle)**

Make sure the pointer looks like this ✛.

☞ **Drag the text box to the bottom right corner of the picture**

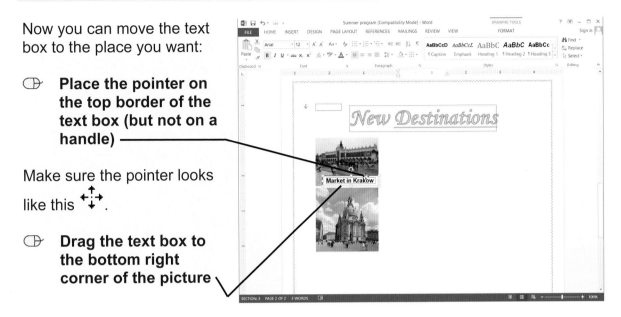

You will see the text appear within the picture.

6.10 Formatting Text Boxes

A text with a white background within a picture is not very pretty. You can make the white background of the text box transparent:

☞ **Click the FORMAT tab**

☞ **By Shape Fill, click ▼**

☞ **Click No Fill**

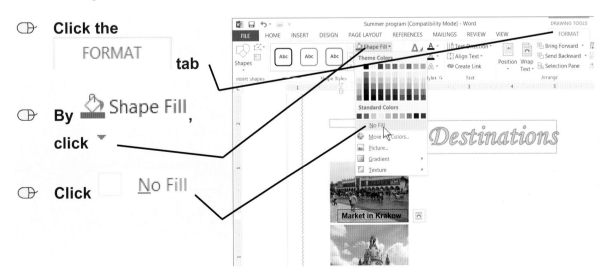

The white area has disappeared. Now you can remove the border of the text box:

⊕ **By** 🖊 Shape Outline ,
click ▾

⊕ **Click** ☐ No Outline

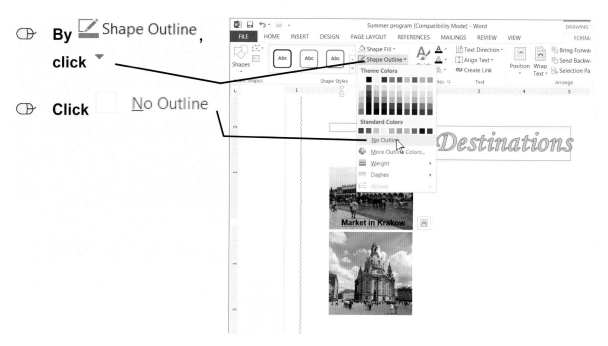

You can also change the color of the letters:

☞ **Change the color of**
the letters to white
✂52

⊕ **Click next to the**
picture ———

Now you will see the final
result:

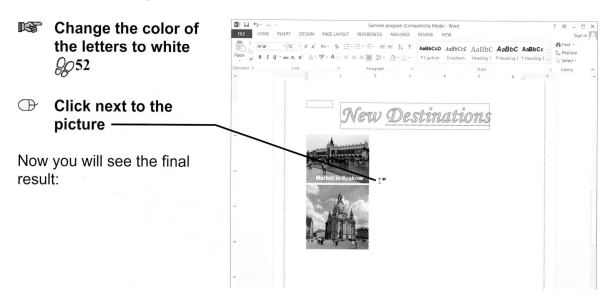

You can always edit a text box later on. When you do this, you need to select the text box first by clicking it and then proceed further.

6.11 Creating a Reply Coupon

You can also use a text box to make a text stand out more by giving it a special border and a colored background. At the bottom of the leaflet, for example, you can add a coupon for a customer to apply for more information. First, you create a new text box again:

☞ **Click the** INSERT **tab,** Text Box ▾, ▤ Draw Text Box

☞ **Drag the scroll box downwards** ⎯⎯⎯

☞ **Drag a rectangle** ⎯⎯

The size of the box does not matter here.

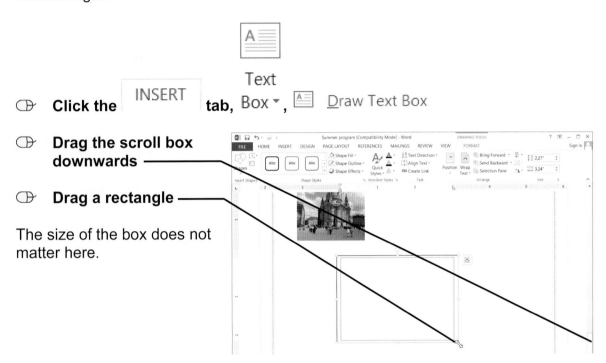

To change the size of the text box:

☞ **If necessary, click** Size ▾

⌨ **By** ↕ ..., **type:** 3 ⎯

⌨ **By** ↔, **type:** 6 . 5 ⎯

☞ **Click the text box** ⎯

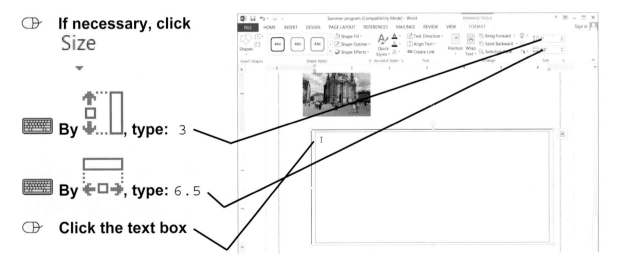

Next you can align the text box to the bottom of the page. Make sure the left-hand side of the text box is aligned with the picture.

☞ **Move the text box to the bottom of the page** 𝕻𝟹𝟽

💡 **Tip**
Stay within the margins
Take good care to ensure the text is placed within the page margins:

If you want, you can open the print preview to check whether the text box is correctly positioned.

This is the correct layout:

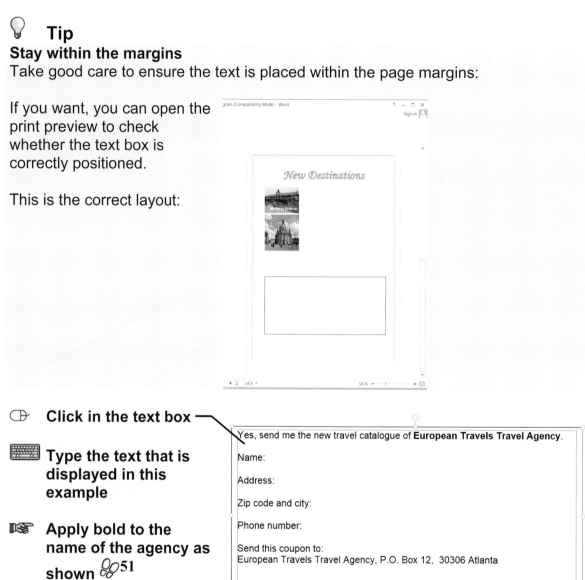

☞ **Click in the text box**

⌨ **Type the text that is displayed in this example**

☞ **Apply bold to the name of the agency as shown** 𝕻𝟻𝟷

Yes, send me the new travel catalogue of **European Travels Travel Agency**.

Name:

Address:

Zip code and city:

Phone number:

Send this coupon to:
European Travels Travel Agency, P.O. Box 12, 30306 Atlanta

To make the coupon stand out more, you can color it:

☞ **If necessary, click the** 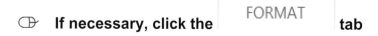 FORMAT **tab**

⊕ **By** 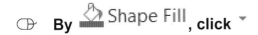 **, click** ▾

Select a light color, in order to make the text stand out, for instance, light green:

⊕ **Click the desired color**

If you are satisfied with the result:

⊕ **Click next to the text box**

The cursor will jump back to the top of the page.

6.12 Shapes

With *Word* you can add simple flow charts, diagrams, and other types of *line art* to your documents. You can use a large number of shapes for this, such as:
- lines and arrows;
- circles;
- rectangles;
- banners.

With these shapes you can create an outline of the travel itinerary. Using shapes is often identical to the way you work with pictures, text boxes, or WordArt.

⊕ **Click the tab** ────

⊕ **Click** ▾ ────

⊕ **By**
Stars and Banners ,
click

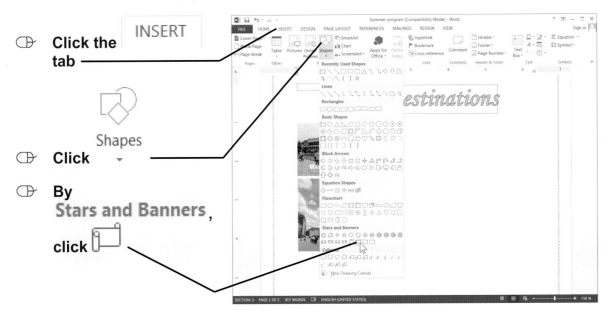

⊕ **Drag a rectangle**

You will see the horizontal scroll:

☞ **Place the horizontal scroll below the title line** 🦶³⁷

⊕ **By** 🔲 **Shape Fill**,

   click ▾

⊕ **Click** ☐ **(white)**

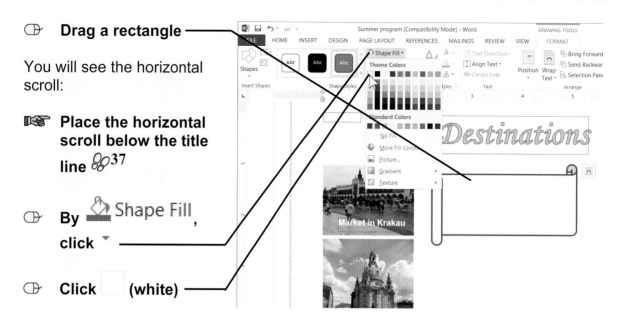

In shapes of this type you cannot enter text directly. You can enter text in the shapes from the *Callouts* group, but there are not as many fun and creative designs. You can solve this problem however, by placing a text box inside the scroll:

☞ **Create a rectangular text box** 🦶⁵³

⌨ **Type:**
   Travel itinerary

☞ **Apply bold** 🦶⁵¹

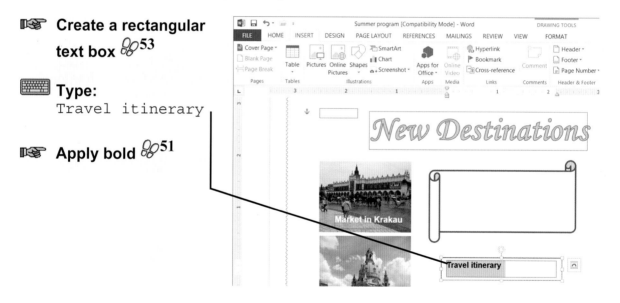

👉 **Select** No Fill **and** No Outline 54, 55

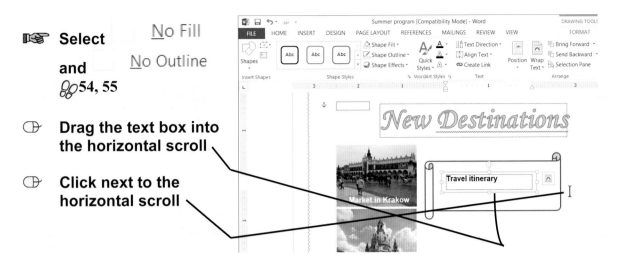

👆 **Drag the text box into the horizontal scroll**

👆 **Click next to the horizontal scroll**

Now the text is placed inside the horizontal scroll.

💡 **Tip**

Corrections
If the text is not in the right place, you can make adjustments by clicking the text first, in order to select the text box. Once selected, you can move the text box to where you want it. If the scroll is too big or too small, then try to click an empty spot in the scroll (next to the text box). If this does not work, then first drag the text box outside the scroll; change the size of the scroll, and drag the text box back into the scroll again.

👉 **Create a rectangular text box below the scroll** 🐾53

👉 **Set the height to 1 inch and the width to 4 inches** 🐾56

👉 **Place the text box below the horizontal scroll** 🐾37

⌨ **Type this in the text box:** The trip starts with a visit to the German city of Dresden. Here you will visit the renovated Frauenkirche, among other things.

🖱 **Click next to the text box**

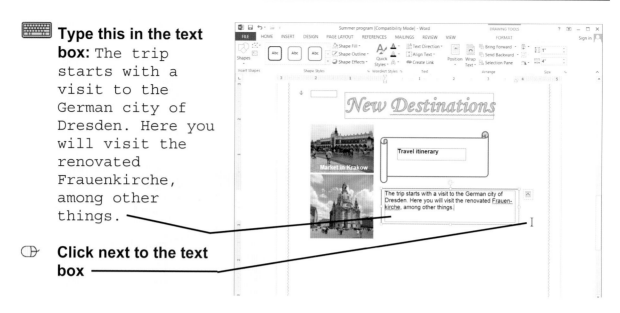

Now you can add the other city names to the itinerary:

☞ **Create a small rectangular text box** 👣53

⌨ **Type in this text box:** Amsterdam

☞ **Apply bold and center it** 👣51, 59

☞ **Adjust the size of the text box to fit the text** 👣35

☞ **Select a light background color** 👣54

🖱 **Click next to the text box**

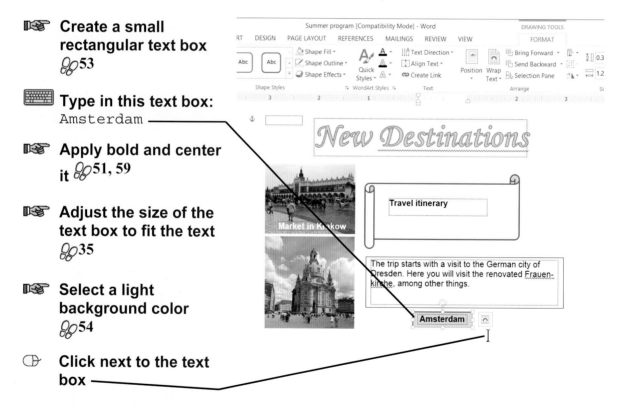

☞ **Create two more text boxes in the same way, with the texts** Dresden **and** Krakow

☞ **Place the *Dresden* and *Krakow* text boxes according to this example** 🐾37

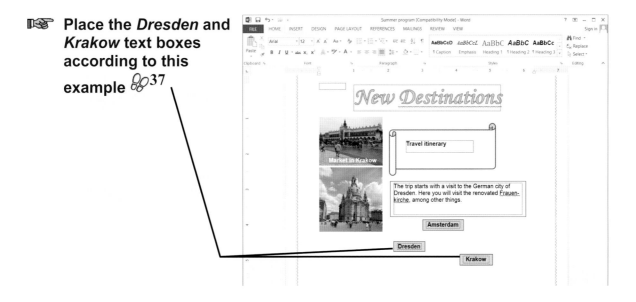

6.13 Lines and Arrows

Now you can draw an arrow between *Amsterdam* and *Dresden*:

⊕ **Click the INSERT tab**

⊕ **Click Shapes**

⊕ **By Lines, click**

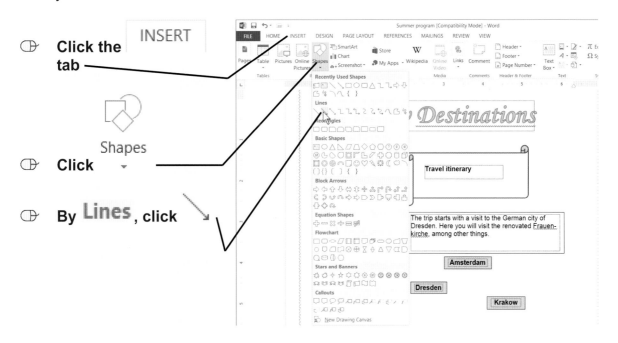

The pointer is now shaped like a ┼:

⊕ **Drag an arrow from the *Amsterdam* text box to the *Dresden* text box**

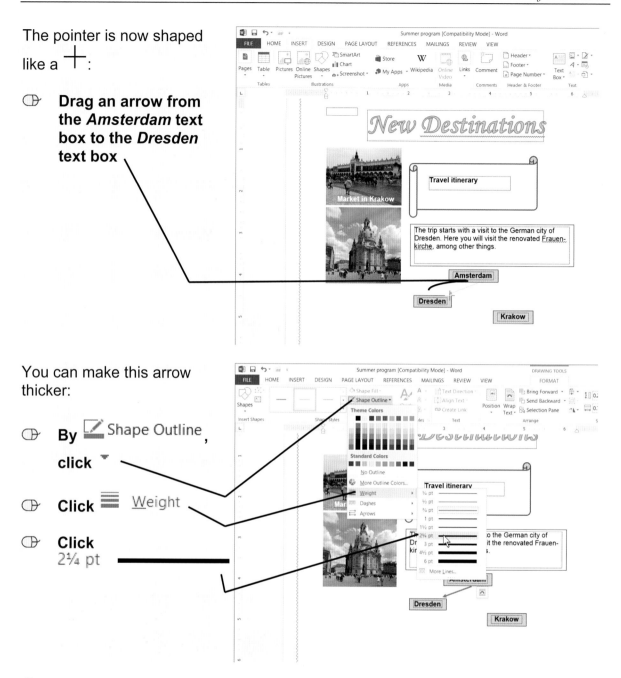

You can make this arrow thicker:

⊕ **By** 🖊 Shape Outline, **click** ▼

⊕ **Click** ▤ Weight

⊕ **Click** 2¼ pt ▬▬▬

💡 **Tip**
Shape options

In the same way you can edit the line even further by 🖊 Shape Outline. For example, you can give the line a different color. You can use the ▤ Dashes option to select a different line style and with the ⇄ Arrows option you can select a different type of arrow.

☞ **Draw arrows from** *Dresden* **to** *Krakow* **and from** *Krakow* **to** *Amsterdam*

☞ **Set the weight of the arrows to** 2¼ pt

⊕ **Click next to the itinerary**

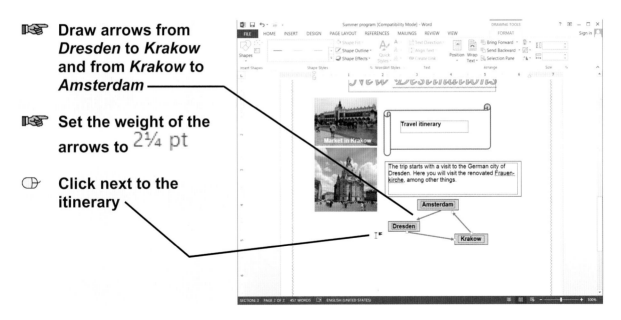

🖐 **Please note:**

If you want to change the arrows afterwards, you need to click the arrow first, in order to select it. Then you can edit or delete the arrow.

⊕ **Click the** FILE **tab, and then** Print

You will see the result:

⊕ **Drag the slider to the left, until you see both pages next to one another**

In *Word 2013*:

⊕ **Click**

In *Word 2010*:

⊕ **Click the** File **tab**

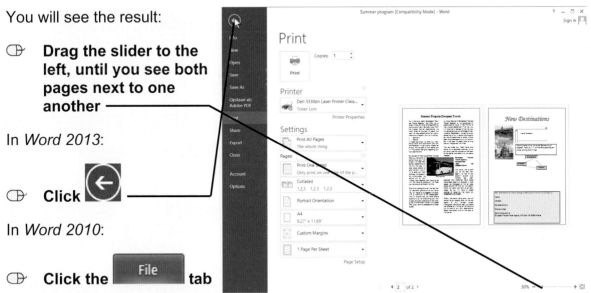

6.14 Linking Text Boxes

You can link text boxes to one another. In linked text boxes, the text will automatically continue into the next text box when the first text box becomes full. If the text in the first box, for example, becomes longer due to edits, the rest of the text will move to the linked text box. If the text is shortened again later on, the text will move back to the first text box. In the following exercise, you can see how this works.

You can create a new text box and link it to the first text box with travel information:

☞ **Create a rectangular text box below the itinerary** 𝒫53

☞ **Set the height to 1.5 inches and the width to 4.5 inches** 𝒫56

☞ **Place the text box below the middle of the itinerary** 𝒫37

👆 **If necessary, click the** FORMAT **tab**

👆 **Click after the period by 'things'**

👆 **Click** 🔗 Create Link

The pointer turns into 🪣.

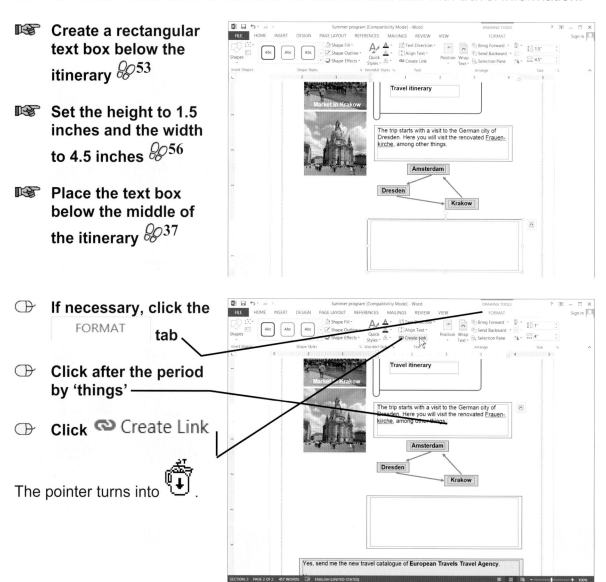

⊕ **Place the pointer on the bottom text box**

The pointer turns into :

⊕ **Click the bottom text box**

⌨ **Type a space after 'things.'**

⌨ **Type:**
```
Next, you will
visit the Polish
city of Krakow
with its famous
Cloth Hall on the
beautiful market
square.
```

When the first text box is full, the cursor will automatically jump to the second text box:

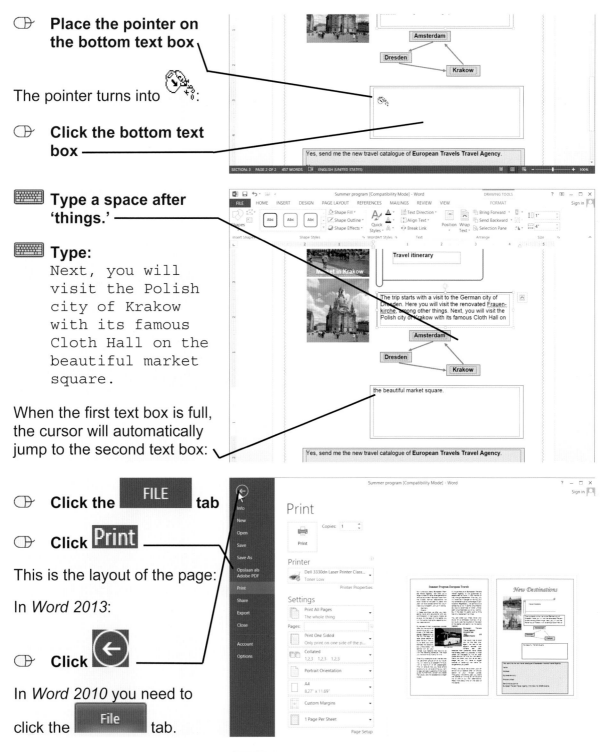

⊕ **Click the** FILE **tab**

⊕ **Click** Print

This is the layout of the page:

In *Word 2013*:

⊕ **Click**

In *Word 2010* you need to click the File tab.

☞ **Close Word and do not save the changes** ₰²

In this chapter you have learned how to work with columns, sections and text boxes. With this knowledge you can create your own leaflets, newsletters, flyers and more.

6.15 Exercises

Have you forgotten how to do something? Use the number beside the footsteps to look it up in the appendix *How Do I Do That Again?* at the end of the book.

Exercise 1: Format a Document

☞ Open *Word*. $\mathscr{S}$**1**

☞ Open the *The Internet connection* document in the *Practice files Word* folder. $\mathscr{S}$**10**

☞ If necessary, enable editing. $\mathscr{S}$**82**

☞ Format the text into two columns. $\mathscr{S}$**57**

☞ Place the title in a single column. $\mathscr{S}$**58**

☞ Justify the text. $\mathscr{S}$**59**

☞ Enable the automatic hyphenation option for the words in the document, and do not hyphenate words with capitals. $\mathscr{S}$**60**

☞ Place a picture in the center of the text. $\mathscr{S}$**33, 36, 37**

☞ Insert a column break. $\mathscr{S}$**61**

☞ Place a caption by the picture. $\mathscr{S}$**62**

☞ Add a section break on the next page. $\mathscr{S}$**63**

☞ Format this new page with a single column. $\mathscr{S}$**57**

☞ Insert a text box. $\mathscr{S}$**53**

☞ Fill the text box with a yellow color. $\mathscr{S}$**54**

☞ Give the text box a blue border. $\mathscr{S}$**55**

☞ Close *Word* and do not save the changes. $\mathscr{S}$**2**

6.16 Background Information

Dictionary

Center	Text or other objects are placed in the exact middle between the left and right margins.
Column	A block of text. Text can be divided over one or more columns.
Crop	Make a picture smaller by cutting off a section.
End marker	A hidden symbol that indicates where a column, page, or section ends.
Justify	Spacing text so the left and right sides of a text block or column have a straight edge.
Paragraph marker	Marker that indicates the end of a paragraph ¶.
Print preview	A view which displays the page as it will look when it is printed.
Section	Parts of a document that can have a different layout or formatting.
Status bar	A bar at the bottom of the window, that provides various types of information about the document. You can determine the content of this bar yourself, by right-clicking it.
Text wrap	The way in which a text is wrapped around a picture.

Source: Word 2013, Word 2010, Windows Help and Support, and Wikipedia

Text boxes

Text boxes can be used for a variety of different purposes. Not just for short pieces of text, as in this chapter, but also for writing things such as an advertisement, for example.

This is useful, because you can set the exact dimensions of a text box, which is often important if you want to publish an ad. The frame (that you can remove later on) will give you a better idea of the layout and formatting of the ad. You can also insert a picture in a text box, if you wish. This is done in the same way as placing a text box on top of a picture like you did earlier in this chapter.

Tables

If you want to format leaflets or ads you can use tables too. It is a good method for placing text and matching pictures on the right spot. This can be very handy if you need to place text right next to a picture, for example. But the downside is that you are a bit more restricted regarding the formatting, compared to using text boxes. You can also combine the formatting of a table with text boxes.

Similar methods

Text boxes, WordArt texts, photos and other types of pictures can be handled in an almost identical manner, when it comes to:
• moving;
• resizing;
• formatting.

Sometimes the borders or handles may look a bit different, but the way in which you work with them is almost identical.

Remember that you always need to select the object first before you begin the following action.

6.17 Tips

 Tip

Place text in columns
If you intend to use columns to format your text, it is generally easier to type the text first, without using columns. Afterwards you can select the text and set the number of columns. *Word* will automatically create the necessary sections. In this way it is easier to create a document with different column layouts.

 Tip

The Columns window
In this chapter you have worked with a two-column layout. But you can use more columns, or apply columns with different widths. You can find these settings in the *Columns* window, together with many other options:

⊕ **Click the** PAGE LAYOUT **tab**

Columns
⊕ **Click** ▾

⊕ **Click** ☷ More Columns...

Set the number of columns:

Set the width and spacing of the columns:

Place a line between columns:

Set equal column width (or not):

Apply the column settings to the section where the cursor currently is, or from this point onwards:

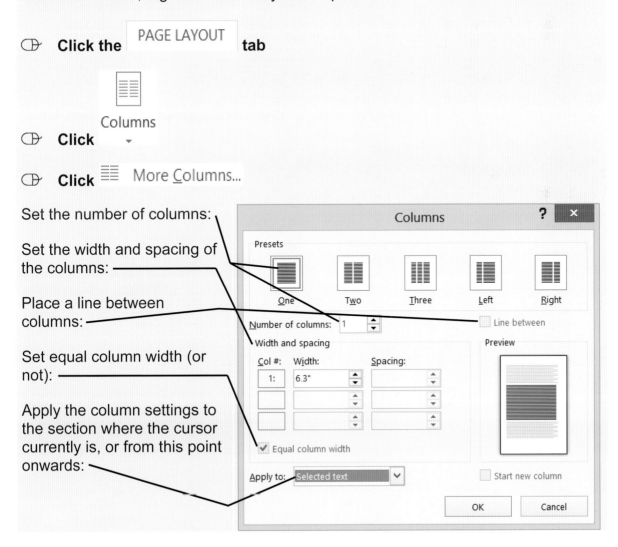

Tip
Evenly distribute text over columns
If you type text in columns, the text will not always be long enough to fill the entire column. This may result in an unattractive final column which is only half filled with text. In this case you can 'balance' the text within the columns:

Click at the end of the text

Now the cursor is placed at the end of the last column:

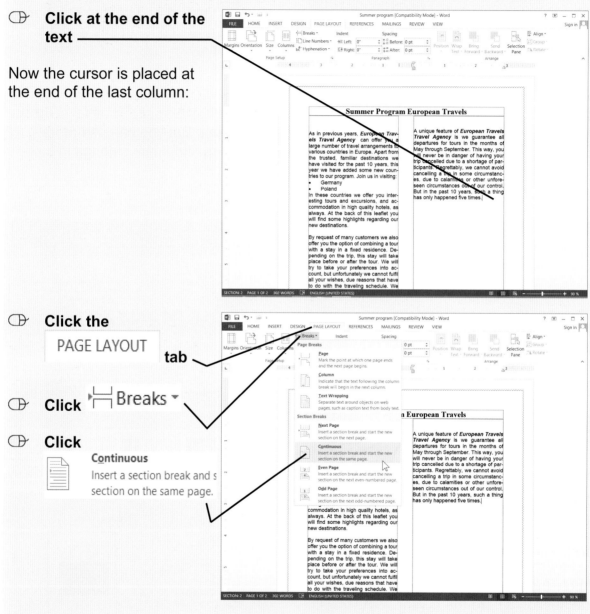

Click the **PAGE LAYOUT** **tab**

Click ⊢Breaks ▾

Click

Continuous
Insert a section break and s section on the same page.

Now the text in the columns will be evenly distributed.

7. Mailings and Mail Merge

Many organizations, neighborhood groups and clubs use mailings to contact their customers or members. They use a standard letter into which the address information and perhaps some other data is inserted, in order to create a more personal document.

With *Word* it is easy to make mailings based on a document (letter, address label) and a list of addresses. Furthermore, the search and selection options can help you set up mailings for a specific target group. You can create address files in *Word* as well as other *Microsoft* programs such as *Excel* or *Access*.

In this chapter you will learn how to:

- link a document to an address file;
- insert an address block and separate fields;
- display addresses;
- adjust the address block;
- select addresses from the address file;
- sort the address list;
- edit address information;
- search for addresses in the address file;
- merge the mailing letter with the address file;
- adjust the mailing;
- create labels.

7.1 Address File

To see how to merge a mailing with an address file, you will use an address list from a table created in *Word*. This is the easiest way of creating your own address file. Other programs such as *Excel* can also be used to create an address file. In the *Background Information* at the end of this chapter you can find more information about this subject.

☞ **Open *Word*** 🦶¹

☞ **Open the *Address list* document in the *Practice files Word* folder** 🦶¹⁰

☞ **If necessary, enable editing** 🦶⁸²

You will see a simple table with address information:

You will be using this table in the next couple of sections of this chapter.

Title	First name	Initial	Surname	Address	Zip code	City	State/Province	Country
Mr.	Patrick	P.	Voice	13920 Hoover Street	92683	Westminster	California	United States of America
Mr.	Steve	S.	Verne	91 Floppy Street	6160	Fremantle		Western Australia
Mrs.	Ivy	Y.	Hulling	3 Disk Avenue	32824	Orlando	Florida	United States of America
Ms.	Chris	C.	Holyoak	56 Website Street	V5K 2G5	Vancouver	British Columbia	Canada
Ms.	Rilana	R.	Groot	23 Line Avenue	50801	Creston	Iowa	United States of America
Mrs.	Lidia	L.	Denby	23 Text Road	27706	Durham	North Carolina	United States of America
Mr.	Hank	H.	Bolen	1177 Finchley Road	NW11 0AA	London		England
Mrs.	Marie	M.	Bitton	822 Correction Lane	94123	San Francisco	California	United States of America
Mr.	Alex	A.	Witt	78 Pictogram Lane	45011	Hamilton	Ohio	United States of America
Mrs.	Ruby	R.	Bee	14 Screen Street	10011	New York	New York	United States of America

☞ **Save the *Address list* document with the new name *New address list* in the *Practice files Word* folder** 🦶¹⁶

☞ **Close the *New address list* document** 🦶³

💡 **Tip**

Create your own address table
If you want to create a table with addresses yourself, it is a good idea to start with a test table first, and experiment a little with mail merging documents. In this way you can find out whether you have included all the necessary data in your table.
In your table you should type the information in the exact way you want to use it later on, for example, in your letters, labels, or other mailings. Pay attention to capital letters, punctuation and possible abbreviations. For example, think about using full first names or initials, or possible prefixes of surnames (d') and the titles with which you want to address the people in your mailing. It is often best to include all data in

- Continue on the next page -

the address file. Then you can select the items you want to use for each individual mailing. For an official letter you may want to use the initials instead of the full first name. For a mailing of a more personal nature you could use the full first name. If the test table is not satisfactory you can easily edit it. Then you can enter all the data into your final table.

7.2 Linking Documents

When you are putting together a mailing you will need to link your address file to the mailing document. The latter could be a label, a letter or an envelope. You can use a blank page or an existing document as a mailing document. In this example we have used an existing document:

☞ **Open the *Mailing letter* document in the *Practice files Word* folder** 🐾**10**

☞ **If necessary, enable editing** 🐾**82**

You will see a letter that is sent to the customers of a travel agency. You can insert a manual link between the address file and this document:

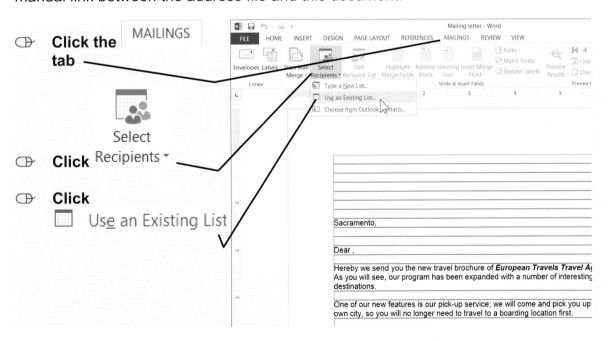

☞ **Select the *New address list* file in the *Practice files Word* folder** 🐾**10**

Now the address list has been linked to the mailing letter. You may see all sorts of lines around the text. This is caused by the text boundaries you have inserted in *section 3.1 Aligning Text with Tabs*. You can remove these lines by disabling the text boundaries function, like this:

☞   **Click the** FILE **tab, and then** Options

☞   **Click** Advanced

☞   **Drag the scroll box downwards**

By
Show document content :

☞   **Uncheck the box** ☑ **by** Show te**x**t boundarie

☞   **Click** OK

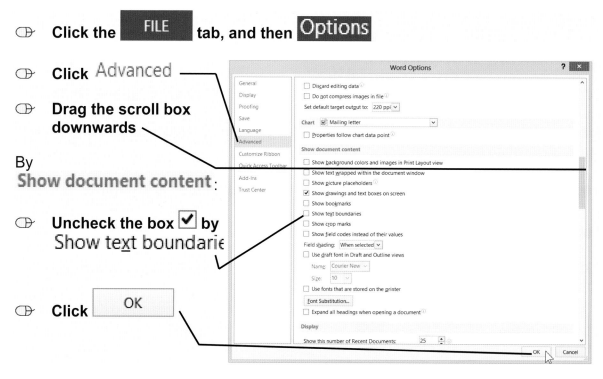

➤ Please note:

After you have created the link, you will see a warning message every time you open the *Mailing letter* document:

Click Yes to continue.

If you click No , the *Mailing letter* will no longer be linked to the *Address list*.

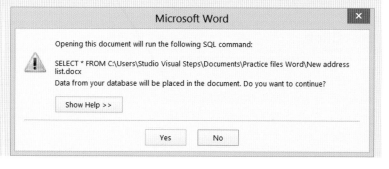

7.3 Inserting an Address Block

In the next step you need to indicate the position of the address information in your mailing letter. In this example, you will place the address at the top of the letter:

Press ⬇ **three times**

Now the cursor is on the spot where the address information will be printed.

Click Address Block

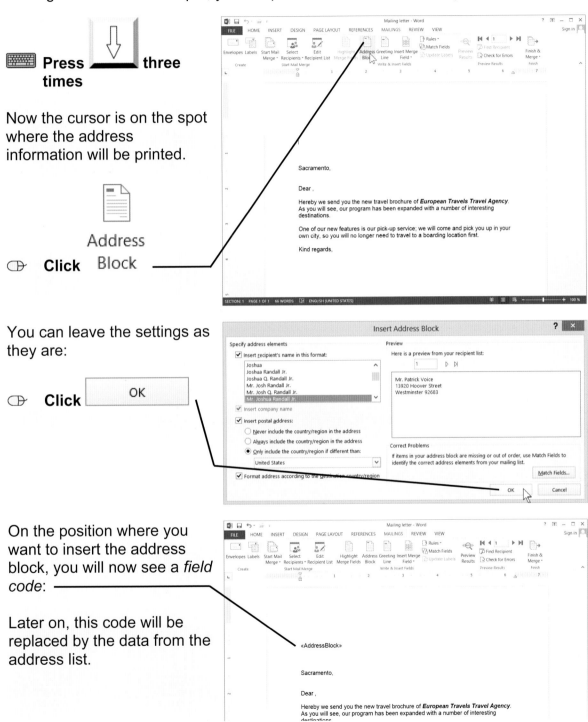

You can leave the settings as they are:

Click OK

On the position where you want to insert the address block, you will now see a *field code*:

Later on, this code will be replaced by the data from the address list.

7.4 Inserting Separate Fields

You can also insert data from each individual column in your address list, besides inserting an entire address block. Each column can become a separate *field*.

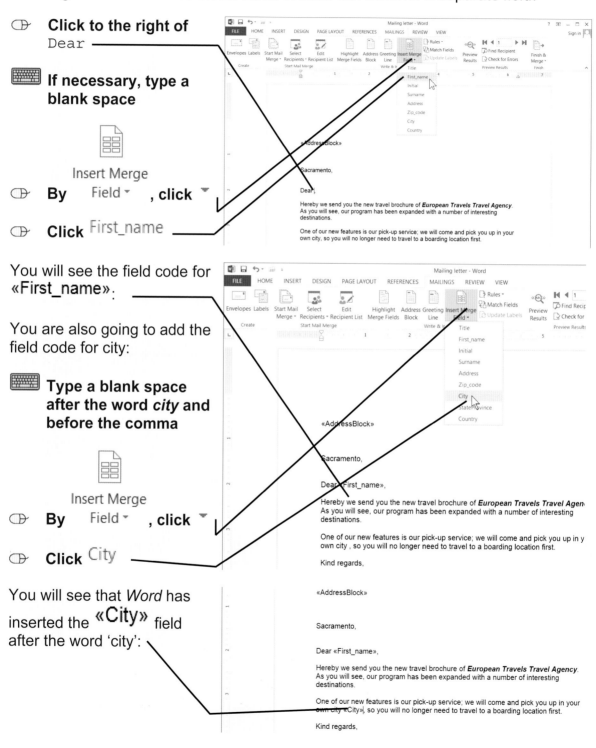

Click to the right of Dear

If necessary, type a blank space

By Field ▾ **, click** ▾

Click First_name

You will see the field code for «First_name».

You are also going to add the field code for city:

Type a blank space after the word *city* and before the comma

By Field ▾ **, click** ▾

Click City

You will see that *Word* has inserted the «City» field after the word 'city':

7.5 Displaying Addresses

In order to check if the field names are correct, you can enter the data from a single *record* in the address file:

Preview

☞ **Click** Results

The data from the first record is already entered:

In an address file, a record is each individual row of data. The first record in the *Address list* document contains the following data:

Mr.	Patrick	P.	Voice	13920 Hoover Street	92683	Westminster	California	United States of America

Now the letter has been completed with the data from the first record in the address file. You can jump to the next record:

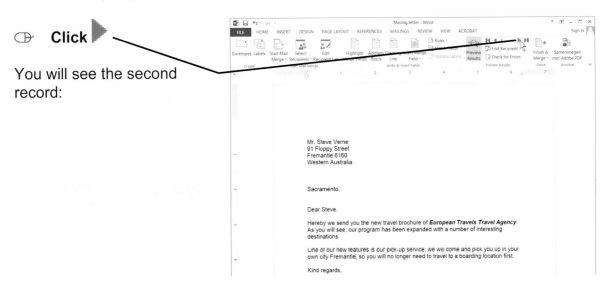

☞ **Click** ▶

You will see the second record:

You can jump through the records as follows:

- With ▶ you go to the next record
- With ◀ you go to the previous record
- With ▶❙ you go to the last record
- With ❙◀ you go to the first record

If you type: 5

Then press Enter

You will see the fifth record:

> Ms. Rilana Groot
> 23 Line Avenue
> Creston 50801
>
> Sacramento,
>
> Dear Rilana,
>
> Hereby we send you the new travel brochure of *European Travels Travel Agency*. As you will see, our program has been expanded with a number of interesting destinations.
>
> One of our new features is our pick-up service; we will come and pick you up in your own city Creston, so you will no longer need to travel to a boarding location first.
>
> Kind regards,

 Tip
Do not send to all recipients
You can also send a standard letter to a single person, or to just a few persons such as new customers or members. After the letter has been completed with the correct data, you can print the page right away.

7.6 Adjusting the Address Block

In the previous section you have seen that the state (or province) had not been entered into the letter. Here is how you can solve the problem:

☞ **Click** Match Fields

Word fills in the data on the basis of the information in the address list. If the field name in the address list has a close resemblance to the name used by *Word*, the data will be correctly entered right away.

Have you used a different field name in your address list, other than the names that *Word* usually uses? Then you will need to link the field names:

☞ **Drag the scroll box downwards**

By **State** it says **(not matched)**. This means no field name has been found:

☞ **By State, click** [⌄]

You will see all the existing field names in the address list:

☞ **Click StateProvince**

The link has been made:

☞ **Click** [OK]

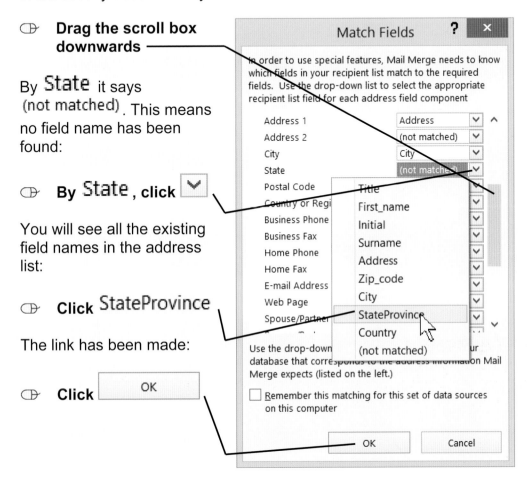

Now the state or province code (if that applies) has been entered in the correct position.

 HELP! I still do not see the state.

If you still cannot see the address block, then click in the document.

7.7 Selecting Addresses

Instead of leafing through an address file, you can also select records in the address list. You can do this manually or on the basis of specific search criteria. You do it manually as follows:

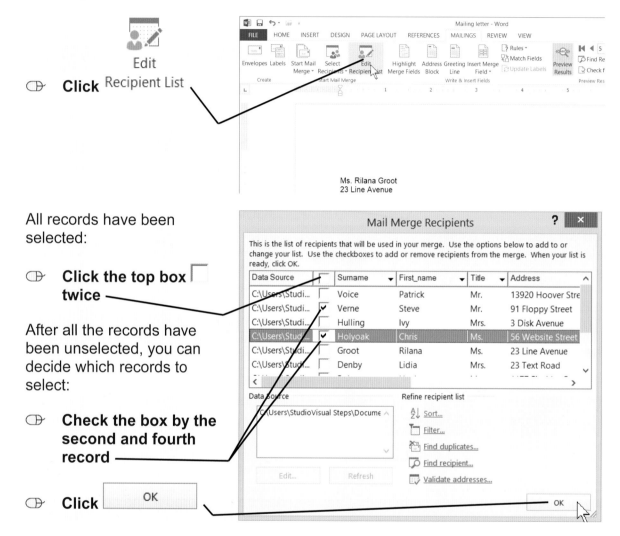

Edit

☞ **Click** Recipient List

All records have been selected:

☞ **Click the top box twice**

After all the records have been unselected, you can decide which records to select:

☞ **Check the box by the second and fourth record**

☞ **Click** OK

☞ **Jump up and down through the records** ✂64

You will only see the selected records. You can also select records that match certain criteria. You could decide to send the mailing to all men only:

Edit

☞ **Click** Recipient List

↺ **Click the top** ☐ **twice**

Now all records have been selected:

↺ **By** Title **, click** ▼

↺ **Click** Mr.

Only the records with the title of 'Mr.' will be selected:

↺ **Click** OK

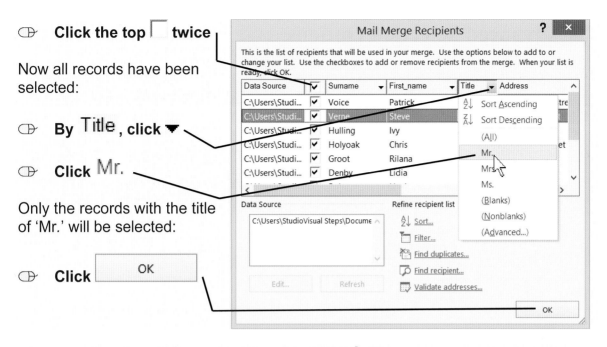

☞ **Jump up and down through the records** 🐾**64**

You will only see the records of the men. If you want to see all the records again:

↺ **Click** Recipient List

↺ **By** Title **, click** ▼

↺ **Click** (All)

Now you will see all the records again:

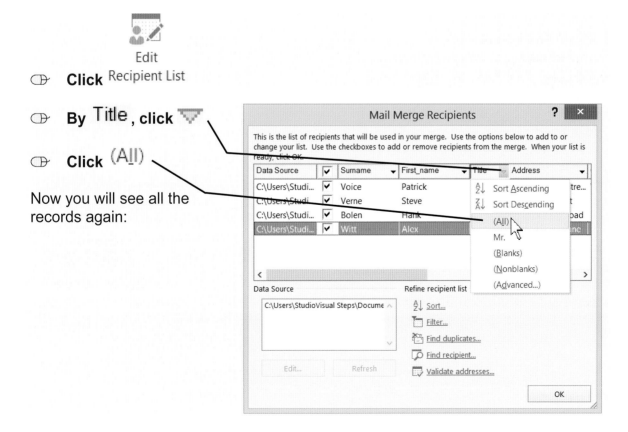

7.8 Advanced Selection Options

But there is a problem if you want to select all the women. In this case, the title can be either 'Mrs.' or 'Ms.'. With the *Advanced* selection options you can still select both titles:

☞ **By** Title **, click** ▼

☞ **Click** (Advanced...)

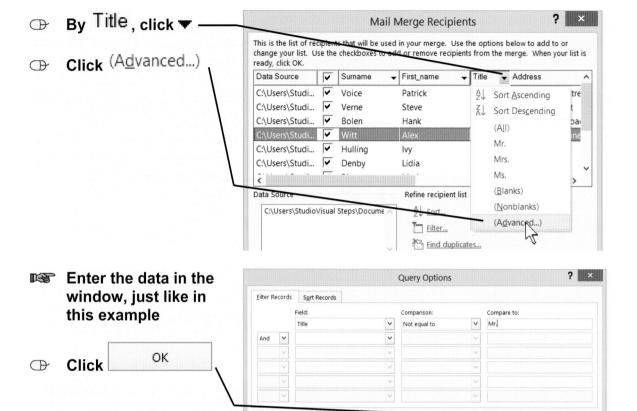

☞ **Enter the data in the window, just like in this example**

☞ **Click** OK

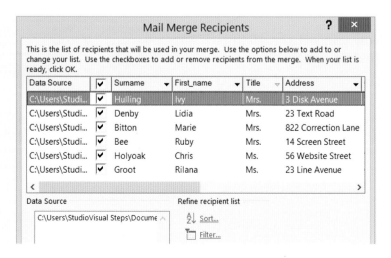

Now you will see the records with both the 'Mrs.' and 'Ms.' titles:

💡 Tip

Selected field

Now you will see a blue arrow ▽ next to Title . This tells you that the records have been selected according to this field.

You can enter six selection criteria. These can be 'and/or' combinations with multiple fields, for example, all the records with the title 'Mrs.' and the city 'San Francisco'.

You can clear the selection criteria again:

☞ **By** Title **, click** ▼ ─────

☞ **Click** (A_dvanced...)

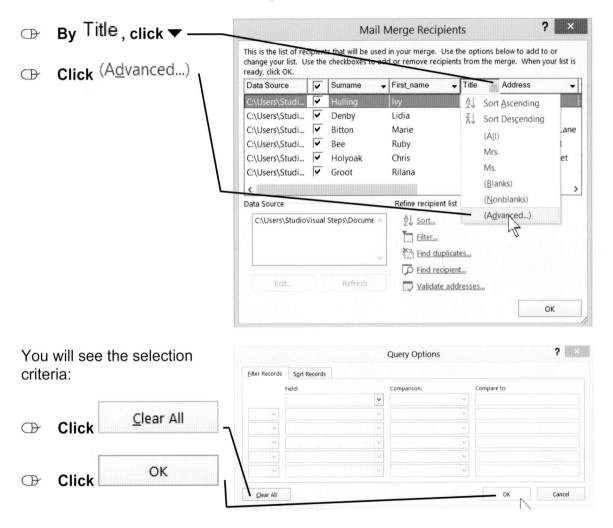

You will see the selection criteria:

☞ **Click** C_lear All

☞ **Click** OK

Now you see all the records again.

7.9 Sorting

If you have large numbers of records it can be very useful to sort them first, for example, according to their surname:

☞ **By** Surname , **click** ▼

☞ **Click** (Advanced...)

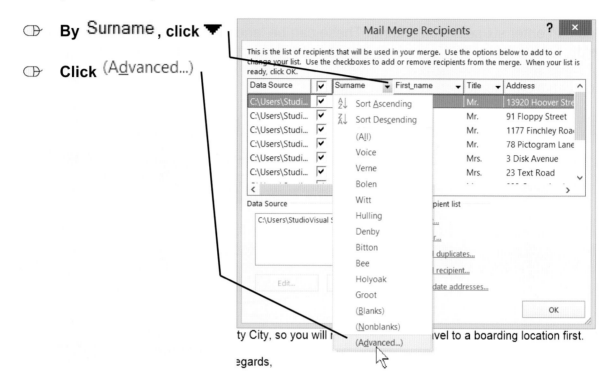

ty City, so you will n.....vel to a boarding location first.

egards,

☞ **Click the** Sort Records **tab**

☞ **By** Sort by , **select** Surname

You can either sort in ascending (A-Z) or descending (Z-A) order. *Ascending* is enabled:

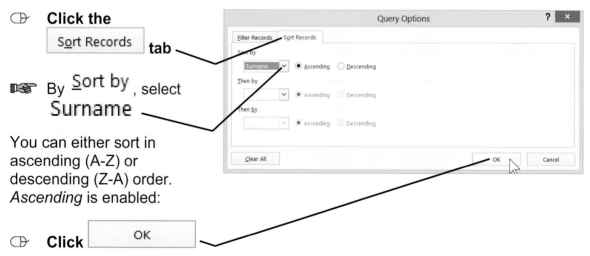

☞ **Click** OK

Now the records have been sorted by the surnames of the addressees.

7.10 Editing Records

If any records need to be changed, or new records need to be added, you can do this either in the address list or in the mailing letter. To do that in the mailing letter:

☞ **Click**
C:\Users\Studio Visual Ste

☞ **Click** Edit...

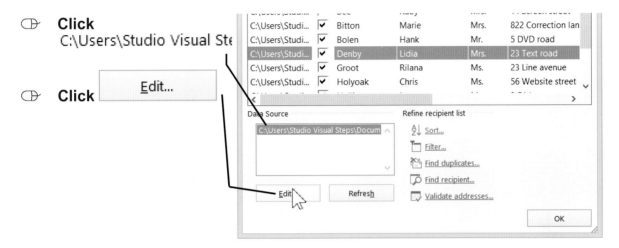

For instance, you want to change the surname 'Witt' to 'Bitt'. If you have a large address file, it is best to use the search function to find a record:

☞ **Click** Find...

⌨ **By** Find what: **, type:**
witt

☞ **By** In field: **, click** ⌄

☞ **Click** Surname

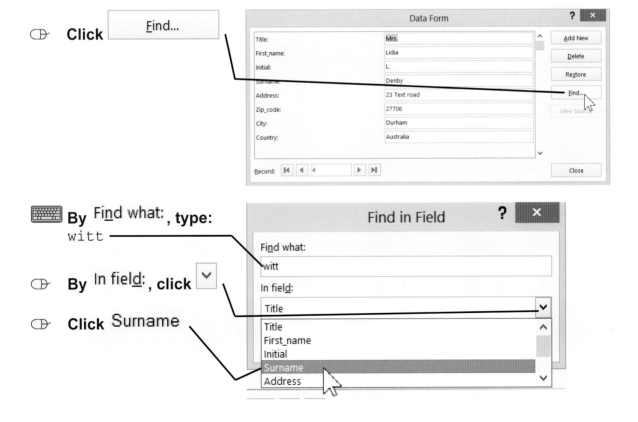

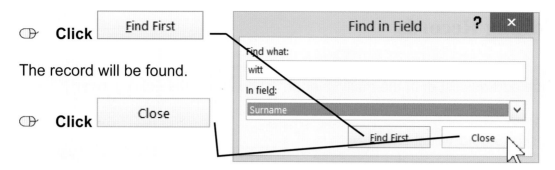

Click Find First

The record will be found.

Click Close

Now you will see the record you were searching for:

 By Surname: **, type:**
Bitt

Click Close

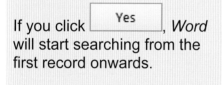

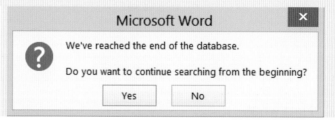

HELP! Nothing is found.

Word will start searching from the record that has been selected, until it reaches the end of the list. If the record you want to find is listed before the selected record, you will not find anything. You will see this message:

If you click Yes , *Word* will start searching from the first record onwards.

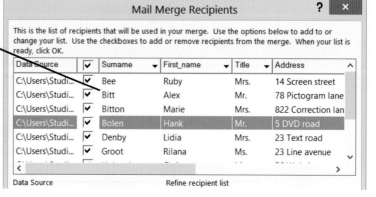

You will see the name you have changed in the address list: ———

The address list has been sorted once again.

At the bottom of the window:

Click OK

Data Source	✓	Surname	First_name	Title	Address
C:\Users\Studi...	✓	Bee	Ruby	Mrs.	14 Screen street
C:\Users\Studi...	✓	Bitt	Alex	Mr.	78 Pictogram lane
C:\Users\Studi...	✓	Bitton	Marie	Mrs.	822 Correction lan
C:\Users\Studi...	✓	Bolen	Hank	Mr.	5 DVD road
C:\Users\Studi...	✓	Denby	Lidia	Mrs.	23 Text road
C:\Users\Studi...	✓	Groot	Rilana	Ms.	23 Line avenue

Data Source   Refine recipient list

You will see the letter again.

 Tip

Need all the zip codes from 10000 up to 90000?

It is very easy to sort the records according to their zip codes, and useful for your mailings.

This is what you need to enter in the window:

If you sort your records by their zip codes, you may be able to send your mailing for a reduced fee.

 Tip

Edit the address list

You can add new records with ⬛ **Add New** :

You can delete selected records with ⬛ **Delete** :

If you want to undo an edit, then click ⬛ **Restore** right after you have changed something: ───

7.11 Merging

In the previous sections, you learned how to use a number of options for selecting and sorting records in an address file. You can send the mailing letter to all the records in the list or to just a few selected records. In this section, you will be merging all the records with the mailing letter:

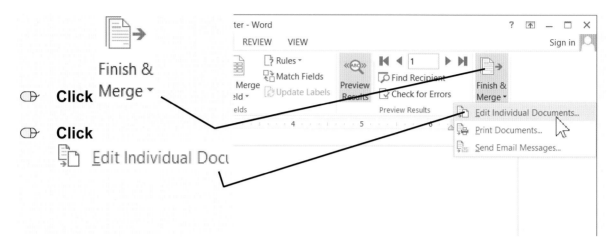

Click Finish & Merge ▾

Click 📄 Edit Individual Docu

➦ Please note:

Do not click 🖨 Print Documents... to merge directly to the printer. Your mailing will be printed right away without having a chance of checking it first.

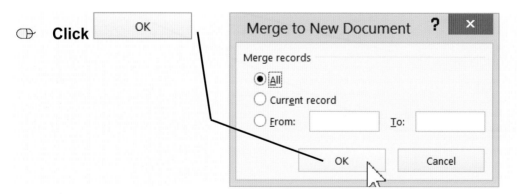

Click OK

Now a letter is created for each record in the address file. In order to do this, *Word* will create a new document in which all the letters are placed on a separate page, one below the other. If you have 200 addresses, this means they will be placed in a single document of 200 pages.

Word automatically creates a name for this document:

The addresses have been filled in:

Here you see page 1 of a total of 10 pages: —————

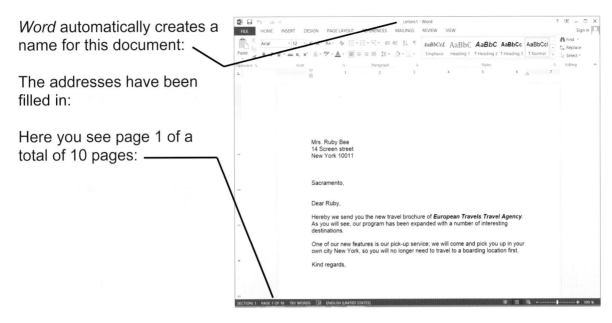

> **Please note:**
>
> If your letter takes up two pages, the number of pages will be twice as much as the number of records.

7.12 Editing and Printing the Mailing

Before you start to print, it is important to take a good look at one or more of the letters. Check the following: is the layout correct; is the country name printed in case of a foreign address; is the date correct, etc.

If you need to edit something in all of the letters, then try to use the *Replace* function for this. This is a quick and easy way of replacing a certain item in all the letters at once. For example, you can replace the words *new travel brochure* in the mailing by *summer travel brochure*:

The HOME tab is opened:

☞ **Click** ᵃᵇ⁄ₐ꜀ Replace

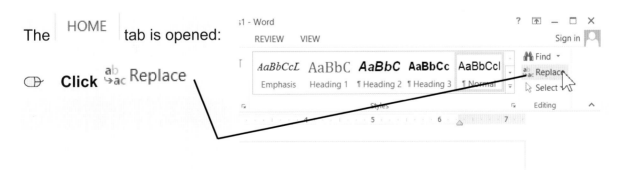

By Fi<u>n</u>d what:, **type:**
new travel

By Replace w<u>i</u>th:, **type:**
summer travel

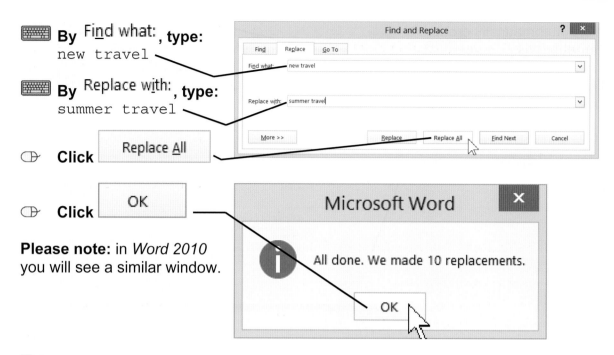

⊕ **Click** | Replace A<u>l</u>l |

⊕ **Click** | OK |

Please note: in *Word 2010* you will see a similar window.

Please note:

Pay attention to the number of replacements in this window. If this number is higher than the number of addresses, *Word* may have replaced more words than you intended to replace. You can undo the search/replace action by clicking ↰.

In the *Find and Replace* window:

⊕ **Click** | Close |

You will see the first of the edited letters:

If you are satisfied with the result, you can print the letters:

☞ **Print the letters, if you wish** 🐾11

Please note: if you actually do this step, you will be printing all ten letters.

It is better not to save the *Letters 1* document, because this document is not linked to the address list. If you happen to edit the address list later on, these edits will not be applied to this document. It is a better idea to merge the *Mailing letter* document with the address file once more, if you want to send the mailing again. This way, you will be sure to use the current address file.

☞ **Close the *Letters1* document and do not save the changes** ✂³

Now you see the original mailing letter. You will need to save this document if you want to use it for other mailings later on:

☞ **Close the *Mailing letter* document** ✂³

First you will be asked whether you want to save the edited *address list* document:

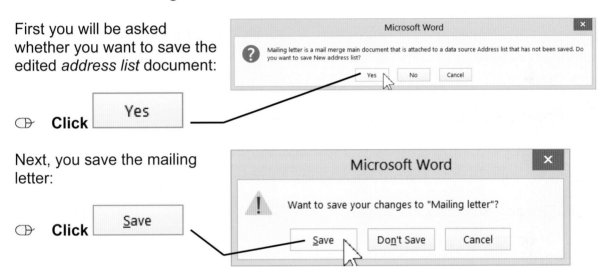

☞ **Click** Yes

Next, you save the mailing letter:

☞ **Click** Save

7.13 Subsequent Mailings

If you want to use the *Mailing letter* document again later on, you will see that this document is already linked to the *New address list* document:

☞ **Open the saved *Mailing letter* document** ✂¹⁰

You will see this message:

☞ **Click** Yes

You will see the letter with the data already entered in the correct places.

To display the field codes:

☞ **Click the**   MAILINGS
   tab

☞ **Click** Preview Results

Now you could edit the letter and merge it again later, with a current address file.

☞ **Close the *Mailing letter* document and save the changes** ³

«AddressBlock»

Sacramento,

Dear «First_name»,

Now you can enable the text boundaries again. In *section 3.1 Aligning Text with Tabs* you can read how to do this.

7.14 Creating Labels and Envelopes

The *Mail Merge* function in *Word* is very useful. You can use it with an existing address list as a data source for creating address labels, among other things. An address list made in a table in *Word* is suitable for this purpose, but you can also use an address list made in other *Microsoft* programs such as *Excel* or *Access*.
In the next few steps, you will be using the same address list that was used earlier in this chapter.

➥ **Please note:**

If you are creating your own address list with a table, make sure that the entire table does not contain any superfluous blank spaces. If the table contains extra blank spaces, the address data on the labels will not be neatly aligned.

Now you are going to create labels with the *Address list* document from the *Practice files Word* folder.

☞ **Open a new, blank document** 🦶**65**

Click the tab   MAILINGS

Click   Start Mail Merge ▾

Click   Step-by-Step Ma

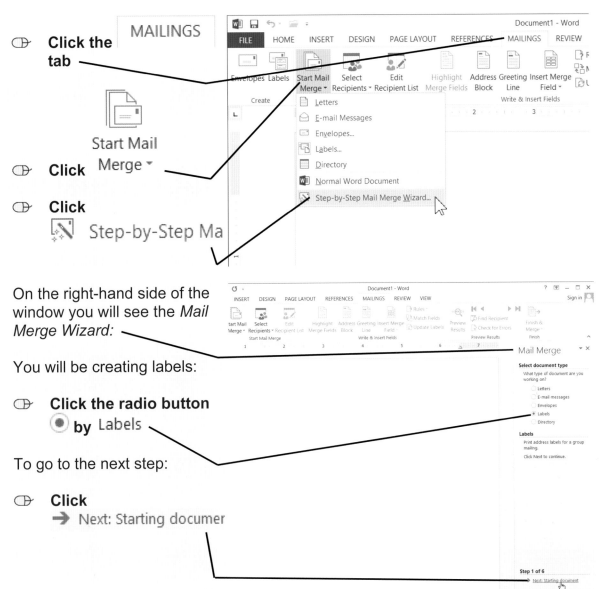

On the right-hand side of the window you will see the *Mail Merge Wizard:*

You will be creating labels:

☞ **Click the radio button ◉ by** Labels

To go to the next step:

☞ **Click**   → Next: Starting documer

The next step is the selection of the label:

👆 **Click** ▦ Label options...

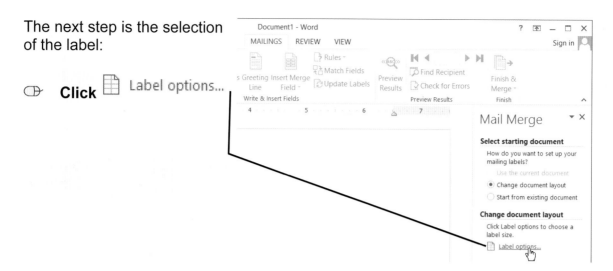

Word contains information for labels of a number of well-known brands. In this example we have chosen a label from the *Avery* brand:

👉 **By** Label vendors:, **select the size called** Avery US Letter

👉 **Select the product number** 8160 Easy Peel Address Lab

👆 **Click** [OK]

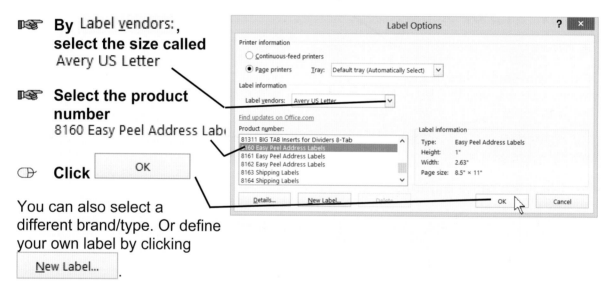

You can also select a different brand/type. Or define your own label by clicking [New Label...].

Now you will see the sample labels.

✚ **HELP! I do not see any sample labels in this window.**

If you do not see the sample labels, the *View Gridlines* option may have been disabled. To enable this option:

👆 **Click the** LAYOUT **tab**

👆 **Click** ▦ View Gridlines

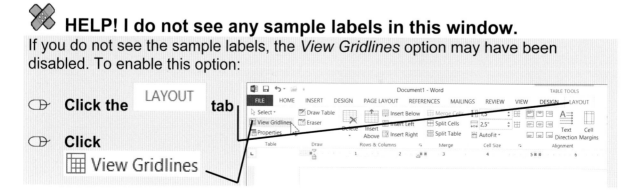

The next step in the wizard is the selection of the addresses:

In the bottom right-hand corner of the window:

☞ **Click**

→ Next: Select recipients

In this case, you are going to use an existing list:

☞ **If necessary, click the radio button ⦿ by**

Use an existing list

☞ **Click** ▦ Browse...

You will see the *Select Data Source* window:

☞ **Open the *Practice files Word* folder** 𝄞4

☞ **Click** ▦ Address list

☞ **Click** Open

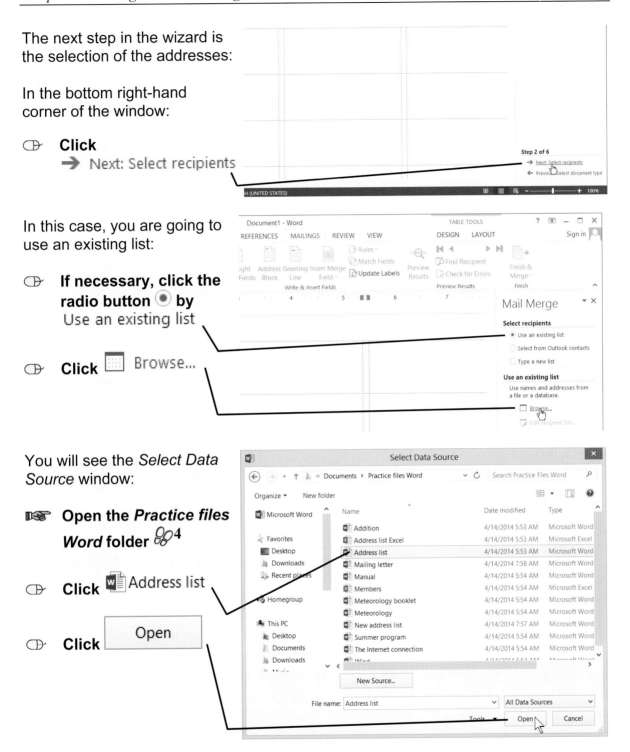

You will see the data in the window:

The rows that are checked will be used for the labels. If you do not want to use specific rows (records), uncheck the box by these rows.

Click   OK

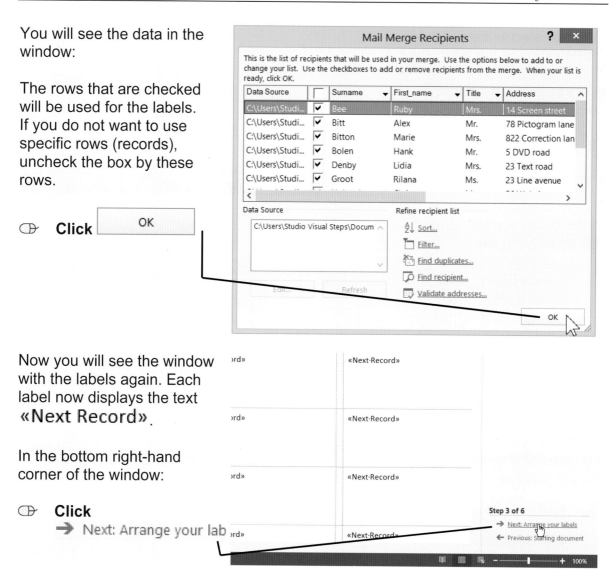

Now you will see the window with the labels again. Each label now displays the text **«Next Record»**.

In the bottom right-hand corner of the window:

Click
→ Next: Arrange your label

The next step is to indicate what exactly you want to print on your label. This could be just the name and address. Or you could insert a title before the name, such as Mrs. or Mr. You start as follows:

Click the top of the first label

Click ⊞ More items...

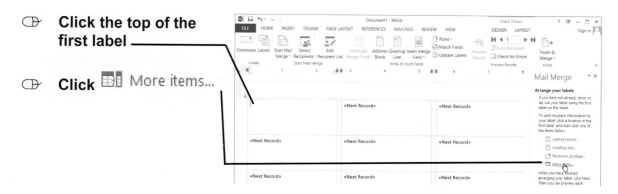

In this window you can see
which fields are present in
your address list. Although
you may need to select the
⊙ Database Fields option:

Each column header in your
table is a separate field. You
can insert a selected field:

Start with the Title field:

☞ **Click** Title

☞ **Click** Insert

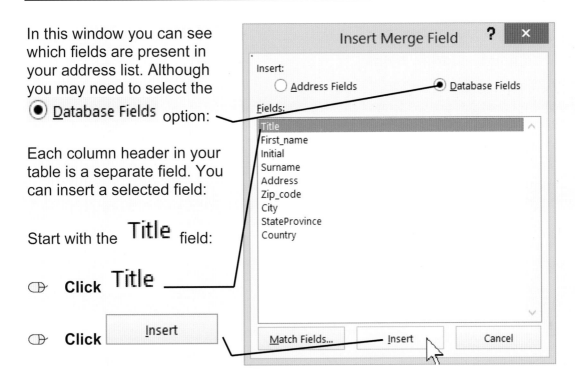

In the first label you will see Title appear. You can fill in the other fields in the
same way. You can decide for yourself whether you want to use the first name initial
or the full first name on the label. If you only have addresses in your own country,
the Country field may be superfluous.

☞ **Insert all the desired
fields**

After you have finished:

☞ **Click** Close

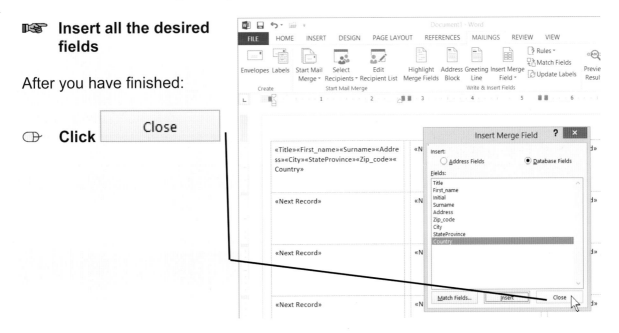

💡 Tip

Enter the complete address block

By <u>**Arrange your labels**</u> you will also find the 📄 Address block... option. This option will let you insert the whole address block at once. You do this in the same way as you did in *section 7.3 Inserting an Address block.*

Now label 1 contains all the fields you have inserted. But you will still need to insert blank spaces between the fields. For example, between the «Title»«First_name» and «First_name»«Surname» fields. You want to move the «Address» field to the next line. The «City», «StateProvince», «Zip_code» and «Country» fields need to go to the next lines and blank spaces need to be added between these fields. Start as follows:

👉 **Click between** «Title» **and** «First_name»

⌨️ **Type a blank space**

👉 **Place a blank space between** «First_name» **and** «Surname» **too**

👉 **Add a comma after** «City» **and a blank space before** «StateProvince» **and before** «Zip_code»

In this example, it looks as if the «Surname» and «StateProvince» fields have moved along to the next line. On small labels you cannot yet see what the final printed label will look like at this stage. You will see that everything will be fine once you have inserted enough blank spaces, commas and new lines in the right places.

Next, move the «Address» field to the next line, just like the «City» field and the «Country» field, by pressing the Enter key:

👉 **Click between «Surname» and «Address»**

⌨ **Press** Enter

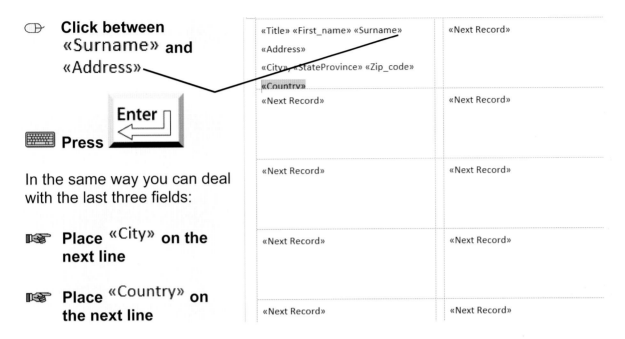

In the same way you can deal with the last three fields:

👉 **Place «City» on the next line**

👉 **Place «Country» on the next line**

You can see that «Country» falls partly outside the label. You can change the spacing so everything fits on the label:

👉 **Select the text in the first label**

👉 **Click the** HOME **tab**

👉 **By** Paragraph **, click** ⌐⌐

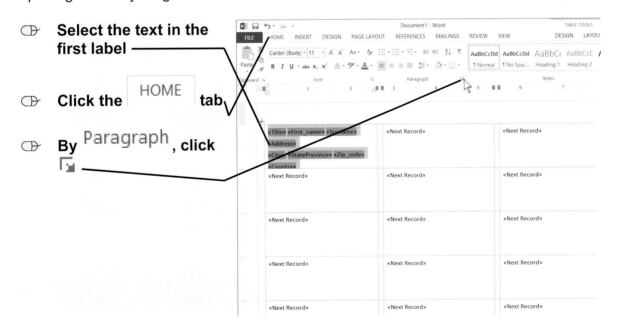

The default spacing before the text is set to 5.55. You are going to change this:

⌨ **By** <u>B</u>efore: **, type:** 4 . 3

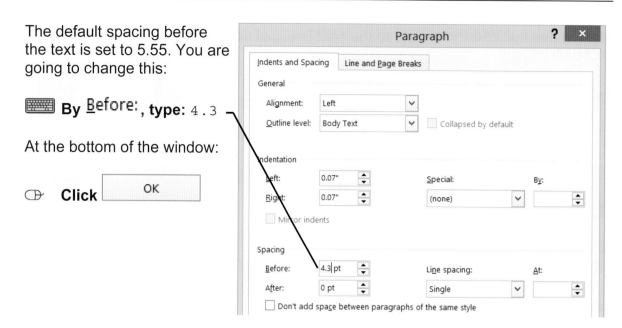

At the bottom of the window:

☞ **Click** OK

Now label 1 is completely as it should be. You can apply this label layout to all the other labels:

☞ **Click** Update all labels

Now all labels have the same layout. Continue with the next step:

☞ **Click**
➔ Next: Preview your labe

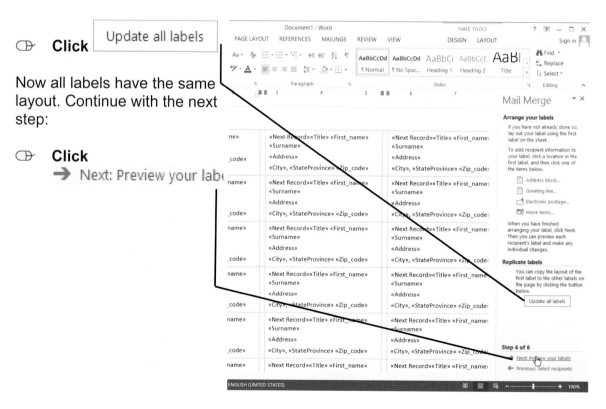

You will see an example of what the labels will look like after you have printed them. Do you see a mistake somewhere? You can still go back to the previous step(s) of the wizard by clicking

 Previous: Arrange your labels

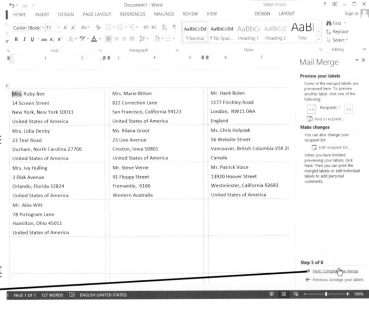

If you are satisfied with the result, you can complete the merge operation:

⊕ **Click**

→ Next: Complete the merge

Now the merge has been completed. You can print the labels directly from this window. But you can also transfer all the labels to a new document that can easily be edited and saved, in order to use it again later on.

⊕ **Click**

Edit individual labels...

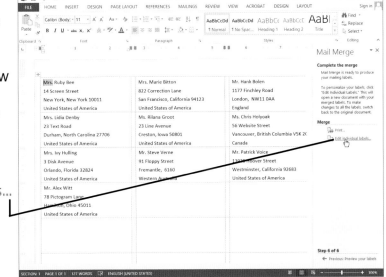

 has already been selected:

⊕ **Click** OK

Now the wizard is closed. You will see the labels in a new *Word* document. You can still edit the text and layout of the labels. For example, you can adjust the font, the font size, font color, add bold or italics and more. Or you can center the text on the label. You can even insert a picture in one or more labels. Afterwards you can print the labels the same way as you print other documents.

☞ **Print the labels, if you wish** 𝒬𝒬¹¹

You can save this document, if you want to use it again later on:

☞ **Save the document, if you wish** 𝒬𝒬¹⁵

If you use the label's product name and number in the file name, it will be easier to find the matching sheets of labels later on.

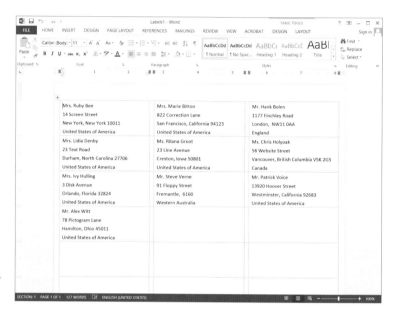

☞ **Close the *Labels1* document without saving the changes** 𝒬𝒬³

You will see the merge document again. You can close this too.

☞ **Close the merge document without saving the changes** 𝒬𝒬³

☞ **If necessary, close *Word*** 𝒬𝒬²

In this section you have learned how to create labels from a table you created in *Word*. If you want to print addresses on envelopes, you need to select the Envelopes option by **Select document type** in the *Mail Merge Wizard*. Next you click ▭ Envelope options... and you select the size of the envelope.

In the *Tip Address file in Microsoft Excel* you can find more information about creating labels and envelopes with an *Excel* file. In the exercises you can practice the actions you have learned.

Tip

Insert a picture

If you click a label, you can insert a picture. This is done in the same way as inserting a picture in a regular *Word* document. You can reduce the size of the picture so that it fits on the label. With the select, copy and paste options you can easily and quickly place the picture on the other labels. Make sure the wrap text option is set to *Square*, so the picture does not move along with the text.

 Tip

Test print

It is recommended to print the first page on regular paper, to test the labels. You can use this test page to see if the text will properly fit on the label sheet. And you can also find out how to feed the label sheets into the printer.

In this chapter you have learned how to merge different types of documents with an address file.

7.15 Exercises

Have you forgotten how to do something? Use the number beside the footsteps to look it up in the appendix *How Do I Do That Again?* at the end of the book.

Exercise 1: Create Labels with an Address List in Excel

☞ Open *Word*. 𝒪ℓ**1**

☞ Open the *Step-by-Step Mail Merge Wizard*. 𝒪ℓ**66**

☞ Click the radio button ⦿ by Labels .

☞ Go to the next step. 𝒪ℓ**67**

☞ Select the label Avery US Letter 8160 Easy Peel Address Labels . 𝒪ℓ**79**

☞ Go to the next step. 𝒪ℓ**67**

☞ Click Use an existing list

☞ Click ▦ Browse... .

☞ If necessary, select All Data Sources ⌄ in the *Select Data Source* window.

☞ Open the ⊞Address list Excel file in the *Practice files Word* folder.

☞ Select ▦ 'Sheet 1$' and click OK .

☞ Click OK .

☞ Go to the next step. 𝒪ℓ**67**

☞ Click the first label.

☞ Click ▦ More items... .

☞ Select the desired fields. 𝒪ℓ**68**

☞ Place the fields on the labels in the correct order.

☞ Update all labels. 👣**69**

☞ Go to the next step twice. 👣**67**

☞ Click 📄 Edit individual labels… and click [　　OK　　].

Now you will see the labels in a new *Word* file.

☞ Close *Word* and do not save the changes. 👣**2**

7.16 Background Information

Dictionary

Field	A field is a temporary placeholder for data in a document where different data can be filled in. It is also an indication for the data that can be used for creating standard letters and labels in mail merge documents. Fields of this type are also called *field codes*.
Field code	See *Field*.
Field name	The name of a type of field, for instance, 'First name' or Address'.
Record	A group of matching data in a data file. For example, a record in an address file could consist of the name, the address, city, state and phone number of a single person.
Space	A blank space between words.
Wrap text	The way in which a text wraps around a picture.

Source: Word 2013, Word 2010, Windows Help and Support

Address files and programs
You can use various programs to create address files. The program best suitable for your purposes will depend on the number of addresses (records) you want to store, among other things:

- For smaller numbers, you can easily use *Microsoft Word*.

- If there are large numbers of records (hundreds or a couple of thousands), then it is best to use *Microsoft Excel* to create the address file.

- If there are really very large numbers involved (many thousands of records), then a genuine database program is the best choice, such as *Microsoft Access*.

- Continue in the next page -

Besides the number of addresses, there are other factors to take into account. The selection and sorting options of *Microsoft Excel* and *Access* are much more robust and extensive than they are in *Word*, for example. *Microsoft Access* has a lot of extra options for creating your own input screens for entering data, creating reports, et cetera, which also makes it more complicated to use. For merging address data and mailing documents, both programs can be used with *Microsoft Word's* mail merge options as discussed in this chapter.

7.17 Tips

 Tip

Printing envelopes
Keep a close eye on your printer when you are printing an envelope. Some printers will wait until you feed the envelope into the printer by hand.

This often means that a light will start to blink and the printer will wait until you enter the print command.
You can do this by pressing a button on the printer.

☞ **Check your printer manual to find out how to print documents when you enter the sheets of paper or envelopes by hand**

 Tip

Create a label with a single address
In this chapter you have created labels by using an address list. But there is also another way of creating a label with a single name/address:

⊕ **Click the** MAILINGS **tab**

⊕ **If necessary, click** Create

⊕ **Click** Labels

Enter the address
information: ⎯⎯

A single label or a full page of
labels:

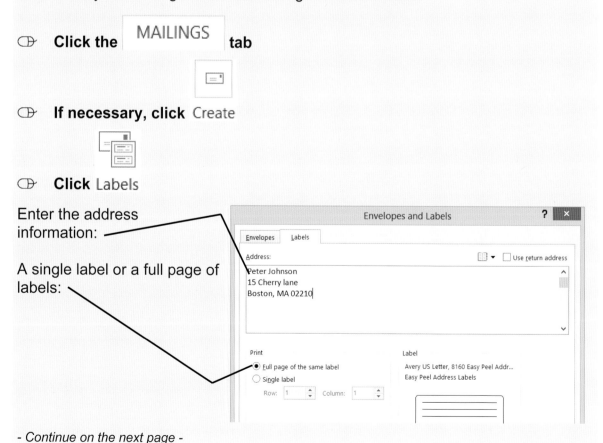

- Continue on the next page -

It is important that you match the settings in *Word* with the size of the labels you want to print. For this, you need to click **Options...**:

Here you select the brand of the labels:

Here you select the type of label:

If your label is not shown in the list, you can enter the correct size yourself, by clicking **New Label...**:

When you are finished:

☞ **Click** OK

Now you can print the labels:

At the bottom of the window:

☞ **Click** Print

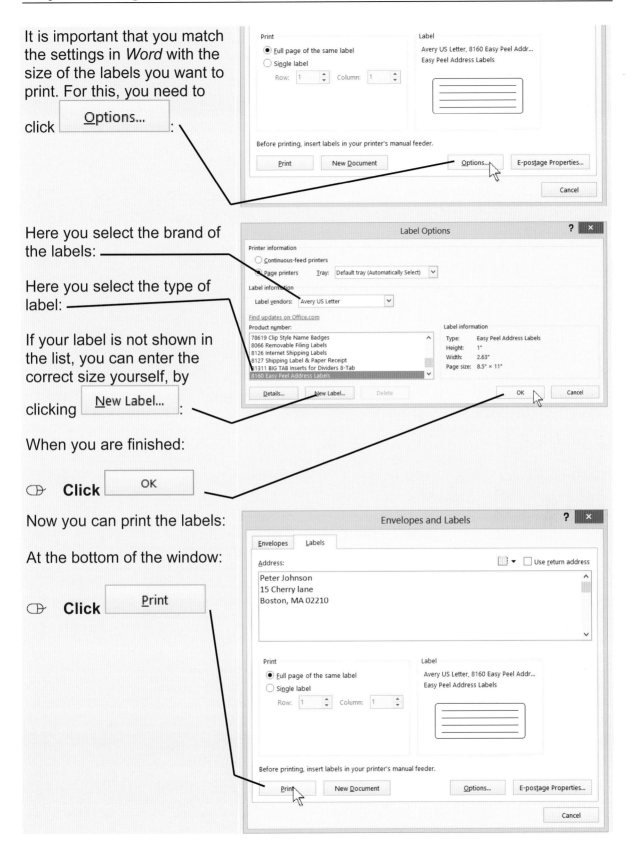

Tip

Outlook data
If you use the *Outlook* mail program and have addresses stored in the *Contacts* list, you can select the Select from Outlook contacts option in step 3 of the *Mail Merge Wizard.* If you do this, the *Outlook* address data will be used as a source for merging the document.

 Tip

Set the label size yourself
If your own vendor or type of label is not displayed in the list, you can set the correct size yourself:

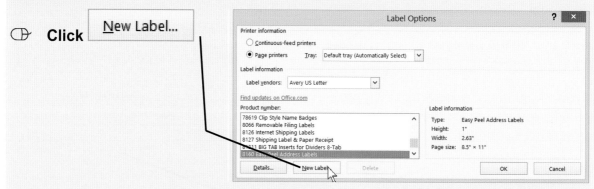

☞ **Click** New Label...

Now you will see a window in which you can set the exact sizes for your own label:

Use a ruler to measure the size of your label sheet, or check the wrapper to find out what size the labels are.

☞ **Enter the dimensions**

It is important to be precise. A small difference can result in significant shifts, after you have printed a couple of pages.

☞ **Enter a name**

The label will be included in the list. You can use it the next time you want to use this type of label.

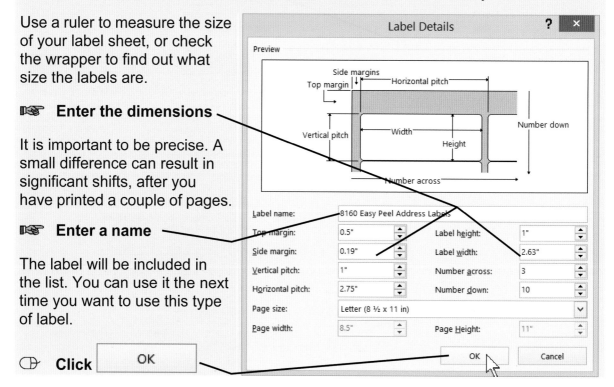

☞ **Click** OK

💡 Tip

Mailing via email

If you include a separate field for the email address in your address file, you will also be able to create email mailings directly in *Word*. But you will need to have the *Microsoft Outlook* program installed on your computer (this option will not work with *Outlook Express*, *Windows Mail* or *Windows Live Mail*).

First, create the mailing letter in the usual manner. Continue with the following steps if you want to send your mailing through email:

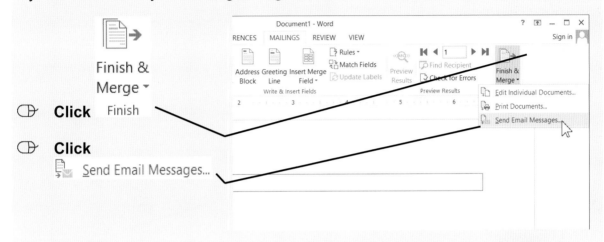

☞ **Click** Finish

☞ **Click**
   📧 Send Email Messages...

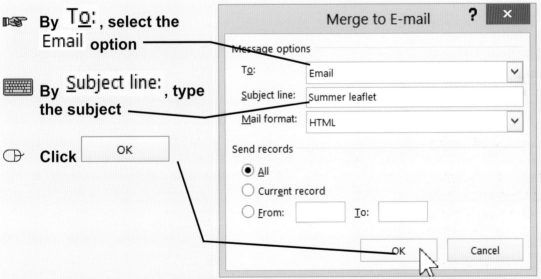

☞ **By** To:, **select the Email option** ──

⌨ **By** Subject line:, **type the subject** ──

☞ **Click** [OK]

Word now creates an email message for all the email addresses. They will be placed in the *Outbox* of *Microsoft Outlook*, ready to send. You can send the email messages in *Outlook* in the usual manner.

Tip

Address file in Microsoft Excel
If you have created an address file in *Microsoft Excel*, the method is the same as when you are linking an address list made in *Word*. Only, now you need to select the *Excel* file when linking the files:

☞ **Click the *Excel* file**

☞ **Click** | Open |

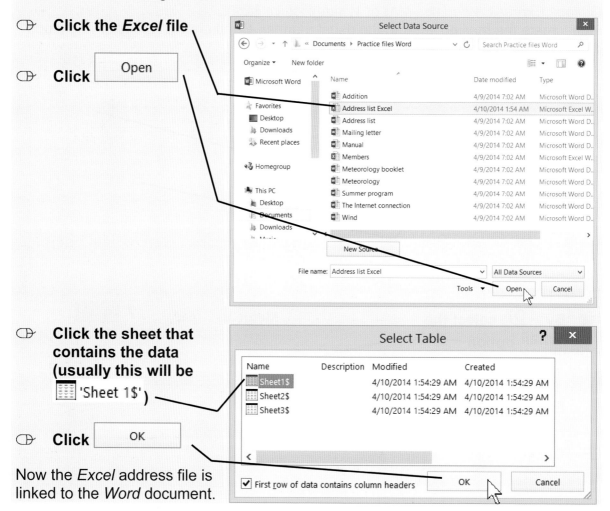

☞ **Click the sheet that contains the data (usually this will be 'Sheet 1$')**

☞ **Click** | OK |

Now the *Excel* address file is linked to the *Word* document.

Tip

Multiple address files

You can merge a single mailing document with multiple address lists. You can link the document to any address file you want to use, over and over again.

This is handy if you want to send the same letter to recipients in different address files (for example, regions, various types of members/customers, etc.). You can use the same document for all of them. You only need to link the document to a different address file, each time you want to use another address list. The only requirement is that each address file needs to have the same layout. They all need to be identical with regard to the format. This also means that the fields you have used in the mailing letter need to have identical field names throughout all the address files.

The opposite is also true; you can link a single address file to multiple mailing documents (letters, labels, envelopes).

 Tip

Pictures and the Mail Merge function

If you have photos inserted in the *records* of your address file, you can place these photos in a document with the *Mail Merge* function.

In order to do this, you need to insert a field into the document that matches the name of the column with the pictures.

In this example the field name is called **«Photo»**:

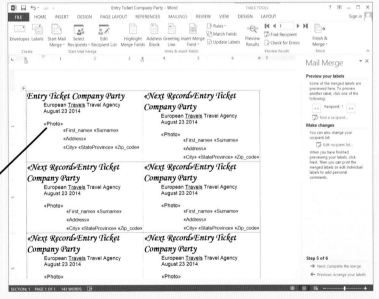

- Continue on the next page -

In this example we have created a personalized entry ticket for a company party:

You could also use this kind of field for club membership, or business cards.

Once you have merged the data, you may need to edit the cards manually in order to place the photos and text in the right position.

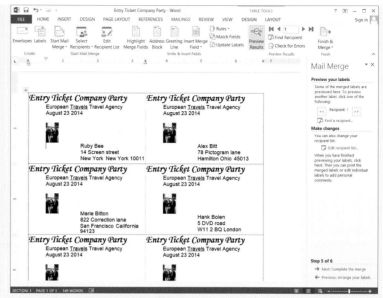

It is important to use the right kind of printing paper for this purpose, that is to say, paper of a heavier quality. You can also laminate membership cards or similar types of cards.

Tip
Other ways of using mail merge documents
A mailing document does not always have to be a letter, a label, or something you send by email. You can also create a document in the shape of an information sheet about your product (with a photo, if you wish), or about your DVDs, photos, etc. Just create a table with all the data concerning your products, DVDs, or photos and you can create a nice summary sheet by merging this data with your mailing document.

8. Table of Contents, Index, etc.

Papers, reports, manuals, and other lengthy documents require a high standard of work. Not only does the text need to look nice and be well-ordered, but the reader should be able to find things without too much trouble. You can make things easier by creating a well-structured table of contents. You may also want to include an index at the end of your document as well, with references to the main subjects and concepts. If it is an official document or paper, you will need to include a bibliography with references to source materials and acknowledgements.

Word offers a number of options that can perform some of these tasks automatically. However, you need to add your own input. You are after all, the only person who should decide what is to be included in the table of contents or index.

In this chapter you will be applying the finishing touches to a booklet created with letter sized paper (booklet is the size of a sheet folded in half, 5.5" x 8.5").

In this chapter you will learn how to:

- automatically create a table of contents with styles;
- update the table of contents;
- mark words to include in the index;
- include cross-references and sub items in the index;
- add foot and end notes;
- insert source references into your document;
- list all the pictures in the document.

8.1 Table of Contents

☞ Open *Word* 𝔔𝔔¹

☞ Open the document called *Meteorology booklet* in the *Practice files Word* folder 𝔔𝔔¹⁰

☞ If necessary, enable editing 𝔔𝔔⁸²

☞ If necessary, close the *Navigation Pane* 𝔔𝔔³²

☞ Show the text boundaries 𝔔𝔔⁸³

You will see the text of a booklet in letter size paper folded in half. The page layout and the margins for this booklet have already been correctly set. Even the extra 'gutter' margin has been taken into account, to make room for folding and stapling the booklet. In the following steps you will add and edit a table of contents for this booklet.

If you have consistently used heading styles in your document, *Word* will be able to automatically generate a table of contents. In this document, the title of the text has been set in the *Heading 1* style and the *Heading 2* style has been used for all the subheadings.

☞ Check if the cursor is positioned at the beginning of the title 'Meteorology'

⊕ Click the REFERENCES tab

⊕ Click Table of Contents ▾

⊕ Click Automatic Table 1

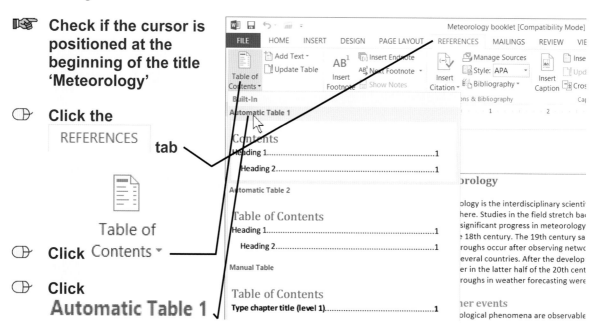

The table of contents is inserted automatically at the top of the page. But you want to place it on a separate page. To do that, you can move the text to the next page:

☞ **Check if the cursor is positioned before the title 'Meteorology'**

⌨ **Press** **Ctrl** + **Enter**

Now the text has moved to page 2. Since the title and the rest of the text have moved to the next page, the table of contents is no longer accurate. This table of contents does not automatically update, you need to do that manually.

☞ **Go to the beginning of the document** ✂ 21

Here you see the table of contents. It says that the text begins on page 1:

👆 **Click** 🗋! Update Table

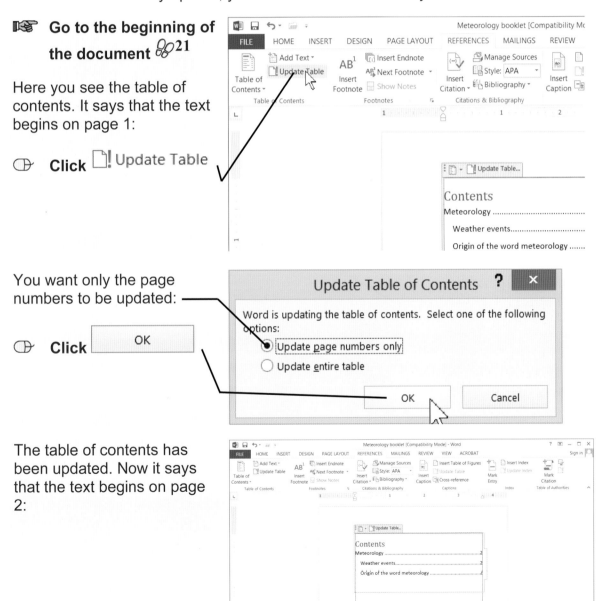

You want only the page numbers to be updated:

👆 **Click** OK

The table of contents has been updated. Now it says that the text begins on page 2:

8.2 Styles and the Table of Contents

The table of contents is created by *Word* on the basis of the heading styles that are used in the document. By default, a *Word* document has four heading styles. *Heading 1* is the most important style and is used for a chapter title, for instance. *Heading 2* can be used for a section, *Heading 3* for a subsection, and *Heading 4* is for a subheading. Note that the formatting of these heading styles depends on the styles that have been applied to the document, and the edits that may have been applied to these styles.

By consistently using these headings, you can quickly and easily create a table of contents, and edit it too. In the following step, you can practice editing the table of contents by inserting new headings into the text:

On the second page:

Place the cursor on the blank line above the third paragraph

Type:
Higher powers

Click the HOME **tab**

By Styles **, click** ▼

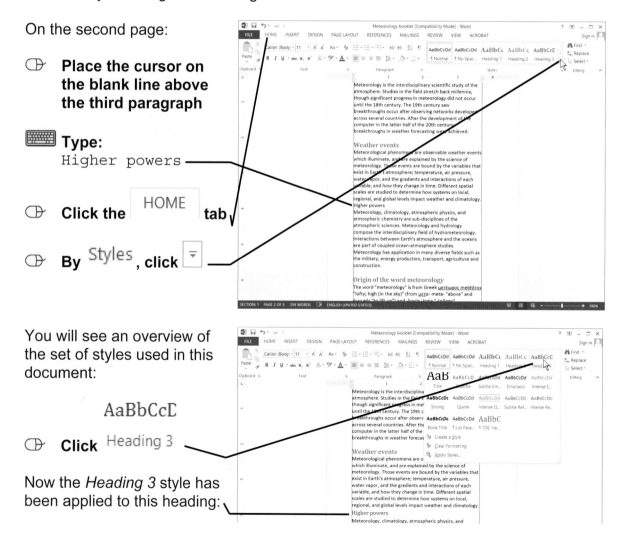

You will see an overview of the set of styles used in this document:

AaBbCcC

Click Heading 3

Now the *Heading 3* style has been applied to this heading:

⊕ **Place the cursor at the beginning of the third page**

⌨ **Type:**
Holy days

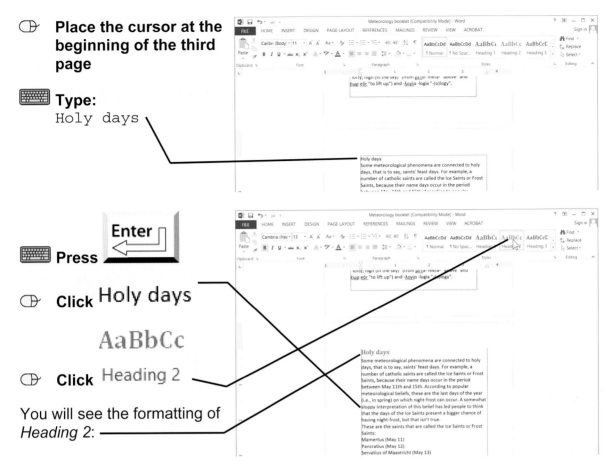

⌨ **Press** **Enter**

⊕ **Click** Holy days

AaBbCc

⊕ **Click** Heading 2

You will see the formatting of *Heading 2*:

By updating the table of contents at this point, you can include the new headings too:

☞ **Go to the beginning of the document** 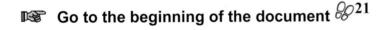21

⊕ **Click the** REFERENCES **tab, and** 📄! Update Table

⊕ **Click the radio button** ⦿ **by**
Update entire table

⊕ **Click** OK

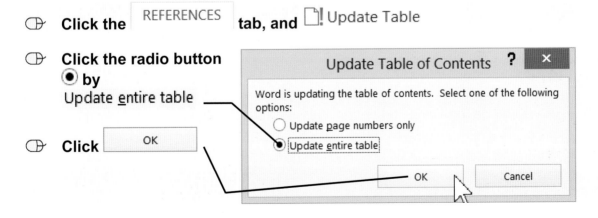

You see that the headings are included in the table of contents, on different levels:

You have just updated the table of contents through the tab, with the

Update Table option.

If you click the table of contents you will also see this option:

8.3 Creating an Index

An index is a list of the keywords and subjects that are discussed in a text or book. In this Visual Steps book you will also find an index at the end of the book. Indexes allow you to easily lookup a specific word and find the page that contains it.

For a large part, *Word* will take care of creating an index automatically. You only need to indicate which words you want to include in the index. In order to do this, you need to mark the words.

➣ Please note:

Only generate the indexes after you have completely finished with the document. If you change the document later on, by adding text, the words in the new piece of text will not be added to the index automatically. You will need to add these words to the index by hand.

♡ Tip

Make a copy
Before you generate an index, it is a good idea to first make a backup copy of your document. After you have closed the document, any index markers are hard to remove later on.

☞ **Go to the beginning of page 2** 👣**21**

👉 **Double-click meteorology**

👉 **Click** Mark Entry

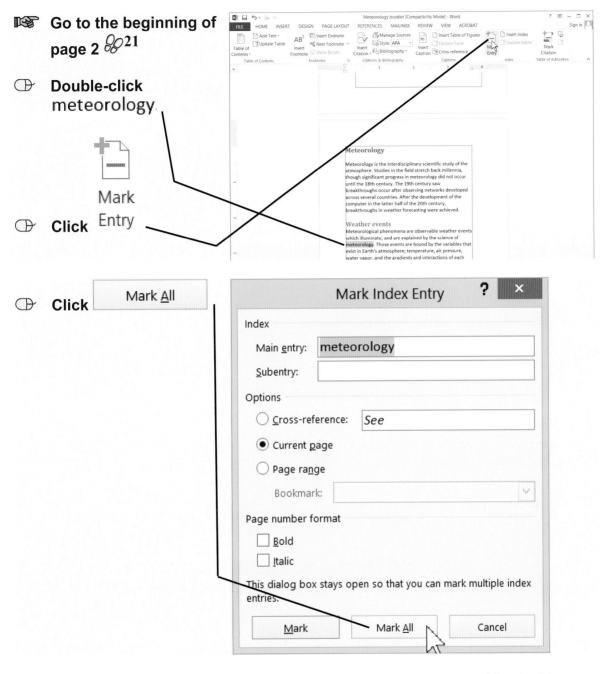

👉 **Click** Mark All

Now *Word* will search the document and mark all the words that are identical to 'meteorology'. At the same time the program will switch to the view in which all the special markers are displayed.

🖐 **Please note:**

The *Mark Index Entry* window remains open, so you can mark other index items. If this window gets in your way, you can drag it to the side.

Next to the word 'meteorology', a field code has been placed between braces { }:

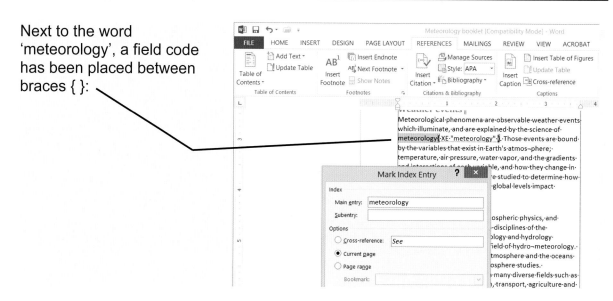

You can include different levels in an index. For instance, you can add all the names of saints in the index, under the word 'saint':

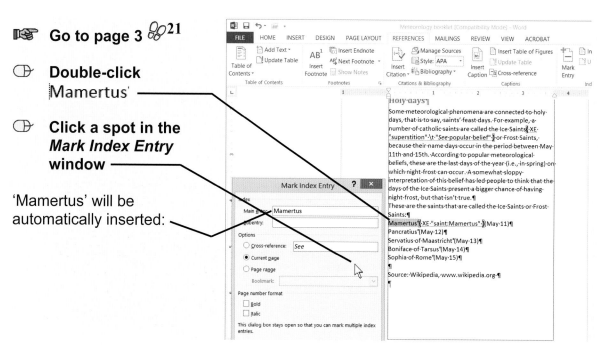

☞ **Go to page 3** 👣**21**

👆 **Double-click** **Mamertus**

👆 **Click a spot in the** ***Mark Index Entry*** **window**

'Mamertus' will be automatically inserted:

Now you need to turn 'Mamertus' into a subentry of 'saint':

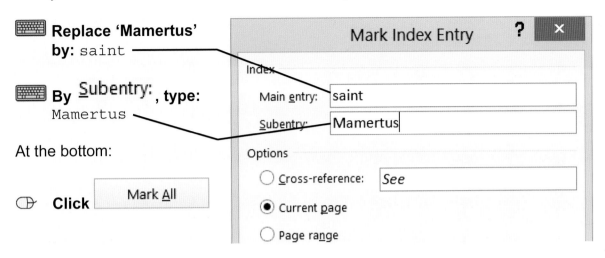

⌨ **Replace 'Mamertus' by:** `saint`

⌨ **By Subentry:, type:** `Mamertus`

At the bottom:

👆 **Click** Mark All

Now *Word* will place the field code {XE "saint:Mamertus"} next to the word 'Mamertus'.

You can also insert so-called cross-references in the text. This way you can refer to another word in the index. For instance, you can refer to 'popular belief' when someone looks for the word 'superstition':

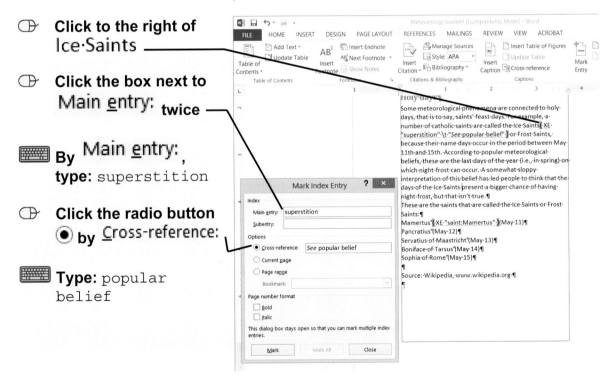

👆 **Click to the right of Ice·Saints**

👆 **Click the box next to Main entry: twice**

⌨ **By Main entry:, type:** `superstition`

👆 **Click the radio button ⊙ by Cross-reference:**

⌨ **Type:** `popular belief`

Click [Mark]

Click [Close]

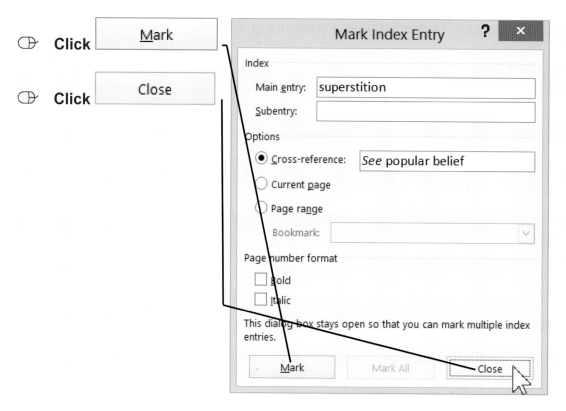

You have indicated which words you want to include in the index. Now you can generate the index. The usual place for an index is at the end of the document:

☞ Go to the end of the document ✂21

To go to a new page:

⌨ Press **Ctrl** + **Enter**

Click 🗎 Insert Index

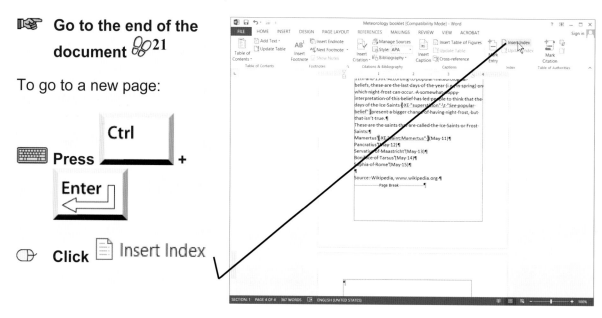

☞ **Check the box** ☑ **by** Right align page numbers

☞ **Click** OK

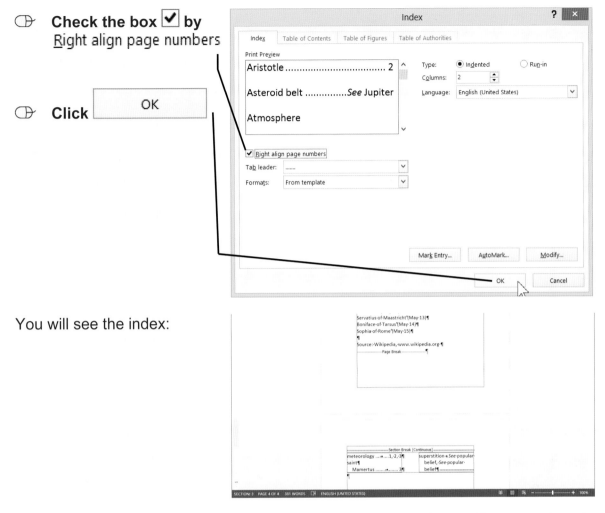

You will see the index:

As you see, creating an extensive index can be quite a lot of work. Every word, and sometimes also various alternatives for a certain word, needs to be marked in order to include it in the index. If you have added words to the index later on, or edited the text in any way, you will need to update the index. You can practice this now:

☞ **Go to page 2** ✌²¹

☞ **Add the word 'weather' to the index** ✌⁷¹

☞ **Close the *Mark Index Entry* window** ✌⁸⁰

☞ **Drag the scroll box downwards to the index**

☞ **Click a spot in the index**

Now the index is selected.

☞ **Click** 🗋! Update Index

The index has been updated. You will see the word 'weather' in the index:

☞ **Click the** HOME **tab, and** ¶

Now the field codes and other markers in the document are no longer visible.

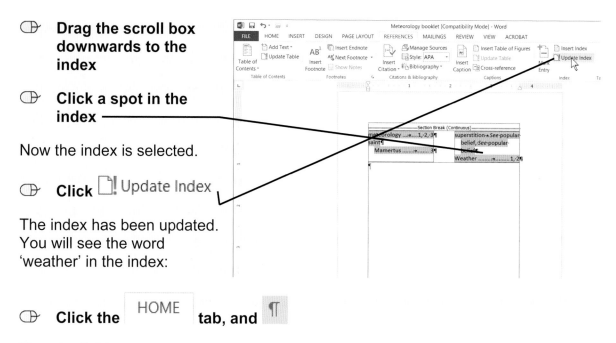

8.4 Footnotes and Endnotes

You can use footnotes and endnotes to insert a comment, addition, or explanation regarding the text at the bottom of the page (footnote) or at the end of your document (endnote). These notes are often used to refer to source materials, such as literature, to indicate the source of certain sayings or quotes.

In order to create a footnote, first you need to select the text to which you want to add a footnote:

☞ **Go to page 2** ✂[21]

☞ **Select the word 'breakthroughs'** ✂[20]

☞ **Click the** REFERENCES **tab**

AB[1]

Insert

☞ **Click** Footnote

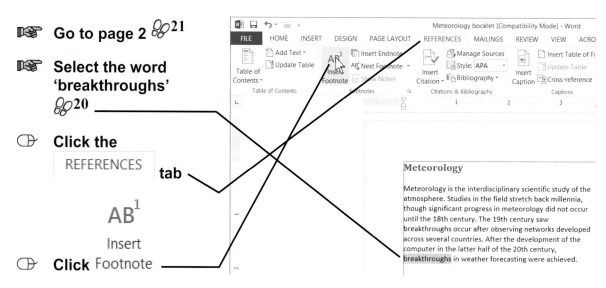

Tip

Insert endnote

If you want to insert an endnote instead of a footnote:

▱ **Click** Insert Endnote

The number of this footnote is inserted at the bottom of the page: ——————

Now you can type the text for this footnote:

⌨ **Type:**
According to various historical accounts

▱ **Click a spot in the text to quit the footnote** ——————

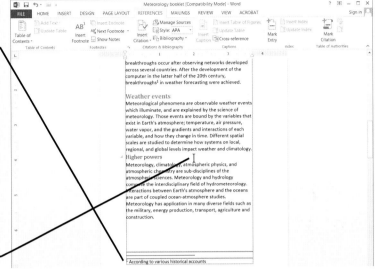

☞ **Go to the beginning of the page** ⌕21

Now you will see a marker by the word 'breakthroughs' with the footnote number, to indicate that footnote number 1 goes with this word: ——————

All the footnotes you enter from this point on are automatically numbered with consecutive numbers.

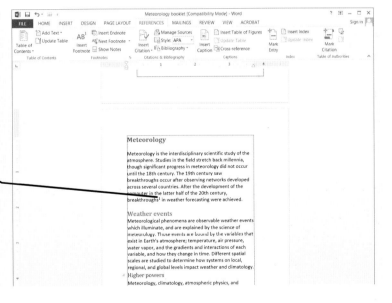

8.5 Source References

Source references are often used in books, reports, and papers, to indicate the source of the information in the text. Actually, the last sentence in the *Meteorology booklet*, 'Source: Wikipedia, www.wikipedia.org' is also a source reference. The difference with a footnote or an endnote is that no markers are inserted into the text.

You can also insert source references with *Word*:

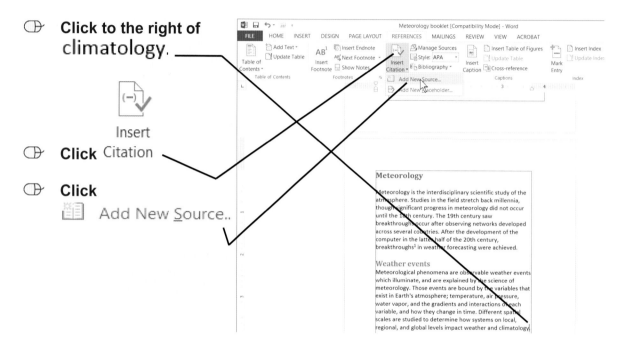

⊕ **Click to the right of climatology.**

⊕ **Click** Citation

⊕ **Click** Add New Source..

You will see the *Create Source* window. Here you can select the type of source, for example: an article in a paper or magazine, a website or a film. In this case you do not need to change the Book source type:

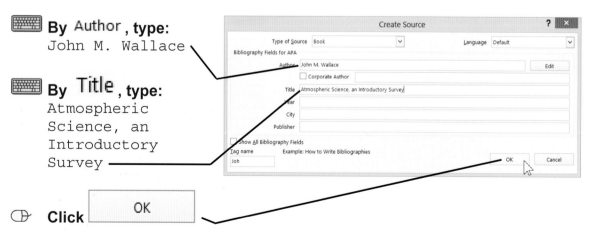

⌨ **By** Author **, type:** John M. Wallace

⌨ **By** Title **, type:** Atmospheric Science, an Introductory Survey

⊕ **Click** OK

The name of the author is now shown inside parentheses below the text:

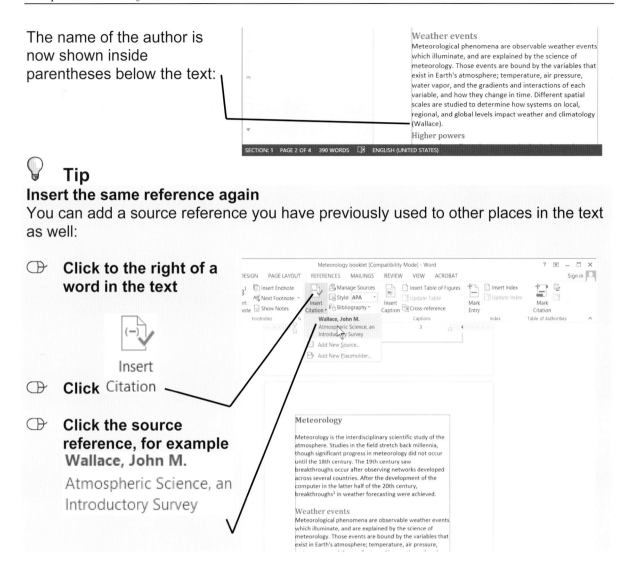

💡 **Tip**

Insert the same reference again

You can add a source reference you have previously used to other places in the text as well:

☞ **Click to the right of a word in the text**

☞ **Click** Citation

☞ **Click the source reference, for example Wallace, John M.**

Atmospheric Science, an Introductory Survey

Repeat these steps to add information for other sources. Then you can insert a bibliography with all the sources at the end of your document:

👉 **Go to the end of the document** 👣**21**

☞ **Click** 📑 Bibliography ▾

☞ **Click** Bibliography

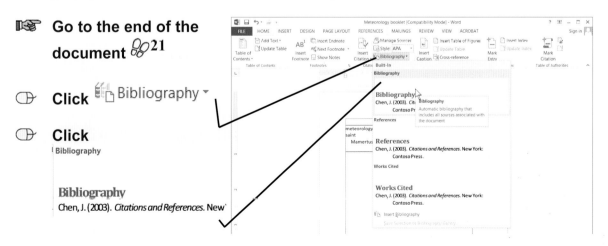

The bibliography has been inserted:

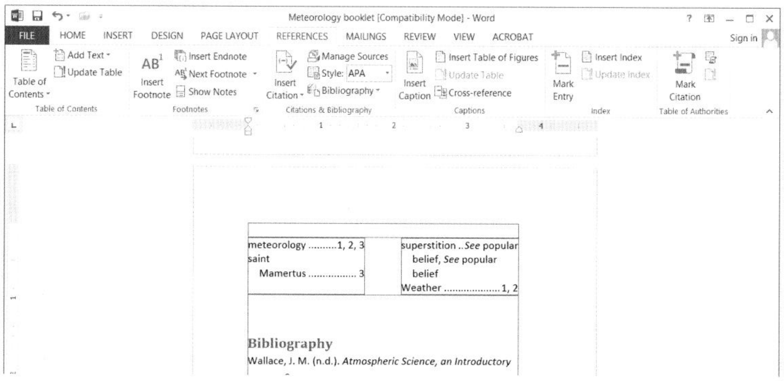
Meteorology booklet [Compatibility Mode] - Word
FILE
HOME
INSERT
DESIGN
PAGE LAYOUT
REFERENCES
MAILINGS
REVIEW
VIEW
ACROBAT
Sign in
Add Text
Update Table
Table of Contents
Insert Footnote
Insert Endnote
Next Footnote
Show Notes
Manage Sources
Style: APA
Bibliography
Insert Citation
Insert Caption
Insert Table of Figures
Update Table
Cross-reference
Mark Entry
Insert Index
Update Index
Mark Citation
Table of Contents
Footnotes
Citations & Bibliography
Captions
Index
Table of Authorities
meteorology 1, 2, 3
saint
Mamertus 3
superstition ..See popular belief, See popular belief
Weather 1, 2
Bibliography
Wallace, J. M. (n.d.). Atmospheric Science, an Introductory

Tip

Layout of the bibliography

If you are not happy with the style for the bibliography, you can change it. Instead of selecting a style, you can also click Bibliography, Insert Bibliography. Then you can format the bibliography yourself.

8.6 List of Pictures

You can also insert a list of pictures, tables, diagrams, etc. at the end of your document. If you want to do this you will need to add a caption to these items.

Place the cursor below the table of contents

Insert the *Spring* picture from the *Practice files Word* folder 33

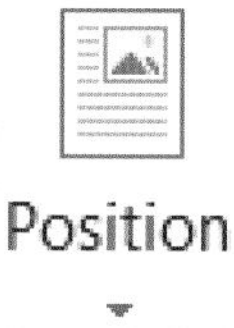
Position

Click

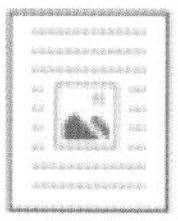

Click

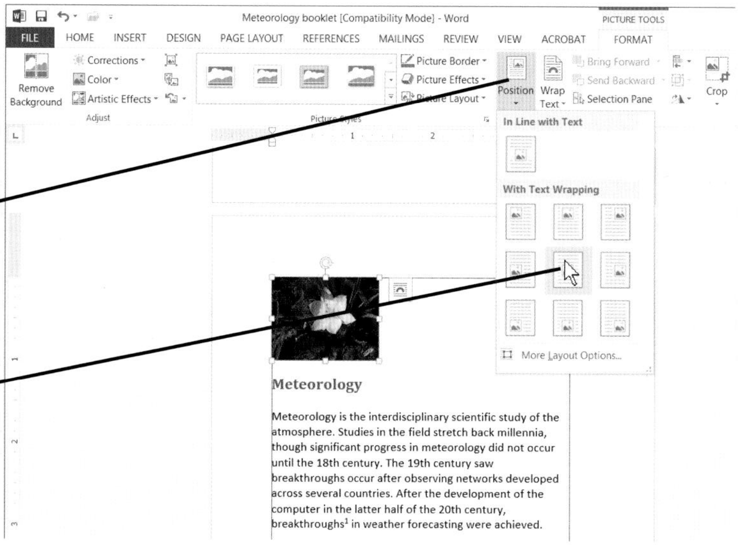
Meteorology booklet [Compatibility Mode] - Word
PICTURE TOOLS
FILE
HOME
INSERT
DESIGN
PAGE LAYOUT
REFERENCES
MAILINGS
REVIEW
VIEW
ACROBAT
FORMAT
Remove Background
Corrections
Color
Artistic Effects
Adjust
Picture Border
Picture Effects
Picture Layout
Picture Styles
Position
Wrap Text
Bring Forward
Send Backward
Selection Pane
Crop
In Line with Text
With Text Wrapping
More Layout Options...
Meteorology
Meteorology is the interdisciplinary scientific study of the atmosphere. Studies in the field stretch back millennia, though significant progress in meteorology did not occur until the 18th century. The 19th century saw breakthroughs occur after observing networks developed across several countries. After the development of the 20th century, computer in the latter half of the 20th century, breakthroughs in weather forecasting were achieved.

The picture is centered:

Click the

REFERENCES **tab**

Click Insert Caption

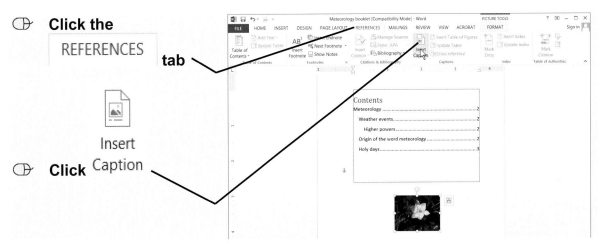

Type a blank space

Type: Signs of Spring

Click OK

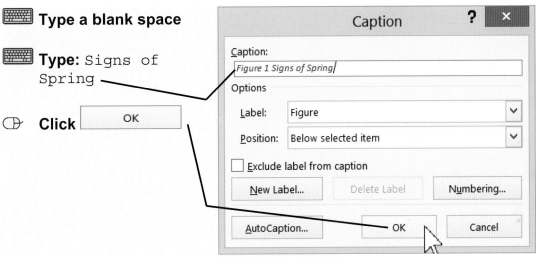

Go to the end of the document 21

Type: Pictures:

Press Enter

Click Insert Table of Figures

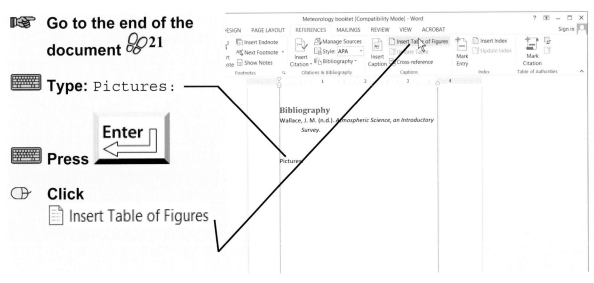

☞ **If necessary, by Formats: , select From template**

In this window you can also adjust some of the other settings, if you wish:

☞ **Click** OK

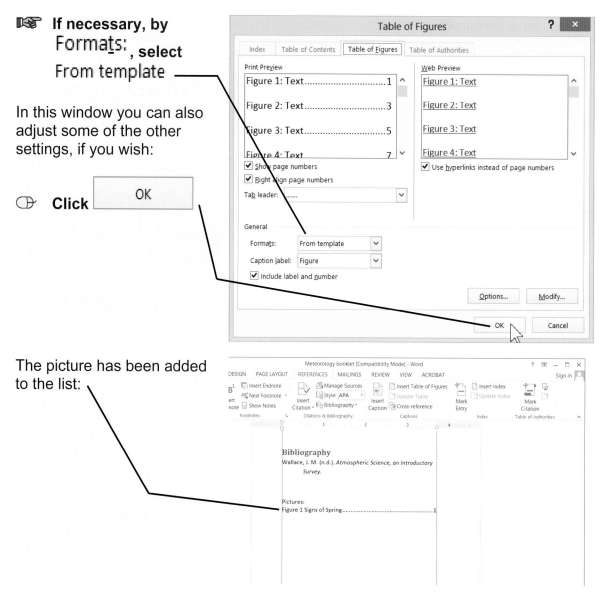

The picture has been added to the list:

Now you have finished creating the booklet. You can print the booklet if you like, to see how it looks.

☞ **Close *Word* and do not save the changes** ✂️²

In this chapter you have learned how to create a table of contents, add an index, footnote or endnote and more items of this type.

8.7 Exercises

Have you forgotten how to do something? Use the number beside the footsteps to look it up in the appendix *How Do I Do That Again?* at the end of the book.

Exercise 1: Table of Contents, Index, and List of Pictures

☞ Open *Word*. **1**

☞ Open the *Manual* document. **10**

☞ Insert a table of contents on the second page of the document. **72**

☞ Place the first heading *Read a document* on the next page. **73**

☞ Change the heading 'Read a document' to `View a document.`

☞ Update the whole table of contents. **74**

☞ Mark the words *PAGE DOWN*, *PAGE UP* and *BACKSPACE* on page 3 for the index. **71**

☞ Close the Mark Entry window **80**

☞ Insert the index at the end of the document. **75**

☞ Insert a caption by the picture on page 3. **62**

☞ Insert a list of pictures at the end of the document. **76**

☞ Close *Word* and do not save the changes. **2**

8.8 Background Information

Dictionary

Bibliography	A list of the sources you have consulted while you were creating the document, or the sources you have quoted.
Center	The picture is placed in the exact center between the left and right margins.
Cross-reference	An entry in the index that refers to another word in the same index.
Endnote	A comment, addition, or explanation regarding a piece of text, placed at the end of the document with a reference to this text.
Field code	A code that is inserted in the text to indicate text that needs to be placed in the index.
Footnote	A comment, addition, or explanation regarding a piece of text, placed at the bottom of the page with a reference to this text.
Heading style	A pre-defined way of formatting a heading.
Margin	The amount of blank space between the border of the page and the text.
Mark	Placing an index marker in the text, in order to include this text in the index.
Paragraph	A paragraph is a part of a text. A paragraph always begins on a new line and ends when you press the Enter key.
Style	A pre-defined way of formatting a text.

Source: Word 2013, Word 2010, Windows Help and Support, and Wikipedia

8.9 Tips

 Tip

Options for the table of contents

You can select one of the default styles for the table of contents. But you can also select a different style of formatting:

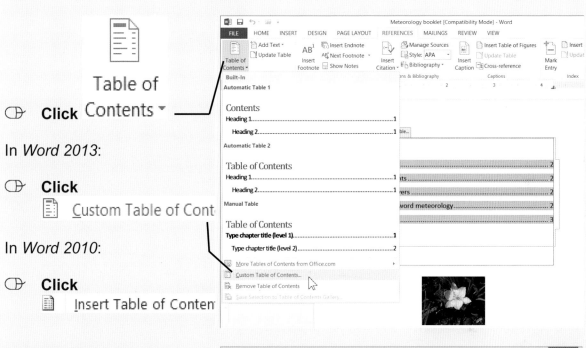

👆 **Click** Table of Contents ▾

In *Word 2013*:

👆 **Click** Custom Table of Cont

In *Word 2010*:

👆 **Click** Insert Table of Conten

In this window you can choose whether you want the page numbers aligned to the right, for example:

And you can select the tab leader, to fill in the blank spaces:

Also, you can select a different default format:

By clicking Modify..., you can change the formatting of the table of contents:

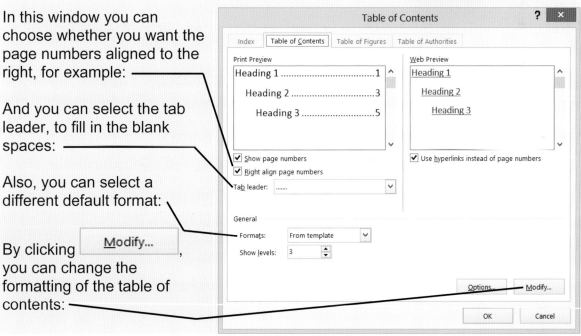

Tip

Options for the index

For the index, you can also select a different way of formatting other than the default:

In this window you can select the number of columns, for example:

You can choose whether you want to right align the page numbers, and you can select the tab leader:

You can select a different default format:

By clicking Modify... you can change the formatting of the index:

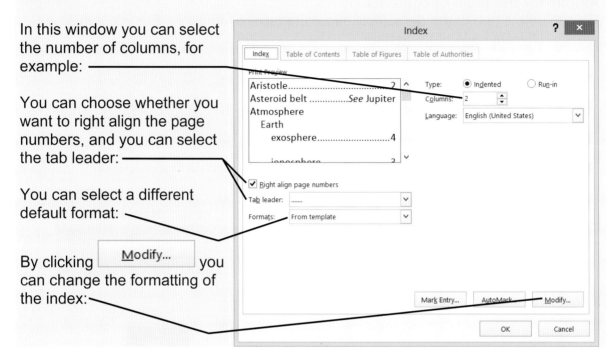

Tip

Options for footnotes or endnotes

In the *Footnote and Endnote* window you have various options. This is how you open the window:

By Footnotes, click

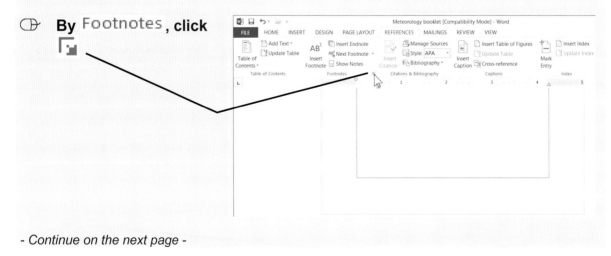

- Continue on the next page -

For instance, you can select whether you want to place the footnote at the bottom of the page or directly below the text:

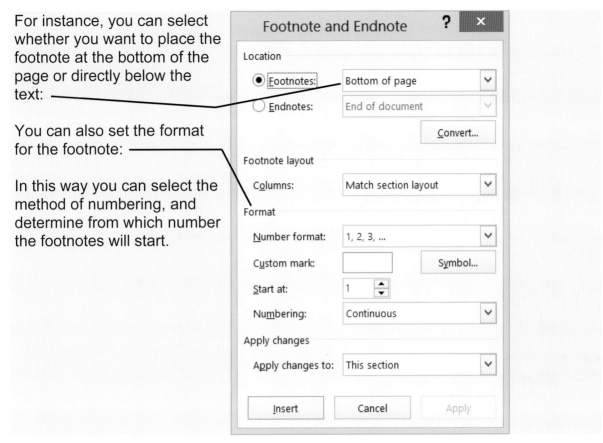

You can also set the format for the footnote:

In this way you can select the method of numbering, and determine from which number the footnotes will start.

 Tip

Printing a booklet on A5 paper size

When you are creating a booklet on the A5 paper size and want to print the cover as well as the back, it will be quite difficult to place the pages in the right position.

The *Book fold* function in *Word* will help you with this. This function makes sure that two A5 sized pages are printed on a single A4 sheet of paper, and this way the pages will end up in the right position. While you are at work you will see the pages in their regular order. Start with a new blank document and set the *Book fold* function, like this:

- Continue on the next page -

Click the **PAGE LAYOUT** **tab**

Click Margins

Click Custom Margins..

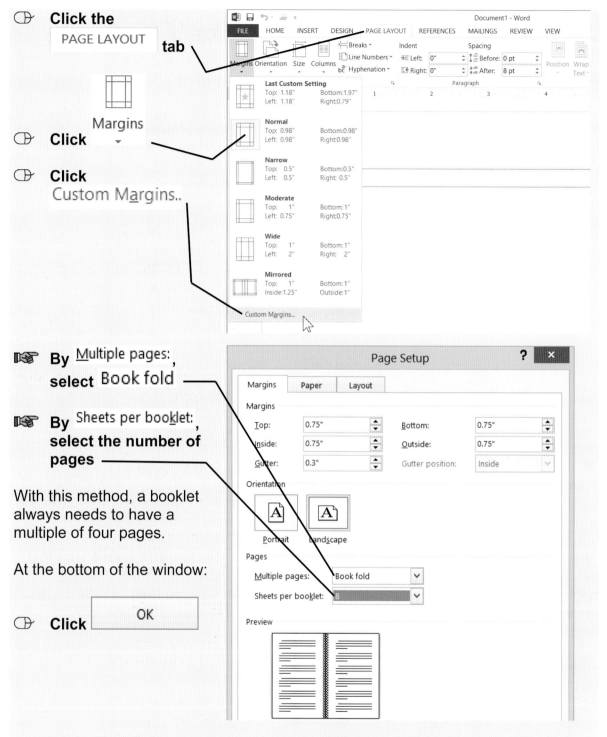

☞ **By** Multiple pages:, **select** Book fold

☞ **By** Sheets per booklet:, **select the number of pages**

With this method, a booklet always needs to have a multiple of four pages.

At the bottom of the window:

Click OK

In order to create a double-sided (duplex) booklet, your printer needs to be able to print in duplex mode. Some printers will automatically do this, but other printers need to be operated by hand. This means you will need to reverse the pages that have already been printed on one side, and put them back in the paper tray, upside down.

Appendix A. How Do I Do That Again?

The actions and exercises in this book are marked with footsteps: 1
If you have forgotten how to do something, you can read how to do it again by finding the corresponding number in the list below.

1 **Open *Word***

In Windows 8.1:
- Click the *Word* tile on the Start screen

Or:
- Move the pointer to the bottom left corner of the screen

- Click ⬇

- Click the *Word* tile

In Windows 7 and Vista:
- Click 🪟

- Click ▶ **All Programs**

- Click 📁 Microsoft Office

- Click 📘 Word 2013 or 📘 Microsoft Word 2010

2 **Close *Word***

- Click ✖ or ✖

Do not save document:
- Click Don't Save

Save new document:
- Click Save

- Select the location for saving the document

- By File name:, type the file name

- By Save as type:, select the file type

- Click Save

Save existing document:
- Click Save

3 **Close a Document**
- Click the FILE tab

- Click Close

Do not save document:
- Click Don't Save

Save new document:
- Click Save

- Select the location for saving the document

- By File name:, type the file name

- By Save as type:, select the file type

- Click Save

Save existing document:

- Click Save

4 **Open the *Practice Files Word* folder**

Only in Word 2013:

- Click Computer

In both versions:

- Click Documents

- Double-click
   Practice files Word

5 **Set line spacing to *Single***

- Click the HOME tab

- Click

- Click 1,0

Or:
- Click
   Line Spacing Options...

- By Line spacing:, click

- Click Single

- Click OK

6 **Set paragraph spacing after to *0 points***

- Click the HOME tab

- Click

- Click Line Spacing Options...

- By After:, click until you see 0 pt

- Click OK

7 **Add a button to the *Quick Access* toolbar**

- Click

- Click the button

8 **Place the *Quick Access* toolbar below or above the ribbon**

- Click

Below the ribbon:
- Click Show Below the Ribbon

Above the ribbon:
- Click Show Above the Ribbon

9 **Remove a button from the *Quick Access* toolbar**

- Click

- Uncheck the box ✓ by the button

10 **Open a document**

- Click the FILE tab

- Click Open

Only in Word 2013:

- Click Computer

- If necessary, click Browse

Next, in both versions:
- Select the folder

11 Print document

- Click the **FILE** tab

- Click **Print**

- Click

  Print

12 Insert symbol

- Click the **INSERT** tab

- Click **Ω Symbol ▾**

- Click the symbol

If you cannot find the symbol in the list:

- Click **Ω More Symbols...**

- Click a symbol

- Click **Insert**

- Click **Close**

13 Start manual hyphenation

- Click the **PAGE LAYOUT** tab

- Click **b𝐜ᵃ⁻ Hyphenation ▾**

- Click
  b𝐜ᵃ⁻ Hyphenation Options...

- Click **Manual...**

14 Insert / do not insert hyphen

Insert:

- Click **Yes**

Do not insert:

- Click **No**

15 Save document

- Click the **FILE** tab

- Click **Save**

- Select the location for saving the document

- By **File name:**, type the file name

- By **Save as type:**, select the file type

- Click **Save**

16 Save document as

- Click the **FILE** tab

- Click **Save As**

- Select the location for saving the document

- By **File name:**, type the file name

- By **Save as type:**, select the file type

- Click **Save**

17 Set the font

If the text has already been typed:
- Select the text first

Otherwise:

- Click the **HOME** tab

- By **Calibri (Body)**, click **▾**

- Click the desired font

18 Set the font size

If the text has already been typed:
- Select the text first

- By 11, click ▾

- Click the desired number of points

19 Show/hide paragraph markers

- Click the HOME tab

- Click ¶

20 Select text
Lines:

- Place the pointer in the left margin, before the first line

- Click and drag the pointer downwards, until all lines have been selected

Word:
- Click the word two times

Part of a text:
- Press and hold the mouse button down, then drag across the desired text

21 Navigate within a document
Go to the beginning of the document:

- Press **Ctrl** + **Home**

Go to the end of the document:

- Press **Ctrl** + **End**

To go to the next page/previous page in Word 2010:

- Click ⬇ or ⬆

Or:
- Drag the scroll box

22 Place left tab
- Check if the left tab is selected on the ruler ∟

23 Enter a blank line

- Press

24 Drag a tab stop
- Click the tab stop, press and hold the mouse button down

- Drag the tab stop to the desired spot

25 Make a list

- Click the HOME tab

- Click

- Type the text

- Press

To end the list:

- Press  once more

26 Change the level

- Click the HOME tab

- By , click ▾

- Click the level

27 Change margin

- Click the PAGE LAYOUT tab

Margins
- Click ▾

- Click the desired margin

Or:
- Click Custom Margins...

28   Insert page break
- Click the spot where you want to insert the page break

- Click the PAGE LAYOUT tab

- Click ⊞ Breaks ▾

- Click

  Page
  Mark the point at which one page and the next page begins.

29   Add header

- Click the INSERT tab

- Click ▭ Header ▾

- Click the desired option

30   Footer with page number

- Click the INSERT tab

- Click ⊞ Page Number ▾

- Click ⊞ Bottom of Page

- Click the desired option

31   Open the *Page Setup* window

- Click the PAGE LAYOUT tab

- By Page Setup , click ⌐

32   Close the *Navigation Pane*
- Click ✕

33   Insert picture

- Click the INSERT tab

- Click Insert ▾

34   Reset picture
To reset original picture only:
- Click 🖼

To reset picture and size:
- By 🖼, click ▾

- Click 🖼 Reset Picture & Size

35   Enlarge/shrink a picture/text box/shape
- Click the object

- Place the pointer on a handle

- Press and hold the mouse button down, drag the handle up or down to the desired size and release the mouse button

36   Wrap text around picture
- Click the picture

- Click the FORMAT tab

  Wrap
- Click Text ▾

- Click the desired method of wrapping the text, for example, ▣ Square

37   Move picture/text box/shape
- Click the object

- Place the pointer on the object and press the mouse button

- Drag the object to the desired position and release the mouse button

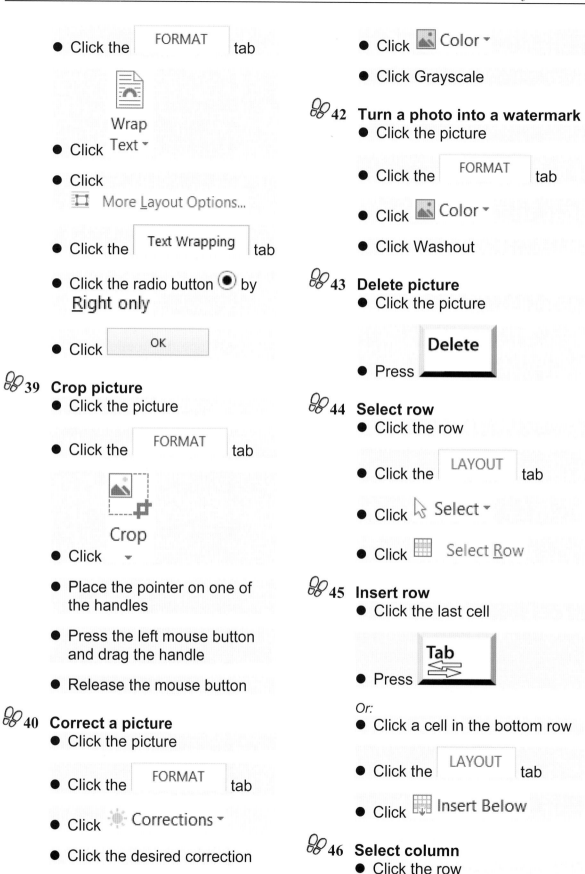

- Click the FORMAT tab

Wrap
- Click Text ▾

- Click
  ⌗ More Layout Options...

- Click the Text Wrapping tab

- Click the radio button ⦿ by
  <u>R</u>ight only

- Click OK

👣 39 Crop picture
- Click the picture

- Click the FORMAT tab

Crop
- Click ▾

- Place the pointer on one of
  the handles

- Press the left mouse button
  and drag the handle

- Release the mouse button

👣 40 Correct a picture
- Click the picture

- Click the FORMAT tab

- Click ☼ Corrections ▾

- Click the desired correction

👣 41 Change picture to black-and-
white

- Click Color ▾

- Click Grayscale

👣 42 Turn a photo into a watermark
- Click the picture

- Click the FORMAT tab

- Click Color ▾

- Click Washout

👣 43 Delete picture
- Click the picture

- Press Delete

👣 44 Select row
- Click the row

- Click the LAYOUT tab

- Click ▷ Select ▾

- Click ⊞ Select <u>R</u>ow

👣 45 Insert row
- Click the last cell

- Press Tab ⇆

Or:
- Click a cell in the bottom row

- Click the LAYOUT tab

- Click ⊞ Insert Below

👣 46 Select column
- Click the row

- Click the LAYOUT tab

- Click Select Column

47 Create table
- Click the INSERT tab

Table
- Click ▾
- Click the box with the desired table size

48 Calculate total sum
- Click the cell where you want to insert the total

- Click the LAYOUT tab

Data
- If necessary, click ▾

- Click *fx* Formula

- Click OK

49 Delete row
- Click in the row

- Click the LAYOUT tab

Delete
- Click ▾

- Click ⇥✗ Delete Rows

50 Rotate picture
- Click the picture

- Click the FORMAT tab

- Click ◿▮ ▾

51 Apply bold, italics, or underlining
- Select the text

- Click the HOME tab

Bold:
- Click **B**

Italics:
- Click *I*

Underlining:
- Click U̲

52 Change text color
- Select the text

- Click the HOME tab

- By **A**▬, click ▾
- Click the color

53 Create text box
- Click the INSERT tab

Text
- Click Box ▾

- Click ▤ Draw Text Box

- The pointer turns into +

- Drag a rectangle

54 Fill a shape
- Click the shape

- By ⬧ Shape Fill, click ▾

- Click the desired fill method and color

55 Shape outline
- Click the shape

- By ✎ Shape Outline , click ▾

- Click the desire outline

56 Set size of text box
- Click the text box

- If necessary, click *Size* ▾

- By , enter the height

- By , enter the width

57 Set up columns
- Click PAGE LAYOUT

- Click Columns ▾

- Click the number of columns

58 Title in a single column
- Select the title

- Click the PAGE LAYOUT tab

- Click Columns ▾

- Click One

59 Aligning text
- Select the text

- Click the HOME tab

Align to the left or right:
- Click ≡ or ≡

Justify:
- Click ≡

60 Automatic hyphenation and hyphenate words in capitals
- Click PAGE LAYOUT

- Click b$\overset{a}{c}$⁻ Hyphenation ▾

- Click
  b$\overset{a}{c}$⁻ Hyphenation Options...

- Uncheck the box ☑ by
  Hyphenate words in CAPS

- Check the box ☑ by
  Automatically hyphenate document

- Click OK

61 Insert column break
- Click the spot where you want to insert the column break

- Click PAGE LAYOUT

- Click Breaks ▾

- Click
  Column
  Indicate that the text following t
  break will begin in the next colu

62 Insert caption
- Click the picture

- Click the REFERENCES tab

- Click Insert Caption

- Click in the box below
  Caption:

- Type the name

63 Insert section break
- Click the spot where you want to insert the section break
- Click the [PAGE LAYOUT] tab
- Click ⊢☐ **Breaks** ▾
- Click

  Next Page
  Insert a section break and start section on the next page.

64 Next and previous records
- Click ▶ or ◀

65 Open new blank document
- Click the **FILE** tab
- Click **New**

  In Word 2013:

- Click Blank document

  In Word 2010:

  Blank
- Click document

- Click Create

66 Open *Step-by-step Mail Merge Wizard*
- Click the [MAILINGS] tab

Start Mail
- Click Merge ▾

- Click Step-by-Step Mail Merge <u>W</u>izard...

67 Go to the next step
- Click ➡ Next:

68 Select fields
- Click the field

- Click [<u>I</u>nsert]

  After all the fields have been inserted:

- Click [Close]

69 Update labels
- Click [Update all labels]

70 Set the style
- Click in the text

- Click the [HOME] tab

- If necessary, by Styles click [▾]

- Click the style

71 Add word to index
- Select the word

- Click the [REFERENCES] tab

  Mark
- Click Entry

- Click [Mark <u>A</u>ll]

- Click the REFERENCES tab

Table of
- Click Contents ▾

- Click **Automatic Table 1**

73 Move text to next page
- Click to the left of the text

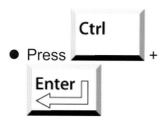

- Press Ctrl + Enter

74 Update table of contents
- Click ▢! Update Table or
  ▣! Update Table

- Click the radio button ◉ by
  Update entire table

- Click OK

75 Add index
- Click the spot where you want
  to insert the index

- Click the REFERENCES tab

In Word 2013:
- By Index, click
  ▤ Insert Index

- Check the box ✔ by
  Right align page numbers

- Click OK

76 Insert list of pictures
- Click the spot where you want
  to insert the list

- By Captions, click
  ▤ Insert Table of Figures

- If necessary, by Formats:,
  select From template

- Click OK

77 Open Internet Explorer
In Windows 8.1, on the taskbar:

- Click

In Windows 7 and Vista:

- Click ⊚

- Click ▶ All Programs

- Click ⅇ Internet Explorer

78 Visit a website
- Click the address bar

- Type the web address

- Press Enter

79 Select label
- Click ▦ Label options...

- By Label vendors:, select the
  Avery US Letter size

- Select the product number
  8160 Easy Peel Address Labels

- Click OK

80 Close program
- Click ✕ or

81 Insert picture
In Word 2013:

- Click de picture

- Click | Insert ▼ |

**82 Enable editing**

- Click | Enable Editing |

**83 Show text boundaries**

- Click **FILE**

- Click **Options**

- Click Advanced

- By
  Show document content
  check the box ✔ by
  Show te*x*t boundaries

- Click | OK |

Appendix B. Downloading the Practice Files

In this appendix, we explain how to download and save the practice files from the website accompanying this book. Downloading means you are transferring files to your own computer.

☞ **Open** *Internet Explorer* 𝒮𝒮⁷⁷

☞ **Open the www.visualsteps.com/word2013 web page** 𝒮𝒮⁷⁸

Now you will see the website that goes with this book. You can download the practice files from the *Practice files* page:

⊕ **Click Practice files**

⊕ **Right-click**
     [Practice files Word.zi|

You will see a menu:

⊕ **Click Save target as...**

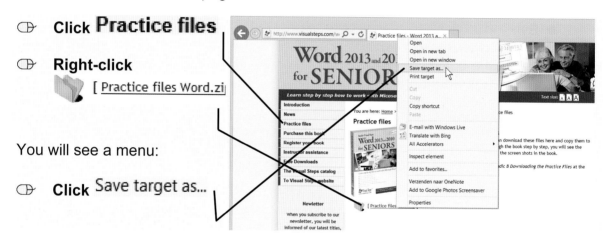

The *Practice Files Word.zip* folder is a compressed folder. You can save this folder in the (*My*) *Documents* folder.

⊕ **Click**
     ▷ 🚪 Documents

⊕ **Click Save**

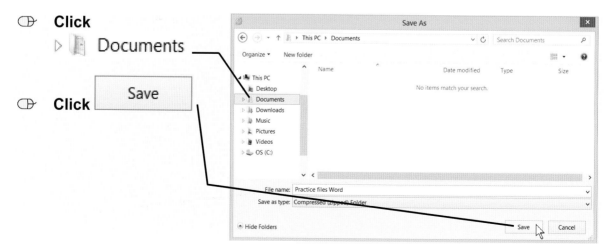

When the file has finished downloading:

⏿ **Click** Open folder

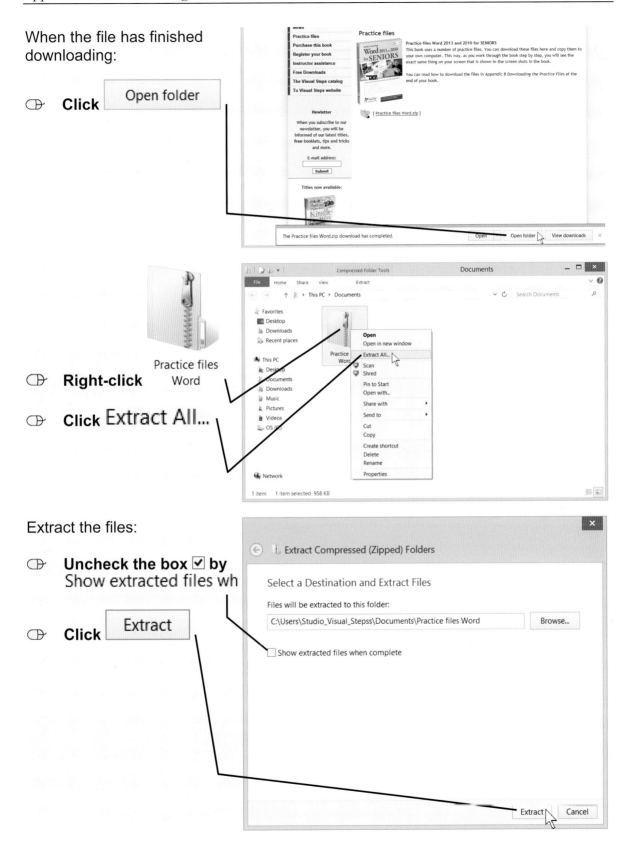

⏿ **Right-click** Practice files Word

⏿ **Click** Extract All...

Extract the files:

⏿ **Uncheck the box** ☑ **by** Show extracted files wh

⏿ **Click** Extract

Now the *Practice Files Word* folder has been saved in the (*My*) *Documents folder*:

You can delete the
compressed folder:

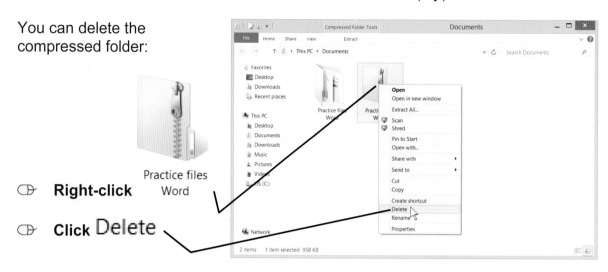

Practice files
Word

☐ **Right-click**

☐ **Click** Delete

In *Windows 8.1*, the folder will be deleted at once. In *Windows 7* and *Vista* you will
see the *Delete Folder* window:

☐ **Click** Yes

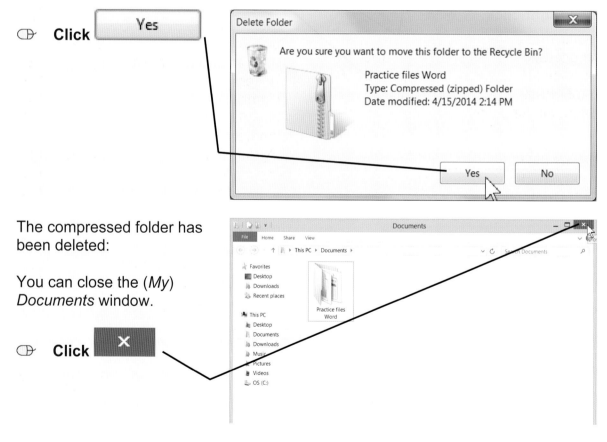

The compressed folder has
been deleted:

You can close the (*My*)
Documents window.

☐ **Click** ✕

☞ **Close** *Internet Explorer* ⠦**80**

Appendix C. Index

Excel 2013 and 2010 for Seniors

Microsoft's well-known spreadsheet program *Excel* is user-friendly and offers a wide range of features and built-in functions for many different uses.

LEARN STEP BY STEP HOW TO WORK WITH EXCEL

The book *Excel 2013 and 2010 for SENIORS* will teach you how to perform such tasks as entering data and formulas, formatting cells, designing charts and graphics, creating address lists, sorting, and filtering. This book also demonstrates how to create an accounting book and explores other topics such as creating estimates, budgets, pivot tables and mailings.

With thorough explanations and step-by-step instructions, this book makes every task discussed easy to perform.

Please note: In order to work with this book, you need to own *Excel 2013* or *Excel 2010* and have it already installed on your computer or have a subscription to Office 365, the online version.

Author: Studio Visual Steps
ISBN 978 90 5905 180 5
Book type: Paperback, full color
Nr of pages: 344 pages
Accompanying website: www.visualsteps.com/excel2013

Full color!

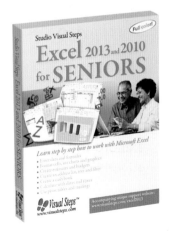

You will learn how to:
- enter data and formulas
- format cells, use charts and graphics
- create estimates and budgets
- create and address list, sort and filter
- create an accounting book
- calculate with dates and times
- use pivot tables and mailings

Suitable for:
Microsoft Excel 2013 and Excel 2010
Windows 8.1, 7 and Vista

Windows 8.1 for SENIORS

GET STARTED QUICKLY WITH WINDOWS 8.1

The computer book *Windows 8.1 for SENIORS* is a great computer book for senior citizens who want to get started using computers. The book walks you through the basics of the operating system *Windows 8.*1 in an easy step-by-step manner.

Use this learn-as-you-go book right alongside your computer as you perform the tasks laid out in each chapter. Learn how to use the computer and the mouse and write letters.

This book also teaches you how to surf the Internet and send and receive e-mails. Be amazed at how fast you will start having fun with your computer with the new skills and information you will gain!

Author: Studio Visual Steps
ISBN 978 90 5905 118 8
Book type: Paperback, full color
Nr of pages: 368 pages
Accompanying website: www.visualsteps.com/windows8

Full color!

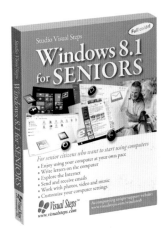

You will learn how to:

- become comfortable and enjoy using your computer
- write letters and memos on the computer
- send and receive messages by e-mail
- explore the World Wide Web
- customize your computer settings

Suitable for:
Windows 8.1 on a desktop or laptop computer

Digital Photo Editing with Picasa for SENIORS

Picasa, a very popular and free photo editing program, is one of the best choices for managing and editing your digital photos.

LEARN ALL ABOUT PHOTO EDITING WITH PICASA

In this book you will get acquainted step by step with some of the many things you can do with photos. You can sort and arrange your photos into albums. Edits can be applied manually or automatically. The contrast, color and exposure in a photo can be adjusted. It's possible to rotate photos, eliminate scratches or blemishes and remove red eyes. You can add effects or even text to a photo and create something unique to print or send. *Picasa* also gives you the option to make collages, view slideshows or create movies from your photos. A great way to share photos with family and friends!

In this book you will work with practice photos. Once you have become familiar with the sorting and editing options available in *Picasa* you can start to work with your own photo collection. At the end of the book you will also learn how to import photos from a digital camera or other device to your computer.

With *Picasa* and this book you will have everything you need to manage, edit and share your photos.

Author: Studio Visual Steps
ISBN 978 90 5905 368 7
Book type: Paperback, full color
Nr of pages: 272 pages
Accompanying website:
www.visualsteps.com/picasaseniors

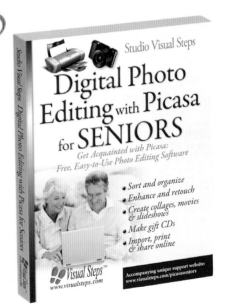

You will learn how to:
- sort and organize photos in albums
- enhance and retouch photos
- create collages and make gift CDs
- create movies and slideshows
- print and share photos online
- import photos

Suitable for:
Windows 8.1, 7 and Vista

HELEN HALL LIBRARY
100 WEST WALKER
LEAGUE CITY, TX 77573

DISCARD